Oliver Paul Gooding

The People's God vs. the Monarchic God

Oliver Paul Gooding

The People's God vs. the Monarchic God

ISBN/EAN: 9783337244958

Printed in Europe, USA, Canada, Australia, Japan

Cover: Foto ©Lupo / pixelio.de

More available books at **www.hansebooks.com**

THE PEOPLE'S GOD

vs.

THE MONARCHIC GOD

OR

The True Story of a World

BY

Gen. Oliver Paul Gooding,

Of the St. Louis, Mo., Bar.

A Graduate of West Point and a General in the Union Army
During Our Late Civil War.

Defends Religion from the True Standpoint,
The Republic of Religion.

PRICE, TWO DOLLARS.

PUBLISHED BY THE AUTHOR.
1892.

Copyright, 1892, by
OLIVER PAUL GOODING.
All rights reserved.

CHAPTER 1.

Reader, if you will fix this book well in your memory by reading it over several times, and afterwards thinking and talking about its contents, it will make you as bright a person, on the general field of intelligence, as there is in the world.

As the late James Freeman Clarke, of Boston, Mass., one of the greatest of American preachers, in his work entitled "The Ten Great Religions," declares that revelation wears out with intellectual people, the first great object of this work will be to prevent intellectual people from running off into infidelity and rejecting the only true religion, that is, the people's religion, when revelation, monarchic religion, shall have worn out with them.

This object to save the only true religion from infidelity, with intellectual people, will be accomplished by proving from the standpoint of science the existence of the true and only God, and that man has a soul capable of immortality.

This will be necessary, as eventually nearly all the people will become intellectual under the educational influences of the public schools and other institutions of learning, the newspapers and public oratory.

The next great object of this work will be to successfully defend the natural inalienable right of the people to self-government, to think and choose for themselves in religion as well as in politics. This object will be accomplished by historically tracing the track of religious as well as political thought around the world, thus showing that the people came into this world with the natural inalienable right of self-government in both religion and politics. This object will also be proven from a scientific standpoint, by showing how the people originally came into the world.

Man knows that he is on this earth, but whence he came and whither he goeth are questions he has been asking ever since the first generation. As long as man shall live on this earth he will be asking these questions, unless they are sooner satisfactorily answered. This work will give satisfactory answers to these questions, or tell the true story of a world. Preliminary to this, however, the history of the efforts man has made all around the earth to arrive at satisfactory answers to these questions will be given, then satisfactory answers to them will be made in the true story of a world concerning the birth, the life and the death of a world, at the end of this book. Such is the plan of this book, to arrive at the truth, as to whence came man and whither goeth man, and thus put the mind of man at rest; that he may worship God intelligently of his own free will in the great republic of religion as well as in the great republic of politics all around the earth, to the end that he may think and choose for himself in religion as well as in politics, and work out his own salvation in both, without dictation from any source in either.

As religion, like politics, is either republican or monarchic, and man came into existence with the natural inalienable right of self-government in religion; as well as in politics, he can not remain free in either permanently unless free in both. This book will therefore defend religion from the true standpoint, *i. e.*, the republic of religion, or "The People's God *vs.* The Monarchic God," and prove that the people's account of creation, life and salvation is the truth, and that the monarchic account of creation, life and salvation is false.

This book will also show how politics and religion affect all humanity for weal or woe, and how in wars over them millions have been slain; and that the truth of history proves that perils never come to a people from republicanism, but on the contrary that they invariably flow from the violation of the principles of true republicanism; that is, from the practice of some monarchic idea either in politics or religion in a republic or a monarchy; and that a strict adherence to the principles of true republicanism, in both politics and religion, will always undoubtedly prevent all troubles of a political or religious nature.

This book gives the history of all the principal gods that have ever been worshiped by the people.

In the preparation of this work the author consulted Clarke's "Ten Great Religions," Rawlinson's "Religions of the Ancient World," Savage's "Belief in God," Pressense's "Ancient World and Christianity," Johnston's "Oriental Religions," "Sacred Mysteries Among the Mayas and Quiches," by M. Le Plongeon, "Morals and Dogmas," by Albert Pike, and "Kent's Commentaries."

CHAPTER 2.

CHINA.

The first generation of people having no parents of whom to inquire, naturally asked of each other on meeting, whence they came.

Thus soliloquized the first man: Here I am all alone, O! so lonely.

Thus soliloquized the first woman: Here I am all alone in this beautiful world, but, O! so lonely.

What is that I see, said the first man; a beautiful creature so nearly like myself. O! what joy. I am no longer alone. At first she looked overjoyed when our eyes met, now she appears to be bashful and timid. I will go to her, but she runs and hides behind a tree. The man chased her, caught her, and thus by looks and signs, having no language, they talked.

Looking deep down into the glorious black eyes of the beautiful brunette, with flowing black hair, who stood before him, the man said: Beautiful creature, whence came you?

Blushingly looking up into the flashing eyes of

the gallant man, who stood before her, the first woman said: Grand, handsome creature, I am here: I know not whence I came. Whence came you?

I am here, but I know not whence I came, answered the man. By looks and signs, kisses and caresses, they courted and soon married. There was neither minister nor priest, nor legal authority to tie the knot; nature alone brought them together. They multiplied, and thus the Chinese nation began, who originally were like all other races, roving children of nature, in contradistinction to our present conventionalities of life. Many centuries they multiplied and lived a roving life, existing on tropic fruits, under a patriarchal government, where the old grandfather ruled his descendants. Finally, for protection against the hostile neighbors, two or more patriarchal communities united into a tribe, and elected their chief. The tribal government was therefore undoubtedly republican government, as they elected their chief. For centuries the tribes led their roving lives, roving over the plains and mountains, through the valleys, and camping on the streams, and in time went to living on game and fish. And then catching the wild cattle and sheep, tamed them, and led the lives of shepherds tending their flocks. And finally finding wheat and other cereals growing wild, and learning that they were good food, and would sustain human life, they carried along the seed with them, and finding game scarce, sowed them, and thus became a farming community, with plenty of stock. And in time other industries grew, and thus civilization began, and republican government continued for centuries.

In time one man went with another man's woman. Jealousy caused the husband to kill the offender. This having happened so often, caused great trouble in the community, to prevent the recurrence of which two of the Ten Commandments were established: Thou shalt not adult. Thou shalt not kill.

After while man acquired personal property, and his fellow-man stole it. This gave rise to the commandment: Thou shalt not steal. In a similar way came the other commandments, and thus the moral law was established.

Experience proved that those who lived in accordance with the moral law, as a rule, kept out of trouble, and were happy, which state they called happiness, which was finally called heaven, while those who lived contrary to the moral law were, as a rule, in trouble and unhappy; mentally confined to a dark cave, called hell or hades, so at first their ideas of hell and heaven were confined entirely to this life. So they urged the importance of living in accordance with the moral law, if people wanted to be in a mental heaven in this life and keep out of a mental hell in this life. Hell was a dark cave in the earth called hades, in which the greatest criminal in the community was confined. They called him the Devil because he deviled or tormented the people so. Other criminals were confined in hades, where the devil tormented them.

NATURE WORSHIP.

They looked off into space at the sun, moon and the stars, and wondered what they were. Observing that the sun caused the vegetation to grow, in gratitude they worshiped the sun. As the moon gave them light when the sun was gone away, in gratitude they worshiped the moon. As the stars gave them light, and were so beautiful, they worshiped the stars. Seeing the earth bearing the grain and the other food, in gratitude they worshiped the earth, and called it Mother Earth. Such was Nature worship.

In time they conceived the idea that it was not the sun that caused the vegetation to grow, but an invisible power back of the sun, which they called the Sun God. In the same way they arrived at the idea of a Moon God. And so on they conceived the idea of different gods for all the separate objects of nature. Finally they conceived the idea that there was a supreme God over all these plural gods.

CREATION BY EVOLUTION.

Seeing everything coming and going, according to the laws of nature, they concluded that with all life it was simply a question of conditions. And also seeing the different chemical elements uniting to form new objects, they concluded that the earth had come into existence from matter passing through different conditions, from chaos to the perfect world; and therefore believed in creation by evolution. In time dreams started the idea of a future life.

FUTURE LIFE.

Before they began to bury dead bodies, man saw the dead body of his fellow-man decay and become invisible, and subsequently dreamed of seeing him as he appeared in life. Having seen the body decay and become invisible, he thought that it could not be the body appearing to him in a dream, so he concluded that the body must have had a spirit in it that presented to him in a dream the same appearance that the body presented to his eyesight when it was alive. Hence his belief in a soul.

They at first believed that the spirits they had seen in their dreams remained in the neighborhood, as they saw them there in their dreams. They called them ghosts, and were afraid of them. And thus started the idea of a spirit life after the death of the body. After while they found out that they did not remain in the neighborhood, as they could not see them when they were awake, so they concluded that they only came there when they appeared unto them in dreams. And as they could not see them about, concluded that they must have gone into space—that the spirits of the good people must have gone up into space to a place of light and happiness, which they called heaven, from comparison to their idea of heaven in this life, where the supreme God would bless them, and that the spirits of the bad people must have gone down into a place called hell, from comparison to the dark cave called hades or hell here on earth, where there was a devil to receive and torment the spirits of the bad people. And thus came their ideas of the soul, of heaven, of hell, of God, of the Devil. And thus came natural religion. And for many generations they enjoyed liberty, both in politics and religion, but their cunning old chief, observing the great superstition of the people, played on them the monarchic trick.

THE MONARCHIC TRICK.

Being very ambitious to have his chieftainship descend to his progeny indefinitely, for the glory of his own family, the old chief pretended to have received a revelation from the supreme God telling him that he was the son of God, although he had a Chinese mother, and commanding that he and his progeny should rule over the Chinese and live at their expense forever, and that he would deliver the orders of God unto them. And whosoever disputed them was in revolt against the will of God. The ignorance and superstition of the people caused them to submit, and the cunning old chief was worshiped as the son of God, and was not only the temporal but was also the spiritual ruler.

It was a sharp trick the old chief played on them, politically and religiously. And thus man was first deprived of his natural right of self-government, both in politics and religion. Thus was monarchy, in both politics and religion, established on the overthrow of free government by that lying trick of pretended revelation in favor of that fraud called divine right monarchy. It was the overthrow of all liberty, political and religious. Other chiefs got the idea and played the trick on their tribes, in most cases using priests for the purpose.

For centuries the Chinese Emperor pretended that he descended from God, and away back, not now, was worshiped as a descendant of God, and was religious as well as political ruler, as a lineal descendant of God. The Chinese claimed that they had thirteen Emperors who were lineal descendants of God.

Since the Chinese people have become so highly educated and intelligent, they now put it fine by simply saying their Emperor is of celestial origin, which is only a new way of putting the old idea, God being the only celestial being in heaven. So it is the same old lie.

While under free government, their natural right, they enjoyed perfect liberty, both political and religious, thinking and choosing for themselves, both in politics and religion, and believed in natural creation, creation by evolution.

But the old arbitrary chief thought his dynasty was more likely to be perpetuated if all free thought, both in politics and religion, was suppressed. Hence he told them that he would let them know what the truth was in regard to creation, that he had gotten it from God. And told them that their idea of creation by evolution was all wrong. That instead of nature creating them, and everything else, God had created nature, created them, the earth, the stars and everything else. That God having created them, he alone had a right to rule them. That they had no right to rule themselves, for all authority comes from God, and that God had authorized him to deliver his commands to them, and they must obey them, or he would punish them in this life, and after death God would punish them in hell forever. From all of which we see that religion, like politics, is either republican or monarchic. That under free government religion was republican, and under monarchy it was monarchic. That under free government politics and religion were separate and distinct. That by the trick of pretended revelation, overthrowing free government, politics and religion were united in monarchy, and free thought among the people suppressed in both, thus raising the issue of the People's God *vs.* the Monarchic God, and thus bringing into the world all the trouble that has occurred over politics and religion.

CHINESE BIBLE.

The religion of the Chinese was oral, and carried entirely in their memories for many centuries before any of it was reduced to writing.

The first Bible writings of the Chinese were called Sacred Books, or Kings, and were ancient even in the days of Confucius. Confucius passed his last years editing these books, which are called the Yih-King, the Shoo-King, the She-King, and the Le-Ka King, and they constitute all of the ancient literature of the Chinese that has come down to posterity.

The four books of Confucius which contain his doctrines were not written by him, but were written by others after his death.

CHINESE PHILOSOPHY.

The Chinese also had their philosophers outside of their Bible writers, who tried to account for everything, from creation to salvation. Chinese philosophy originated with Fuh-He, who lived about 3327 B. C. He was the man who substituted writing for the knotted strings which had before formed the only means of record.

The Chinese were the first to begin to record history, and were advanced in the sciences and the arts as early, if not earlier, than any other people on the earth. Their great wall which bounds China on the north, twelve hundred and forty miles long, twenty feet high, with towers every few hundred yards, crosses mountain ridges, valleys, and is carried over rivers on arches. It was built two hundred years before Christ, to repel the attempts of the Huns, who then occupied what is now Siberia, to conquer China.

The mariner's compass, gunpowder, and other useful inventions came from China.

The immense canals of China are wonders. Europeans and Americans are surprised at the splendid libraries in China. Our civil service law was borrowed from China.

CHAPTER 3.
ARYANA.

West of China, just north of India, and east of the Caspian Sea, lie the great elevated plains of Central Asia, the center of which region was called Bactria, but I will call the entire region Aryana, as it was the original home of the Aryans. On these plains, perhaps one hundred thousand years ago, were evoluted into existence the most remarkable people the earth has ever known—*white* people, from whom have descended most of the different white peoples of Europe, America and of the whole world. Those primitive white people were called Aryans, the meaning of that word being *honorable people*. That being the meaning of the word, it is evident that the Aryans are now almost extinct. The Aryans, like all other races, had a story of a first couple, an Adam and an Eve. With them, as with the Chinese, government was at first republican, and religion was also free.

History informs us that more than ten thousand years ago these people were a pastoral and agricultural people on those plains, living in houses that had windows, doors and fire-places. They had oxen, cows, horses, sheep, goats, hogs and domestic fowls, the plow, the mill for grinding grain, cereals, the hammer, hatchet, auger. They were acquainted with several metals, among which were gold, silver, copper and tin. They knew how to spin and weave, and were acquainted with pottery. They boiled and roasted meat and used soup. They had lances, swords, the bow and arrow, shields, but not armor. They had family life, some simple laws, games, the dance and wind instruments. They had the decimal numeration, and their year was three hundred and sixty days.

NATURE WORSHIP.

The Aryans, seeing the grain and all vegetation grow under the influence of the sunlight, believed that the sun was the cause of all life. Accordingly they worshiped the sun. Seeing that fire, like the sun, imparted heat and helped to preserve life in winter, worshiped fire. Seeing that the earth helped the sun to produce the vegetables, grass for the cattle and so on, worshiped the earth. Seeing how beautiful the heavens were, that the stars and moon gave them light by night, in gratitude worshiped the heavens. From the changes they saw going on, producing new objects, the Aryans believed in creation by evolution, and therefore worshiped nature, the sun, the moon, the stars and the earth.

There were seven tribes of Aryans, all white, that afterwards became the Hindoos, the Persians, the Greeks, the Romans, who emigrated south-west from the original ancestral home in Central. Asia, and the Kelts, the Teutons and the Slavi, who entered Europe on the northern side of the Caucasus and the Caspian Sea.

Himmel, the German word for heaven, was derived from Himalaya, the name of the range of mountains that lie east and west and constitute the dividing line between India and Aryana, thus proving that the German tribe of Aryans must have had some imaginary gods before they left Aryana, and must have thought that their imaginary gods resided in the Himalaya mountains.

Greek soldiers under Alexander the Great fought their way to Aryana, the original home of their ancestors, where they remained, and for centuries were a power.

The Russians are now building a railroad into Aryana, to be able to send her army down there rapidly and threaten England's possession of India. Thus do some of the posterity of the ancient Aryans go back to the land of their ancestors. The Russians are also building a railroad through Siberia to the Pacific ocean, just north of China, on about the same parallel of latitude as the Canadian Pacific railroad across our own continent.

CHAPTER 4.
INDIA.

When the Aryans, who afterwards became Hindoos, got down into India, they found natives there, who had been evoluted into existence in the days of evolution, and were dark people, but not negroes. Being dark, the white Aryans thought they had a right to make them their lowest caste, and accordingly reduced them to that condition. Here the Aryans built cities. Here the imaginations of the Aryans created a great many gods for the different objects of nature they had worshiped in Aryana, on the plains of Central Asia. For the atmosphere, their imaginations created a god, whom they called Indra; for the ocean of light, or the heavens, a god, they called Varuna; for fire, a god they called Agni; for the sun, a god they called Savitri;

for the moon, a god they called Soma; for death, a god they called Yama. And in turn, their imaginations created separate gods for the earth, food, wine, months, seasons, day, night and dawn. Here they built magnificent temples in which to worship their different gods. Here they even hewed out magnificent temples in the solid rock.

Here the imaginations of the Aryans ran till they concluded that all was spirit, and there was no such thing as matter in all space. That we think we see matter in the shape of stars, the earth, houses and other objects, but in reality we do not see them, that they are only illusions, that they are all spirit. That universal spirit throughout space they called Brahman. This view could only have been taken by regarding all the invisible matter in space as spirit, and all the globes and other objects as simply condensed spirit. But this view would prove it all simply matter, most of it invisible matter and the rest visible. This latter was the Buddhist view at first. Brahmanism declared everything spirit, and Buddhism declared everything matter.

Brahmanism taught that this life was no account, and the sooner a person got out of it the better. So many of them suicided to get into the spirit land as soon as possible. To stop that ridiculous extreme, Buddhism taught the religion of humanity, that this life, or the body, was some account, and should be preserved and made as happy as possible. That people should not neglect the happiness of this life, and at first denied that there was any such thing as spirit, or a future life.

Buddhism broke down all castes, and is a religion of humanity. It was a revolt against the castes, aristocracy, of Brahmanism and the extreme spiritualism. Buddhism wanted to save people from hell in this life.

The greatest personal god of the Brahmans was called Brahma. They claimed that he was the first born of creation ; that he was born from the self-existent being, which was in the form of a golden egg. That by the power of prayer he became the creator of all things.

Some of the Brahmans worshiped a god they called Vischnu, and claimed that he was the greatest god. Other Brahmans worshiped a god they called Siva, and claimed that he was the greatest god. When the war came on between the Brahmans and the Buddhists for religious supremacy the different factions of the Brahmans found it necessary to settle their differences as to which was the greatest god ; so they agreed that Brahma was the Creator, Vichnu the Preserver, and Siva the Destroyer, all three in one Supreme God. And thus the Indian triad, or trinity, was created. The civil war between the Brahmans and the Buddhists resulted in the expulsion of the Buddhists from India. The struggle between them lasted during nine centuries, from A. D. 500 to A. D. 1400, resulting in the total expulsion of the Buddhists, and the triumphant establishment of the triad as the worship of India. What a ridiculous civil war, in which the Brahmanists and Buddhists fought each other for nearly a thousand years over the dispute as to whether it was all spirit or all matter, when all of them ought to have had sense enough to know that it was part matter, as they saw it with their own eyes every time they looked at the sun, the moon, the stars, and the earth. Long prior to this occurred the civil war between the Solar and Lunar Monarchies, resulting in victory to the Solar Monarchy. How these monarchies came by these names is plain enough. The chief of one tribe must have claimed that he was the son of the Sun-God, and ploclaimed himself king, and accordingly his would be called the Solar Monarchy. In a similar way the name of the Lunar Monarchy came.

The Buddhists left behind them about nine hundred temples excavated in the solid rock in the sides of mountains in the Bombay Presidency in India.

The Buddhist rock-cut monasteries are also numerous in India, although long since deserted. The Buddhist monks, then as now, took the same three vows of celibacy, poverty and obedience, that are taken by the members of all the Catholic orders.

The Catholic Church, in its ritual, confession and general outline, is supposed to be a copy of the Buddhist Church. In its forms the Buddhist religion resembles the Catholic Church and in its spirit, Protestantism. The Buddhist religion is now the popular religion of the Chinese and the Japanese, Siam, Anam, Nepaul, Ceylon, nearly all of Eastern Asia.

BIBLE OF THE BRAHMANISTS.

The religion of the Brahmanists was entirely oral for many centuries. For centuries it mostly consisted of hymns, which were carried in their memories. Finally they were reduced to writing, and the volume was called the Vedas, and that age was called the Vedic age. Subsequently came the Laws of Manu. The Vedas and the Laws of Menu constituted the Brahmanistic Bible. The Buddhists had a separate Bible.

Buddha was the son of the last King of the Solar Monarchy. The Buddhist calls his heaven Nirvana, and considers it a place of perfect rest from all worry.

INDIAN PHILOSOPHY.

Independent of the Bible writers, the priests, there were philosophers in India who tried to account for the existence of everything, from creation to salvation. They had three systems of philosophy, called the Sankhya, the Vedanta and the Nyasa. It is not known who were the authors of these systems of philosophy. The Vedantists held that there was but one God, and that the worship of the plural gods was necessary to those who could not rise to the sublime monotheism. All three of these philosophies agreed on certain points, and differed on others. They all three agree in asserting the transmigratian of souls, and that the cessation of that brings final deliverance. A ridiculous idea. They will not be pursued in this chapter any farther. The poets also wrote poems about creation, the gods and salvation. The Brahmanists sacrificed human beings to their gods. The Buddhists did not practice that outrageous murder of human beings.

ORDER OF SACRED MYSTERIES.

In the days of nature worship some of the smartest

men assumed the office of priest of the people. In time they organized themselves into a secret society, called "The Order of Sacred Mysteries." This order was organized for the study of nature—the sun, the moon, the stars and the earth, and through that study finding out the origin of all things, gaining light, further light, even unto the finding of God. This was the beginning of scientific knowledge, and from it came chemistry, geology, geometry, trigonometry and astronomy. This order was generally divided into three degrees. The secret rites and ceremonies of these degrees were called "Sacred Mysteries." In the first degree they were given some light; in the second degree they were given further light, and in the third degree they were told which was the true God.

At first nobody but the priests of the nature worship were allowed to enter "The Order of the Sacred Mysteries." Some of the priests were only allowed to enter the first degree; others were only allowed to take the second degree, while but few were ever allowed to take the third degree, that is to be introduced to the true and only God.

The people were kept in profound ignorance of the secret ceremonies of "The Order of Sacred Mysteries," and the great secret, who the true God was; and the priests only imparted very little of the knowledge they gained by the study of nature to the people. Their object seemed to be to get all the knowledge they possibly could for themselves, but at the same time keep the people in ignorance, that they might play on their superstition and control them to their own purposes. They let the poople go on worshiping the sun, the moon, the stars and the earth, and subsequently the imaginary gods, who were supposed to preside over those objects in nature, while they in "The Order of Sacred Mysteries" concealed from the people and worshiped the true God, whom we now worship publicly.

LODGE ROOM OF SACRED MYSTERIES, AND INITIATION.

In India the degrees in the Sacred Mysteries were at first conferred in dark caves in the earth. The cave was supposed to be divided into three rooms—first, second and third, the last being called the Holy of Holies. The candidate, who was invested with a cable-tow, having long wandered in darkness in the cave, truly wanted light, and he was given light finally in the worship of the true God in the Holy of Holies. In the last degree he was admitted into the Holy Cavern, which blazed with light, called the Holy of Holies, where, in costly robes sat, in the east, west and south, the chief officers of the lodge called Hierophants, and who represented the Indian triune deity. The ceremonies in this degree began with an anthem to the great God of nature. In this degree he was told the truth—who the true God was. He was then required to promise that he would be obedient to his superiors, that he would keep his body pure, govern his tongue, and observe a passive obedience in receiving the doctrines and traditions of the order, and the firmest secrecy in maintaining inviolable its hidden and abstruse mysteries. Then he was sprinkled with water (whence our baptism); certain words, now unknown, were whispered in his ear, and he was divested of his shoes, and made to go three times around the cavern.

CHAPTER 5.
PERSIA.

The Persians were Aryans, and it is not known just how long they retained republican gevernment, electing their chief, but it is known that they allowed their imaginations to run till they thought they had a mythical king they called Jamshid. History informs us that the first King of Persia called himself Gilshah, meaning that he was King of the World; thus evidently trying to make the people believe that he was God. A subsequent King, Darius, neither claimed to be God, nor the son of a god, but called himself an Aryan. Still a later King, Cyrus, conquered Babylon and killed King Belshazzer, the Semitic, the very night of his great feast, when the children of Israel were his captives, and Daniel, the Jew, foretold him his fate by interpreting the mysterious handwriting on the wall.

NATURE WORSHIP.

The Persians brought nature worship with them from Aryana, as is fully proven by their worship of the sun and fire at Persepolis. The lovely valley of Shiraz is situated in the south-western part of Persia.

PERSEPOLIS.

At one end of this valley, fifty feet above the plain, is a crescent formed by rocky hills, within which is a platform partly hewn out of the mountains themselves, and partly built up with gray blocks of marble, from twenty to sixty feet long, so that the joints could scarcely be seen. This platform is fourteen hundred feet long by nine hundred broad. From the plain below they went up marble steps to the platform. On the way up they reached a landing, where stand two immense marble statues, supposed to have represented the sacred bulls of the Magian religion.

Passing these sentinels, they went on up still more marble steps, alongside of which were carved rows of figures, which seemed to be going up by their sides, representing warriors, courtiers, captives, men of every nation, till they reached the platform, where stood gigantic columns, sixty feet high and fifteen feet in circumference, which supported a roof of cedar, which protected the multitudes from the sun of Southern Asia. On that platform, near the tombs of the Kings of Persia, which were cut in the sides of the mountain, was an altar on which the priests kept a fire burning all the time, and suspended above the fire was a ball representing the sun, thus proving they had nature worship. Figures of the Kings were cut on the side of the mountain above their tombs, and above these figures, suspended in the air, were winged, half length figures in fainter outlines of them. The palace of the great Kings of Persia was also at Persepolis, the ancient capital of that kingdom. Outside of Persepolis the Persians had no altars, no temples nor images; and they worshiped on top of mountains. They adored the heavens, and sacrificed to the sun, moon, earth, fire, water and winds. "They did not erect altars, nor use libations, fillets, or cakes. One of the Magi sang an ode concerning the origin of the gods, over the sacrifice, which was laid on a bed of tender grass. They paid great reverence to rivers, and did nothing to defile them. In burying the dead, they never put the body in the ground till it had been torn by some bird or dog. They then covered the body with wax, and put it in the ground."

PERSIAN MYTHOLOGY.

The mythology of the Persians was oral, coming down through the ages from the priests by word of mouth, till a man by the name of Zoroaster put it into a book of manuscripts called the Zend Avesta, which was the Persian Bible. From that and a subsequent writing called the Bundekesch, we learn that the Persians imagined that the Supreme God had created two powerful gods. The first they called Ormazd, and believed that he created all the good people, and everything that was good, and was therefore the God of Good. The other they called Ahriman, and imagined that he created all the bad people, and everything that is bad, and was therefore the God of Evil; that Ormazd was the God of Light, and Ahriman the God of Darkness; that Ormazd created the world of light, and Ahriman created the world of darkness; that Ormazd created a protecting god for every object in his world of light; that Ahriman created a corresponding world of darkness, with its many gods of evil. So they had a great many gods.

WAR BETWEEN ORMAZD AND AHRIMAN.

To prepare for war with Ahriman, Ormazd armed himself and created for his assistance the whole shining host of heaven—the sun, the moon and the stars, which were supposed to be wholly submissive to him. The stars were simply private soldiers in the army of Ormazd, and were divided into four troops, commanded by four Generals. Twelve companies were arranged, in the twelve signs of the zodiac. These were divided into four divisions, which were stationed in the east, west, north and south. The planet Jupiter, called in the Persian language Tistrya, commanded the division in the east, and was named the Prince of the stars; Saturn (Sitairsi) commanded the western division; Mercury (Vanant) commanded the southern division, and Mars (Hapto-Iringa) commanded the division of the north. In the center of the heavens is the great star, Venus (Mesch), that led all of them against Ahriman. The dog, Sirius (Sura), stood guard over the abyss out of which was to come Ahriman.

Ahriman was imagined to have created his forces of darkness to fight the forces of Ormazd. Ormazd being the God of Good, is represented as wanting peace, but Ahriman, being the God of Evil, was true to his evil nature, and would not allow him to have peace, and declared for war.

But blinded by the majesty of Ormazd, and frightened by the Fravashis, souls of holy men, before the terrible word of Ormazd he shrank back into the abyss of darkness, and lay fettered there for three thousand years of the second period.

CREATION OF PEOPLE.

Ahriman did not remain in the abyss, but returned to the earth to do all the harm he could. In pursuance of this purpose he entered the bull, the original animal, and caused him to die. But after his death, the first man, called Kaimorts, came out of his right shoulder, and out of his left shoulder came the soul of the bull, called Goshurun, which then became the guardian spirit of all the animals. They also imagined that all clean animals and plants came from the body of the bull. But mad because good results had followed his killing the bull, he then created the unclean animals.

KAIMORTS.

Ahriman had nothing to oppose Kaimorts, so he concluded to kill him. They imagined that Kaimorts was both man and woman, and that through his death came from him the first human pair; a tree grew from his body, and bore ten pairs of men and women. The first couple were called Meschia and Meschiane. They were originally innocent and made for heaven, and worshiped Ormazd as their creator. But Ahriman tempted them. They injured themselves by drinking milk from a goat. Then Ahriman gave them the forbidden fruit, and they ate of it, and thereby lost a hundred parts of their happiness, so that only one part remained. The woman was the first to sacrifice to the Dævas. They then had two children after fifty years called Siamak and Veschak, and died one hundred years old. For their sins they are supposed to remain in hell till the resurrection. The substance of the commands in the Persian religion was: "Think purely, speak purely, act purely." That religion taught cleanliness of the body also. It also taught that the Fravashis of men who were created by Ormazd and are preserved in heaven, in the realm of light of Ormazd. But that they had to come from heaven to be united to human bodies and go through a probation called the Way of Two Destinies. That those who chose the good in this world are received after death by good spirits, and are guided by the dog, Sura, to the bridge, Chinevat, and that the wicked were dragged there by the Dævas. Here Ormazd holds a judgment day, and determines the fate of souls. The good pass the bridge into heaven, where they are welcomed by the Amshaspands, seven archangels, with rejoicing, while the bad fell into the gulf of Duzahk, where they were tormented by the Dævas, devils. The duration of the punishment was fixed by Ormazd, but some were prayed out by their friends, while others had to remain till the resurrection of the dead. As all were finally released from hell, the Persian religion taught final universal salvation. They think Ormazd will then clothe them anew with flesh. They imagined that Ahriman is to cause a comet to descend onto the earth and cause it to be just like a stream of melted iron, which will rush down into the realm of Ahriman, and that all beings will have to pass through this stream; to the righteous it will feel like warm milk, and they will pass through to the dwellings of the just; but all sinners will be borne along by the stream into the abyss of Duzahk. There they will burn three days and nights, then, being purified, they will invoke Ormazd, and be received into heaven. Subsequently Ahriman himself and all in Duzahk shall be purified by this fire, all evil consumed, and all darkness banished. They imagined from this extinct fire there will come a more beautiful earth, pure and perfect and destined to be eternal.

Clarke declares that Zoroaster did not invent the Persian religion, but that it grew like all other religions. Small bodies of Parsis, disciples of this ancient faith, are still in Persia and Asia.

CHAPTER 6.
EGYPT.

History proves that the earliest Egyptians on the lower Nile were Semitics, who mixed with the surrounding African tribes, not negroes. The Egyptians recognize no relationship with the negroes. The negroes only appear on the monuments as slaves. How long the Egyptians retained the republican government, electing their chiefs, is not known, but it is known that in their ancient monarchy their king claimed to be the son of God by his mortal mother, and compelled his sons and daughters to marry each other under the pretense of keeping his divine blood in his royal family. So in Egypt that fraud was also played on the people.

NATURE WORSHIP.

The earliest worship of the Egyptian people was Nature Worship, the worship of the sun, the earth, the air, fire and water. From that to the worship of the imaginary gods that represented them. These were the gods of the people. The greatest of these they named Osiris. They then imagined that the imaginary Osiris had an imaginary wife, they named Isis, and that they begot an imaginary son they named Horus. They also imagined ridiculous stories about their gods. They imagined that Osiris was killed by Typhon, another imaginary god, and after his death his soul begot a son by Isis. Nowhere did their imaginations ever provide for any marriage ceremony between the gods and goddesses. They were all natural marriages. They continued to imagine till their imaginations had created three orders of imaginary gods. But as it is not the purpose of the author to give the names and imaginary history of all the imaginary gods, nothing further will be said on that subject now, except to state that they imagined Osiris, after his death, came back to sit in judgment on the souls of the dead and contend with the imaginary Satan, they called Set, for the possession of the souls; and that their Sun-God was called Phra, from which the name Pharaoh was derived, which indicates that King Pharaoh must have claimed that he descended from Phra, the Sun-God.

ANIMAL WORSHIP.

The Egyptians carried their worship of nature even to the worship of the animals. They worshiped what they called a sacred bull they named Apis. They imagined that he was the representative of Osiris. He is said to have been a bull with black hair, a white spot on his forehead, and other special marks. He was kept at Memphis in a splendid temple. They held a festival in his honor, which lasted seven days, when great multitudes of people assembled. When he died his body was embalmed and buried with great honor, and the priests searched till they found another Apis, that was taken to Memphis and honored as the dead one had been. The sacred bulls were buried near Memphis in an arched gallery, hewn in the rock, two thousand feet long and twenty feet high, and twenty feet in breadth. On each side is a series of recesses, each containing a large granite sarcophagus, fifteen feet long and eight feet wide, in which the body of a sacred bull was deposited. In 1852 they had already found thirty of these sarcophaguses containing dead bulls. In front of this tomb is a paved road, on each side of which are arranged stone lions, and before this is a temple with a vestibule. The bull was not the only sacred animal in Egypt. The tombs are full of the mummies of dogs, wolves, birds, and crockodiles that were embalmed and buried by the priests. It is strange that they preferred to worship animals to worshiping human beings. As they wanted to worship nature, they ought to have worshiped its noblest manifestations. But it is said they worshiped the animals because they believed in the transmigration of souls, through the animals up to man. They worshiped flowers, from which fact the Greeks and Romans laughed at them and said: O! sacred nation whose gods grow in gardens.

SACRED MYSTERIES.

In the order of Sacred Mysteries the priests went ahead worshiping the Supreme God, the true and only God, while they continued to teach the religion of the plural gods to the people.

The Egyptians furnished three kinds of Sphinxes. The first was a lion's body with the head of a man on it; the second was the body of a lion with the head of a ram; the third was the body of a lion with the head of a hawk. The Sphinx was the solemn sentinel placed to guard the temple and the tomb, as the Cherubim guarded the gates of Paradise after the supposed expulsion of Adam and Eve. The Cherubim was composed of the figures of parts of a man's body and an eagle's body. The Cherubim consequently had wings. The Persians and Greeks had similar symbolic figures, meant to represent the various powers of the different creatures, combined in one being. The Egyptians also had a Holy of Holies in their temples. The ceremony of the Jewish high priest, placing on the head of the scapegoat the sins of the entire nation, was borrowed from the Egyptians. As Moses was a priest in the Egyptian religion, he doubtless subsequently introduced into the Jewish religion many of the features of his former religion. Many of the customs now in the christian religion can be traced back to Egypt. The Jews derived their custom of circumcision from the Egyptians, and the Egyptians derived it from the Ethiopians. The custom of placing a gold ring on the finger of the bride came from Egypt. There was an Egyptian priest at Thebes, called "Keeper of the Two Doors of Heaven," at least two thousand years before the Pope of Rome assumed to hold the keys. Notwithstanding the plural gods have been knocked out, the doctrines of the natural religions have come into the christian religion. The learned Egyptologist, Samuel Sharp, stated that there are four doctrines common to Egyptian mythology and church orthodoxy. They are these:

1. That the creation and government of the world is not the work of a simple and undivided being, but of one God, made up of several persons, This is the doctrine of the Trinity.

2. That salvation cannot be expected from the justice or mercy of a Supreme Being, Judge, unless an atoning sacrifice is made to him by a divine being.

3. That among the persons who compose the god-head, one, though a god, could suffer pain and be put to death.

4. That a god or man, or a being half a god and half man once lived on earth, born of an earthly mother, but without an earthly father.

The idea of the Madonna and her child, Christ, in her arms was borrowed from the natural religion of Egypt. The Egyptian imaginary goddess, Isis, with her imaginary child, Horus, in her arms, were worshiped as the merciful gods that would save their worshipers from the vengeance of the terrible imaginary judge, or god, Osiris. Isis was, therefore, the Egyptian

Madonna. So Mary, the mother of Christ, was not the first Madonna in this world. The Egyptian Madonna and her child in her arms were imaginary, while the Christian Madonna and her child in her arms were not imaginary, but were sure enough mortals.

TRIAL OF A SOUL BEFORE OSIRIS.

The Egyptians did not believe in confession of sins and repentance, but denied their sins, and tried to purify themselves that way. This is the style of the Christian Scientists of our times.

The Egyptians imagined that the soul was tried before the imaginary Osiris, that some imaginary gods prosecuted the soul, and other imaginary gods defended it and pleaded for it. They had evidently witnessed the trial of a criminal in this life, and consequently imagined that the soul had to go through a similar trial after the death of the body. The most ridiculous part of the trial was where the soul was represented as placing his defenders, lawyers, on the altar to sacrifice them to appease the wrathful Osiris. Lawyers in this life would not allow themselves to be sacrificed in that way for the benefit of their clients. These imaginings proved that there is no telling what ridiculous things the imagination will not imagine. Egypt will be celebrated in history for all time as the land where the children of Israel were first held in slavery for centuries, and on account of their wonderful escape from that bondage. The temples in which the ancient Egyptians used to worship, in the valley of the Nile, were finally buried by deposits from the Nile, and the sands from the desert being blown in over them. They are now being dug up by archiologists, and on their walls they find carved the ancient history, and all the religious beliefs, and representations of the daily life of the Egyptians. There will never be any occasion for any modern city or modern temples to be dug up to find what is going on now in any part of the world, as through the ocean cables the current history, both political and religious, and all other current news of any importance, is being put on record all around the earth. Many inventions that are regarded as modern were in use among the ancient Egyptians.

EGYPTIAN BIBLE.

The Egyptian religion was oral for centuries, but was finally reduced to writing, and was in forty-two sacred books in five classes. The first class consisted of hymns in praise of the gods, and were the most ancient. The other books treated of morals, astronomy, hieroglyphics, geography, ceremonies, the gods, and the education of priests, and medicine. In one of these books is represented, by a picture, a funeral procession, in which the soul of the deceased is represented as the chief mourner, offering prayers to the sun god. Another part of the book represents forty-two gods sitting in judgment on the soul of the deceased, with Osiris as chief justice. Before him are the scales of divine judgment. In one is placed the statue of justice, and in the other the heart of the dead, who stands in person by the balance, while Ambis watches the other scale. The god Horus looks at the plummit to see which way the scale inclines. The god Thoth, the Lord Justifier of the Divine Word, records the sentence.

Learning, the sciences, and the arts reached a very high state in Egypt. In some respects they excelled the moderns. The pyramids are the wonder of the world. Astronomy reached a high state in Egypt, and also in Babylon, and all the ancient Asiatic nations.

CHAPTER 7.
GREECE.

One branch of the Aryans went to Greece, where they found and mixed with a white people called Pelasgians. The country had been known as Pelasgia, but after the mixture of these two peoples it became known first as Hellas and then Greece. From that time the whole people have been known as Greeks, and have played one of the grandest parts in all human history, in both politics and religion. How long they retained republican government, electing their own chiefs, is not known, but it is known that in their ancient monarchy their King claimed to be the son of God by his mortal mother, and compelled his sons and daughters to marry each other under the false pretense of keeping his pretended divine blood in his royal family. So that fraud was also played on the people of Greece. But subsequently the Greeks became a highly cultured people, recovered their natural, inalienable right of self-government, in both politics and religion. It was the Grecian Republic that played the great part in both politics and religion.

The ancient republics of Greece and Rome, both Aryan, are more interesting to us Americans than any other nations on the earth. It was their political troubles that served as warnings to guide our forefathers in framing our National Constitution.

The Greek Republic began its career as a Confederacy of slave States. Some of the States became free, while the others remained slave. Then came the civil war between the free and the slave States, commonly called in history the civil war between the Greek Aristocracy and the Greek Democracy, the people of the free States being called the Democracy, resulting in disintegration.

Our Republic began its career as a Confederacy of slave States. Some became free States, while others remained slave States. Then came the civil war between the free States and the slave States, but, thanks to our central government, disintegration was prevented.

The fact that the Greeks disintegrated, owing to

their having no central government over their States to hold them together when civil war should come between them, suggested to our constitutional fathers the necessity of placing a central government over our States to hold them together when civil war should come between them. The result of our civil war proved the wisdom of their course.

From Greece we received the Greek language, which is still taught in nearly all our colleges.

The greatest struggles man has made to recover and preserve his natural right of self-government took place in Greece, Rome, France and America. After severe struggles, self-government was first recovered in Greece, and a Confederacy was formed, in which white slaves were held. Some of the members of that Confederacy became free States, in which all had equal rights before the law. The other members remained slave States. A civil war of twenty-seven years' duration naturally followed between the free States and the slave States, which has generally been called in history the civil war between the Greek Aristocracy and the Greek Democracy. The free State of Athens, the home of culture and refinement, led the Democracy. Sparta led the Aristocracy, conquered the Democracy, and forced on Athens the rule of the Thirty Tyrants. But the Athenians soon drove the Tyrants from the city and restored the Republic. Seeing the disintegrated, crippled condition in which the civil war had left the Greeks, King Philip, of Macedon, became ambitious to rule them. And accordingly intervened in a subsequent civil war between two States of the Confederacy: forced and bribed his way into the Amphictionic Council, the Grecian Congress, as a member of the same, over the resistance of Athens, led by the immortal Demosthenes, who, to his immortal honor let it be remembered, was proof against all King Philip's efforts to bribe him.

Then came the great struggle between King Philip and Demosthenes. It was Republicanism vs. Monarchy. Demosthenes, with the power of his oratory, tried to rally all the Greeks, but owing to the bitterness engendered by their late civil war, and the general demoralization resulting from corruption in public affairs, few responded. The Aristocracy either held back or aided King Philip on account of their hatred of the Democracy. And many of the Democracy held back because of their disgust over corruption at elections, thus practically disintegrating the Confederacy.

Classic Athens gallantly led the forlorn hope, but in the battle of Cheronea King Philip conquered, and became the master of the Greeks. Demosthenes subsequently led a movement to release Athens, but was defeated, and committed suicide to avoid death at the hands of his enemies. Thus ended the first great struggle between Republicanism and Monarchy.

From this career of stoic Greece, it is plain that disintegration led to the death of Republicanism in that historic land.

Moral: The people of a Republic should always avoid disintegration and never resort to civil war, lest ambitious monarchists intervene and conquer all.

Twenty-five hundred years after these troubles were occurring in Greece similar troubles came on our own continent. During our great civil war a civil war came on in the Republic of Mexico. The ambitious monarchist, Napoleon III, of France, took advantage of the troubles in Mexico, as well as in our own Republic, to intervene in Mexico, overthrow the Republic and establish a monarchy there, sending Maximilian over from Europe to be Emperor of Mexico. He and the monarchists of England then thought of intervening in our Republic, conquering us all, adding the South to

Maximilian's empire in Mexico and the North to England's possessions in Canada. Only the fear of a revolt against it on the part of the people of France and England, who sympathized with our Union people who were struggling to maintain the supremacy of the Republic and establish universal liberty, prevented them from making the attempt. These facts lend additional force to the above moral, that the people of a Republic should avoid disintegration and never resort to civil war, lest ambitious monarchists intervene and conquer all.

During the administration of President Monroe our Government assumed the position that no European monarchy should ever intervene in the affairs of this hemisphere to establish monarchy. This was called the Monroe Doctrine. During our civil war we were in no condition to enforce it, but as soon as our war was over our Government ordered Nepoleon to take his French army out of Mexico and let the Mexican people determine for themselves what government they wanted. Napoleon withdrew his army at once, and the Mexicans killed Maximilian and re-established the Republic. To the everlasting honor of our Southern soldiers let it be remembered that they were anxious to join the Union soldiers and drive Maximilian and his French army out of Mexico, but no occasion offered. It is plain that we repeated the career of the Greek Republic, because we started out with the same conditions under which that Republic began its career. As human nature is the same in all generations, this proves that like political conditions will always produce like political results unless special care is taken to prevent.

Athens, in the free State of Athens, was the most cultured city in all Greece.

RELIGION.

Here their imaginations created separate gods for everything in nature or the universe, till they had hundreds of gods, and names for all of them. In fact, so many gods that a Greek knew not to which god he ought to pray when he wanted a particular relief. In that case he erected an altar to some unknown god and prayed to him for relief. What a great relief the one only God with full power to grant any and all relief would have been to the overburdened memory of the Greek. They also had goddesses for everything in nature. Strange as it may appear to us, they also imagined that these imaginary gods and goddesses had amours and children. They imagined that they had three generations of gods; that the first generation were nature gods, and that the third generation were spiritual gods, but just like men and women, and dwelt on Mount Olympus, on the northern border of Greece. They imagined that those human-like gods and goddesses lived on imaginary foods called nectar and ambrosia, and were thereby made immortal.

The brains of the Greek Aryans traveled over about the same line of religious thought that had previously been gone over by the Hindoo Aryans in India. To Greece they brought nature worship, the worship of the sun, the moon, the stars, the earth, the sky, the ocean, the atmosphere, the storms, fire, &c. From this start they went on and imagined that some of these objects in nature which were first worshiped as gods married and produced a second generation of gods, myths, they called Titans, and that some of these Titans married and produced a third generation of imaginary gods, called Olympian Gods. And also the Nymphs of the Ocean. Most of the names of the Greek gods they borrowed from the imaginary gods of the Egyptians, not using the Egyptian word, but using the corresponding Greek word. As Egypt and Greece were but a few hundred miles apart, and sailing ships were constantly carrying commerce from one to the other, the former very naturally influenced the latter, as it was then just beginning to develop. The Greeks allowed their imaginations to run till they imagined that each tribe of them had its separate god; that each family had its separate household god, and that each individual had an invisible spirit always hovering about him to look after his welfare, which they did not dignify with the name of God, but they called it his Genius.

GREEK BIBLE.

Among the Greeks the priests were not as great men as they were in other nations. In other nations they and the prophets wrote the Bibles for the people, but they did not do so for the Greeks. The Greek Bible was written by two Greek poets, Hesiod and Homer, and is to be found in their poems, called Hesiod's Theogeny and Homer's Iliad. In his poem Hesiod first gives his idea of creation, or how the earth and the heavens came into existence, and then goes on to give an account of the imaginary birth and life of each of the three generations of their imaginary gods. He represents them as no better than the meanest of mortals. Tells how the Greeks imagined that they feasted, got drunk and did all kinds of mean things. He represents those imaginary gods as carrying on wars among themselves; and even represents the Mythical Goddesses as fighting each other. The imaginary children of the imaginary Titans were called Olympian Gods, as the Greeks imagined that they resided up on Mount Olympus on the northern border of Greece.

HOMER'S ILIAD.

Homer represented the Olympian Gods as living together on Mount Olympus, feasting, making love, making war, playing the hypocrite with each other, getting angry and making up. He represents them as feeding on nectar and ambrosia, which imaginary foods, the Greeks imagined, made the gods immortal. He even represents them as getting drunk on nectar and becoming very boisterous at their feasts; feasting all day long and going to bed at sundown; as fighting among themselves, and some times with mortals, and getting whipped by the mortals, and then going back to Zens, their Supreme God, on Olympus, to complain to him about it like a boy going to his father to complain that some other boy had whipped him. He also represented them as taking part in the siege of Troy on both sides.

GODS OF THE ARTISTS.

To the imaginary gods the Greek sculptors also paid their attention. They chiseled out of marble representations of the personal appearance of the gods as they supposed they would appear if they could only be seen by the mortal eye. These marble busts, and some times statues, were by some called idols, and the separate temple of each god had his marble bust set up in it for his worshipers to look at. Some accused the worshipers of worshiping the idol, or bust, instead of the imaginary god it represented. The same god represented in marble presented different appearances according to the different conceptions of how he would appear could he be seen by the different artists who chiseled him out. The artists, in painting, also represented the supposed appearance of the different gods in paintings on the walls inside of their temples. These paintings also represented different appearances of the same god according as the different artists had different conceptions of how they thought the god would appear if he could only be seen.

These different representations of the same god told at once as to whether the artist considered the god a fierce god or a mild and gentle god. If the artist was of a fierce nature he would give that appearance to the bust or painting of the god, and if he was of a gentle nature himself he would give a gentle appearance to the painting or bust of the god.

Similarly men now in expressing their opinions of God give their own attributes to him. If they are tyranical in their own natures they attribute that nature to God; if on the contrary they are not tyranical in their own natures, but are gentle and kind, they represent God as a kind and forgiving father. This fact that men always attribute their own natures to God is what caused the great infidels to declare that every man is the creator of his own god. They should have said, every man is the creator of his own idea of God.

GODS OF THE GREEK PHILOSOPHERS.

The Greeks produced some infidels, who were persecuted because they denied the existence of the imaginary gods. Protagoras was sentenced to death and his writings were burned because he denied the existence of the imaginary gods. Now we all know they had no existence. Diogenes was denounced as an atheist because he denied the existence of the imaginary gods, and a reward of a talent was offered to any one who should kill him. About this time came Socrates, the great Greek philosopher, who, while he did not deny the existence of the imaginary gods, taught the existence of the Supreme God. He looked upon the imaginary gods as not gods, but simply angels, archangels and saints. In other words, Socrates in his philosophy abolished them as gods, reduced them to the ranks of angels, archangels and saints, and left only the Supreme God to worship, and thus arrived at the monotheism, the one only God.

Socrates started out from the standpoint of nature to search for the origin of everything, even to the finding of God. Socrates believed in and argued in favor of the immortality of the soul. Plato, that other great Greek philosopher and monotheist, assumed the existence of God, and declared that everything came from him as creator. Aristotle was not as pronounced a monotheist as was Plato.

STOICAL SYSTEM.

The Greek stoics believed that there was but one being, and that from him flowed the universe, and to him returned everything in regular cycles. That everything is either God or a manifestation of God.

They believed that the soul exists after death of the body, in a future state, much better than this for a time, but in a certain cyle it is absorbed into the Divine Being. That in that better world there would be a judgment day held on the conduct of each person; there friends and relations would recognize each other and dwell together during the cycle preceding absorption.

EPICUREANS.

The Greek Epicureans believed that the imaginary gods had an existence, and that they enjoyed themselves very highly, and that they were immortal; but they did not believe in any future state for mortals, and rejected prayer and all religion, regarding it as a curse to man. Such were the principal theological beliefs of the Greek philosophers.

The sacred mysteries were practiced in Greece. The Greek religion was established by law, and was the national religion in a republic.

CHAPTER 8.
ROME.

As long as time shall last the history of Rome, in both politics and religion, will be intensely interesting and instructive.

Led by Junius Brutus, man recovered self-government in Rome, but denied it to his fellow-man in the establishment of a Patrician Republic.

The Patricians, a rich and privileged class, who owned many slaves, were, by provisions of the Constitution, the ruling power in Rome, so much so that the government could, very appropriately, be described as a *government of the Patricians, by the Patricians, and for the Patricians*. The Patricians comprised about one-tenth of the Romans. The other nine-tenths consisted of Plebeians and white slaves.

This being the situation in Rome, a struggle began

for *equal rights before the law*. The leaders of the people, the brothers Gracchi, for daring to ask equal rights for the people, were slaughtered by the Patricians and their property confiscated. The people's party, however, subsequently gained power under Cinna, the father-in-law of Julius Cæsar, by his first wife, and Marius, the uncle of Cæsar, when the Patrician leaders were in turn put to death, and equal rights before the law established in their Constitution for all Romans; but the struggle continued between the Patricians and Plebeians for the control of the government. And in retaliation, Sylla, the great Patrician general, returned from Asia with his army, and in sight of Rome destroyed the people's army, putting all prisoners to death. Sylla then dictated a Constitution providing for the perpetual rule of the Patricians, and to make sure that that rule should be in no danger of overthrow, executed five thousand leading men of the people's party.

But in spite of the Sylla Constitution and that great slaughter of leaders, the people's party again gained control, this time under Cæsar, Pompey and Crassus, and strange as it may seem, no retaliation was made on account of the Sylla slaughter.

ROME.   65

After the expiration of Cæsar's consulship, he led his army into Gaul, which country he conquered and reconciled to Roman rule. But after the death of Crassus, the Patrician leaders, desiring to regain control, seduced Pompey, then First Consul of Rome, into a movement against Cæsar, demanding his retirement from the army, and the dismissal of his troops to civil life and poverty after nine years' service in Gaul.

In justice to his army, himself and the people, whose greatest leader he was, he declined to comply with their demand. Civil war came, and finally the contending forces met at Pharsalia, Cæsar in command of the army that represented the cause of the people and the Tribunes, and Pompey in command of the army that represented the cause of the Patricians and the Senate. A great many of the Patrician leaders, Senators and their sons, were on the field with Pompey, and many of them were slain in that bloody battle, which resulted in a great victory for Cæsar and the people's cause. Pompey fled to Egypt, where he was treacherously murdered. Finally Cæsar destroyed the Patrician army, commanded by the two sons of Pompey at Munda, and returned to Rome conqueror of the Patricians. And was, again, triumphantly elected

First Consul of Rome, Mark Antony, his most intimate friend, being elected one of his associate Consuls. Cæsar was then at the most critical period of his life. Champion in the people's cause, he might have been the first Washington of the world, and loved by all mankind, had he not allowed the siren voice of ambition to whisper in his ear: "*Cæsar, Emperor of Rome!*"

The Patrician Senators, secretly hearing of Cæsar's ambitious designs, at once concluded to be the first to offer him the crown, and on that ground to claim the right to control his administration as Emperor. They accordingly voted him the crown, and had him sounded to see if he would accept. But not being willing to owe it to his hereditary enemies, whom he had so recently conquered, Cæsar declined the proffered crown. But the Patrician Senators, having committed themselves in favor of making him monarch, and secretly knowing that he could rely on most of the army, Cæsar concluded to *sound the people*, and if he didn't meet with too much opposition from them, declare himself Emperor. Accordingly, in the presence of Cæsar and a large concourse in the Forum, by prearrangement a diadem was placed on the head of his statue, which stood upon the Rostra. The people failed to greet it with any signs of approval, and two indignant Tribunes tore it from the statue. Cæsar failed to disclaim any connection with the crowning of his statue, which he would have done then and there had he not been seeking the crown. Riding on horseback, in the street, shortly after, he was by prearrangement hailed as King. Reining up, Cæsar replied: "I am not King but Cæsar." Some Tribunes tried to arrest the hailers, and a fight ensued. Cæsar had the Tribunes punished by the Senate for daring to interfere with his friends. And soon after, on the 15th day of February following, when presiding at the Lupercalia, the ancient Carnival of Rome, Antony, as a last *sounding of the people*, offered him the crown, saying: "The people give you this by my hand." Cæsar hearing no shouts of approval, and seeing marked disapproval in the faces of the people, turned it off, exclaiming: "*Romans have no King but God!*" This sentiment was greeted with shouts of joy.

Cæsar's refusal of the crown when offered by the Patrician Senators, and then soliciting it from the people, caused the Patricians to *suspect* he intended to make himself Emperor and lean toward the people, his old friends, and away from the Patricians, on account of which they concluded to put him to death. And finally the evening previous to the Ides of March, the conspirators met at the house of Caius Cassius, and agreed to assassinate Cæsar the next morning in the Senate chamber.

That night his wife, Calpurnia, dreamed that Cæsar was murdered, and she saw him ascend into heaven and received by the hand of God. Calpurnia, troubled by her dream the next morning, persuaded him not to go to the Senate.

At the same hour the conspirators, who had some gladiators placed in the temple near by, to be called to their assistance if necessary, and Cicero who fully sympathized with the conspiracy, took their seats in the Senate. And as Cæsar came not, sent one of their number, Decimus Brutus, in whom Cæsar had great confidence, to induce him to come to the Senate. On their way a man slipped into the hand of Cæsar a paper, telling him to read it. He neglected to do so. Had he read it, it would have saved him, for it exposed the conspiracy and the names of the conspirators. Arriving at the Senate, Cæsar took his seat as First Consul, when the conspirators approached him under the pretense of submitting petitions. Tullius Cimber's request was refused, whereupon he caught hold of Cæsar's gown imploringly, and at the same time Caius Cassius, from behind, stabbed Cæsar in the throat. Cæsar involuntarily shrieked, and rising, caught Cassius by the arm, when Marcus Brutus stabbed him in the breast. Throwing up his arms to protect his face from threatening daggers, Cæsar sank to the floor in death. Brutus, waving his dagger, shouted: *"Cicero! liberty is restored in Rome!"* All fled from the scene. The conspirators rushed into the streets, shouting to the people: *"The tyrant is dead and Rome is free!"* The excited people crowded the streets, where Brutus and Cassius spoke to them in defense of their act, declaring that they had killed Cæsar to save the Republic. Brutus and Cassius were leaders in the people's party, but as they were acting with the Patrician Senators, the hereditary enemies of the people, the people believed, at that time, that Cæsar was slain more to place the Patricians back in power than to save the Republic.

Through fear the dead body of Cæsar was left alone where it fell till nightfall, when three of his own servants bore it to his home. That afternoon Lepidus marched his troops into the city and stationed them in the Forum. And all that night was passed by the conspirators, including Cicero, in the Capitol, trying to agree upon what should be done next.

Through fear of Antony, now Chief Executive of Rome, Lepidus and his troops, who were Cæsar's friends, and the people, they finally resolved to allow Cæsar's body to receive a respectful funeral, and to ask Antony to meet with them in the Senate.

The next morning the Senate met in the temple of Terra, Antony presiding as Consul. After a short speech from him, Cicero led off in behalf of the conspirators, in one of the ablest speeches of his life, advocating *peace, reconciliation*, and oblivion of the past. The Senate voted pardon and oblivion for the past, and in due course of time Cæsar's body, the dress of which had not been changed, was brought to the Forum and placed on the Rostra from which he had so often spoken to the people. After a reading of the votes of confidence and honors the Senate had recently heaped on Cæsar, and *the oath the Senators had all recently taken to protect him from assassination*, of which he had expressed apprehension, Antony read the will of Cæsar, in which the people were left about five dollars each, and a public park on the Tiber. The will, also, made Octavius his general heir, and Demicus Brutus his heir in case Octavius failed. Antony then exhibited to the people Cæsar's wounds and bloody gown, exciting the people against the conspirators. His funeral oration ended, a funeral pile was made, there in the Forum, from the platform, chairs and articles of clothing thrown upon it by the people, upon which the body of the great Caesar was *burned*. His unconsumed remains were gathered up and buried in the Tomb of the Caesars in Campus Martius. The grief of the common people, who chiefly composed the audience, was great.

Antony's Consulship soon ended, and Cicero became Chief Executive, and for a year after the death of Cæsar through him the Patrician party had control of Rome, when Antony, Lepidus and Octavius united and marched triumphantly into Rome with the entire Western army. Cicero fled before them to his country seat, where he was pursued and beheaded. Antony and Octavius then marched against Brutus and Cassius. They met at Phillippi. A desperate battle was fought. Brutus and Cassius were defeated, and committed suicide to avoid being captured and murdered by their victorious enemies.

In due course of time Octavius Cæsar was installed

Emperor of Rome. And thus, about forty-three years B. C., perished the great Roman Republic, and a Cæsar was on the throne, doubtless as was intended by Julius Cæsar. The conspirators and all who sympathized with them were then put to death.

WHY DID THE ROMAN PEOPLE SUBMIT TO MONARCHY?

History informs us they had seen the public offices go by the power of money instead of the will of the people, for so many years, they thought that true Republicanism had been destroyed already by the corrupt use of money at elections. That no poor man, however worthy, could be elected to office. That the people, disgusted with that state of affairs, felt as though they would as soon see the offices go by hereditary right as by the power of Patrician money, and consequently submitted to monarchy.

From this career of Rome it is plain: *First:* That the civil wars of the Romans were caused by the Patricians denying the Plebeians *equal rights before the law*, and murdering their leaders for daring to ask for the same. *Second:* That the Republic was destroyed by the ambitious desire of the Cæsars to rule over the

Patricians. *Third:* That the bringing about of that result was made possible by the corrupt conduct of the rich Patrician leaders in purchasing voters at the polls.

Moral: Man should never deny to his fellow-man equal rights before the law, and the people of a Republic should always see that their elections express the will of the people and not the power of money.

Our constitutional forefathers framed our Constitution providing for a People's Republic, excepting as to the negroes, whom it left in slavery. Here also man denied to his fellow-man equal rights before the law, and punishment comes for it in civil war.

Our forefathers also framed our Government after the general plan of the Roman Government, the legislative body being divided into a Senate and House, the only difference being that our House is called a House of Representatives, while theirs was called a House of Triunes; but in both cases they were elected by the people. Our President corresponds to the First Consul of Rome, only being called President instead of First Consul.

RELIGION.

As long as human beings remain on this earth the history of the Roman Republic, its religion, its politics and its military career will be studied by mankind. The religion of Rome was established by law as the national religion, although Rome was a Republic. It consisted of a worship, a ritual, a ceremony. A Roman could believe whatever he pleased to believe and the authorities never molested him so long as he observed the external ceremonies of the church. Cicero as First Consul was by law chief pontiff, head of the church, and as such claimed to believe in religion, but as a philosopher he denied the existence of the gods, and made an argument to that effect in his De Natura Deorum. The Roman law permitted any foreigners to come and reside in Rome and bring along with them their gods and worship them according to the law of their own country.

They considered it the duty of Jews in Rome to worship the Jewish god; of the Egyptians in Rome to worship the gods of Egypt; that it was the duty of every man while in Rome to worship the gods of his own country.

As long as the Christians in Rome were looked upon as a Jewish sect, they were not molested by the authorities, but when they came to be understood as a departure from Judaism, they were regarded as hereties to a national faith. They were then also looked upon as enemies to the Roman gods, and were put to death as such. At this time Rome was no longer a republic, but was an empire under the Emperor, Augustus Cæsar.

The religion of Rome was serious and earnest, while that of Greece was sentimental and gay. The gods of Rome were moral and practical, and supposed to be the givers of earthly fortunes. The Roman gods all had official duties to perform, and had no time to indulge in feasts among themselves and to have disgraceful amours, like the Grecian gods of Olympus. While Zeus, the Grecian god, wandered about, having disgraceful adventures, the Roman god, Jupiter Capitolinus, remained at home attending to the duties of his office, which was to make Rome the greatest power in the world, all in the imaginations of the Romans.

HUMAN SACRIFICES.

The Roman worship consisted of sacrifices, prayers and ceremonies. They sacrificed many men and animals. They thought they could bribe their imaginary gods into granting them favors by murdering a human being and giving his flesh to them.

The Roman gladiators who were thrown into the amphitheater to be slain by the wild animals were the Christians and the convicted criminals of Rome.

The Roman people were made up from different branches of the Aryans, who were known in Italy as Latins, Sabines, Etruscans, and Kelts. These different branches brought into Rome their different gods. The Romans believed that some of their imaginary gods inhabited the hills of Rome. The Romans had no Bible. They had no favorite gods, but worshiped each in turn, according to what kind of favor they wanted to ask of him. They believed in one supreme god, they called Jupiter Optimis-Maximis, of whom all the other gods were but qualities and attributes. But more than any other nation they went on and personified and deified every separate power of nature till they had more gods than any one Roman could remember. So some times when they wanted to ask a favor they could not remember which god had the power to grant that kind of a favor, and therefore had to ask it of some unknown god or the supreme god, and some times a new god was created for the special occasion. They had a god of talkativeness and a god of silence. They believed that pestilence, defeat in battle, blight, &c., were dangerous beings, whose hostility could only be placated by sacrifices. They also had gods for Modesty, Prudicitia, for Fidelity, Fides, for Concord, Concordia, and also their household gods. It is supposed that each family had a pet name for its own household god. It was the duty of the pontiffs to create new gods. The Romans had a goddess, pecunia, money, derived from Pecus, cattle, dating from the time when the circulating medium consisted of cows and sheep. When copper money came the pontiffs created a god for that, which they named Æsculaceus, and when silver money was coined they created a god for that they named Argentarius. So they had a separate god for everything.

PLANETS NAMED AFTER THE GODS.

The Roman gods that are most interesting to us are Jupiter, Saturn, Mars, Venus, Saturn and Neptune, because their names were given to the most beautiful planets of our solar system, at which we are so fond of gazing by night. As Jupiter was the most powerful Roman god, his name was given to the largest planet in our solar system. As Venus, the Goddess of Love, was the most beautiful Roman goddess, her name was given to the most beautiful planet in our system. As Mars was the God of War, his name was given to the red planet because its color was suggestive of blood.

PANTHEON.

The Roman pantheon contained three classes of gods and goddesses:

1. The old Italian imaginary divinities, Latin, Sabine and Etruscan, adopted by the government.

2. The imaginary gods created by the College of Pontiffs for moral and political purposes.

3. The imaginary gods of the Greeks, imported with a change of name by the literary admirers and imitators of the Greeks.

As each god had its separate temple in which it was worshiped, the temple called the Pantheon was a building in which all the gods could be worshiped at the same time. The Romans had no busts or statues of their gods and goddesses in the early times, but when they got that idea from the Greeks, they crowded their temples with them.

CAPITOL.

The magnificent Temple of the Capitol at Rome consisted of three parts—a nave sacred to Jupiter, the greatest god, and two wings or aisles, one dedicated to Juno, the greatest goddess, female Jupiter, the goddess of intellectuality, also goddess of womanhood, devoted to matrons and virgins, and the other to Minerva. This temple was nearly square, being two hundred and fifteen feet long, and two hundred feet wide, and the wealth accumulated in it was immense. The walls and roof were marble, covered with gold and silver. Jupiter, Juno and Minerva were called the Trinity at the Capitol, and they represented Power, Affection and Wisdom.

After these three Capitoline deities, Jupiter, Juno and Minerva and Janus, the old Sabine god of beginnings, from whom January, the first month in the year, derived its name. The Romans worshiped a series of imaginary deities, who may be classified as follows:

1. Gods, representing the powers of nature; Sol, god of the sun, a Sabine deity.

2. Luna, goddess of the moon, also a Sabine deity.

3. Neptune, god of the sea.

II. Gods of the human relations:

1. Vesta, the goddess of household fire, who

sanctified the home. When all Rome came to be regarded as one family, she became the goddess of that family home, and her temple, which still stands in Rome, not far from the Forum, in the south end of the city, became the fireside of Rome, in which always burned the sacred fire, watched and kept burning by the vestal virgins. The vestal virgins were honored more highly than any other people in Rome, even more highly than the highest officials. In the worship of the goddess Vesta could be seen the love of home, respect for family life, and hatred of impurity and immodesty. The goddess Vesta was also called Mater Stata, that is, the immovable mother.

2. The Lares and Penates. The Lares were supposed to be the souls of ancestors residing in the home and guarding it. Their images were kept in a room, or little chapel in the house, called the Lararium, and were crowned by the master of the house, to cause them to be propritious. The father conducted the domestic worship, whether it was to pray or make a sacrifice. The Penates were supposed to be beings of a higher order than the Lares, but being supposed to perform about the same offices as the Lares. Thus the Roman considered himself surrounded in his own house by invisible friends and guardians.

3. The Genius. Each person was also believed to have an invisible spirit, called a Genius, always hovering about him, from whom he was supposed to have received his living, power and vital force. Places as well as persons had their Geniuses. On coins are found the Genius of Rome. The Genius of Rome was considered as taking his rank with the highest gods.

III. Gods of the human soul:
1. Mens, god of the mind, intellect.
2. Pudicitia, goddess of chastity.
3. Pietas, god of piety, reverence for parents.
4. Fides, god of fidelity.
5. Concordia, concord.
6. Virtus, courage.
7. Spes, Hope.
8. Pallor, fear.
9. Voluptas, pleasure.

IV. Deities of rural and other occupations.
1. Tellus, god of the earth.
2. Saturnus, Saturn. Saturn was the god of planting and sowing.
3. Ops, goddess of the harvest.
4. Mars, originally an agricultural god, dangerous to crops; afterward god of war.

5. Sylvanus, the god of wood.
6. Faunus, an old Italian deity, the patron of agriculture.
7. Cerres, goddess of the cereal grasses.
8. Liber, god of vine and wine.
9. Bona Dea, the good goddess. The idea of her feast was a chaste marriage, as helping to preserve the human race.
10. Flora. She was the goddess of flowers and blossoms. Great license was practiced at her worship.

These were the principal deities of the Romans, whose worship was popular, although they had many others. This list of gods proves that the Romans worshiped the powers of earth more than they did the heavenly bodies. The Italians cared more for the country than they did for the city, and Rome was founded by country people. From the Romans we got the Latin classics.

PHALLIC WORSHIP.

In Rome, where now stands the Quirinal, the residence of the King of Italy, once stood the temple of Phallic worship—the worship of the reproductive organs. History proves that worship, in ancient times, extended around the globe. The organs were worshiped by many people as the origin of life. They are undoubtedly the origin of people who now come, but the first people who came had no people back of them to reproduce them, and consequently had to come from germs of life by evolution. That worship also became spiritual. In time they claimed that they did not worship the organs, but worshiped an invisible power, the imaginary Phallic god, back of the organs, which they asserted gave their creative power, as the sun-god was supposed to give the sun its power. It is claimed that the christian cross and other emblems came from the emblems of this worship.

CHAPTER 9.

GERMANY.

That branch of Aryans called the Teutonic, that subsequently became known as Germans and Scandinavians, left Central Asia, traveled northwest and spread over Northern Central Europe. Some of them settled in what is now known as Germany and Holland, facing the North Sea, while the others settled all around the shores of the Baltic Sea, peopling the region where now stands St. Petersburg, on the eastern shore in Russia, and what was then called Scandinavia, but is now called Sweden, Norway and Denmark, on the western shore of the Baltic. The Germans went into Europe after the Keltic tribes, and before the Aryan Slavi, who are now known as Russians. The Romans, under Julius Cæsar, tried to drive the Germans out of Germany, but the Germans whipped the Romans, even

GERMANY. 85

under that great General, and held their country. While the Druids prohibited any communication of their beliefs in writing, the German Scalds put all their belief into popular songs, and reverenced literature as a gift from the gods. Still, but little came down concerning these German tribes till Cæsar and Tacitus wrote their account of them.

REPUBLICAN GOVERNMENT.

Tacitus declared that their government was republican, their leaders being elective, and their powers being limited. Their leaders were allowed to decide the less important matters, while the principal questions were settled at public meetings of the people.

These meetings were held regularly, and were presided over by the chief, and decided all public affairs. Tacitus said they were distinguished as a liberty loving people. They were also distinguished from other nations as allowing only one wife to one man.

NATURE WORSHIP.

Cæsar described them as worshiping the sun, moon and fire, but as having no regular priests, and paying little regard to sacrifices. He said that women, whom they reverenced very highly, were their augurs and diviners, as prophets, but they did not convert them into goddesses. That they reverenced chastity, and considered it conducive to health and strength. That they were a pastoral, rather than an agricultural people; that no one owned land, but each had it assigned to him temporarily. This was said to be to prevent amassing wealth and losing warlike habits.

That they were fond of making inscriptions on the rocks and other objects which were called Runic inscriptions.

GERMAN GODS.

Tacitus found in some of their ancient hymns, or ballads, the only historic monuments they had—the names of a god they called Tuisto, a god they imagined had been born from the earth, and the name of a god they imagined was the son of Tuisto, called Mannus. The other gods of the Germans Tacitus called Mars, Mercury and Hercules. They built no temples to their gods, but worshiped them in the groves, which were called sacred groves, after the gods had been worshiped in them. They had neither busts, statues nor paintings of their gods. The German imagination did not create many gods.

They fought with cavalry, supported by infantry. Augustus Cæsar gave up all attempts to conquer the Germans, and only carried on war against them to revenge the destruction of Varnus and his three legions by the famous German chief, Arminius, or Herrman.

The Roman historian, Tacitus, declared that the Germans were as warlike as the Romans, and were only inferior to them in weapons and discipline. He declared that Arminius was the liberator of Germany, although he died at the early age of thirty-seven, unconquered in war. He also declared that the Germans were all a blue-eyed, yellow-haired people, with large bodies, whose wealth was in their flocks and herds. They, like their modern descendants, drank beer and Rhenish wine. Subsequently they, as Goths, Vandals, Lombarge and Franks, destroyed the Roman empire. Most of the Germans who have settled in our country have proven themselves good citizens and a liberty loving people.

CHAPTER 10.
SCANDINAVIA.

The branch of the Teutonic tribes of Aryans that settled in Scandinavia, and thus became known a Scandinavians, made a great history, which has exercised great influence on modern Europe. They, like their German brethren down in Germany, were a liberty loving people. Their General Assemblies, or Things, as they were called, were the origin of the English Parliament.

REPUBLICAN GOVERNMENT.

The old grandfather was the chief of all his descendants, as well as their priest. But all of the men in a neighborhood who were not slaves, captives in war or their children, were called freemen, and met in a meeting they called the Thing, where they decided disputes, laid down social regulations, and determined on public measures. The Thing was, therefore, legislature, court of justice, and executive council all in one body. Once a year, in some central place, there was held a similar meeting to settle the affairs of the whole country, called the Land-Thing, or the All-Thing. At this the Chief Executive was chosen for the entire country, to serve only one year, and he had the power to appoint subordinate officers, called Yarls, to preside over large districts. No matter by what title they called the Chief Executive, he was practically only the President of a Republic, and to call him anything else would be a misnomer.

The people were classified into land-holders, who were called freemen, and slaves, who were captives in war, or their children.

The slaves did domestic services and tilled the soil, while the freemen went to war. Their highest ambition was to die on the battle-field, believing if they died there they would go at once to the halls of Odin. Rather than die in their beds some of them when sick would plunge into the sea. When not fighting they were fond of feasting, and the man that could drink the most beer was regarded as the best man. The custom of drinking toasts came from them to us through our English ancestors. On all public occasions they first drank to Odin and then to other deities, and then to the memory of the dead, in what was called gravebeer. The English first drink to their Queen, as we first drink to our President.

They had a very high respect for the women. They admired them for their modesty, common sense and force of character more than for their facinations.

The wife carried the keys to the house, and some times divorced the husband for some offences, and took back their dowerys. The people highly honored their poets. Their poems described the historic scenes of the Scandinavians.

The Scandinavians were a liberty loving people. Their General Assembly, or Things, as they were called, were the origin of the English Parliament.

In Scandinavia the Teutonic imagination ran till it created many gods, but not till they arrived in Iceland were its creations placed in a Bible.

SCANDINAVIAN BIBLE.

The Scandinavians had a Bible, which consisted of an account of creation, old poems and ballads that had been composed by different ancient Scandinavians, but were put into two books, called Eddas. The first book, or Poetic Edda, which was the fountain of Scandinavian mythology, consisted of thirty-seven poems, old songs and ballads, which had come down from ancient times in the mouths of the people, but were only first collected and committed to writing by Sacmind, a Christian priest of Iceland, in the eleventh century, who did that for the Scandinavians, who had settled in Iceland, and had there preserved the ideas, manners and religion of the Teutonic people in their purity for many centuries, and whose Eddas and Eagas are the chief source of our knowledge of the race. Sacmind was a bard, or scald, as well as a priest, and one of his own poems, the Sun-Song, is in his Edda. As the old grandmothers used to repeat those ballads and poems relating to the gods to their grandchildren by the firesides of the old farm houses in Iceland, and the book now repeats them to the people, they call that book Edda, which word means grandmother.

The poetic Edda consists of thirty-seven poems, and is in two parts, the first containing mythical poems concerning the gods and creation; the second, the legends of the heroes of Scandinavian history.

The first poem in the first part of the poetic Edda is called the Voluspa, or Wisdom of Vala. The Vala was a prophetess, supposed to possess great supernatural knowledge. The Voluspa gives an account of creation, saying that, in effect, everything came from space or chaos. That the first object was created by nature, and evolution was an immense giant they called Ymer; that neither the sun, the moon, nor the stars, nor anything else had any existence before Ymer; that he came as is here described; that there first came a bright shining world of flame to the south, and another, a cloudy and dark one, toward the north. Torrents of venom flowed from the last into the abyss and froze and filled it full of ice. But the air oozed up through it in icy vapors, which were melted into living drops by a warm breath from the south, and from these came the giant Ymer. From him, continues the Voluspa, came a race of wicked giants. Afterwards from these same drops of fluid seeds, children of heat and cold, came the mundane cow, whose milk fed the giants. There arose also, in a mysterious manner, Bor, the father of three sons, Odin, Vili and Ve, who, after several adventures—having killed the giant Ymer, and made out of his body heaven and earth—proceeded to form a man and a woman named Ask and Emlora, Adam and Eve. Chaos having thus disappeared, Odin became the All-Father, creator of gods and men, with earth for his wife and the powerful Thor for his oldest son.

The resemblance between the Greek and Scandinavian accounts of the origin of the gods and men is very striking.

Having given this account of the formation of the world, of the gods and the first couple of mortals, the Edda next speaks of night and day, of the sun and moon, of the rainbow bridge from earth to heaven, and of the great ash tree, where the gods sit in council. It also gives an account of all the different imaginary gods and goddesses and their marriages. These imaginary gods were supposed to dwell on a mountain called Valkola, after the style of the Olympian gods of Greece, and to feast every day with the heroes who had fallen in battle. Like the Olympian gods, they had their adventures in the imaginations of the Scandinavians and Icelanders. For hell they had a female goddess, whom they called Queen Hela. The many stories of the gods will not be related here. According to this mythology the earth will be destroyed by fire and afterwards renewed.

GODS OF THE SCANDINAVIANS.

The Scandinavians believed that this life, in all its departments, was simply a struggle between light and darkness, heat and cold, right and wrong, and so on. Living in such a cold place, their imaginations created a cold place, where people are always freezing, for hell. The Egyptians, living in such a hot climate, thought there must be a hot place, where people would always be suffering from heat.

They had a god of light, a god of darkness, a god of right and a god of wrong, and so on; and they believed these imaginary gods were always at war. They were very fond of war themselves. They regarded Odin as their most powerful god, and also regarded him as the Alfader (All-Father), because he was the the father of all the gods; and as the Valfudir (Choosing Father), because he chooses all those who fall in battle as his sons. The names of their gods in the order of their rank were Odin, Thor, Baldur, Njord, Freyja, Tyr, Bragi, and so on. There were also many goddesses in the Valhalla, of whom the Edda mentions Frigga, Saga and many others. The most singular god of all was their god, called Heimdall, who was also called the White God.

They claim that he was the son of nine virgins, who were all sisters, and that he was a very sacred and powerful deity. Here comes the story of a god being born of virgins long prior to the story of Christ and the Virgin Mary. When such a whopper as this is told, it is time to stop giving any further account of the imaginary gods of the Scandinavians.

The resemblance between the Scandinavian mythology and the Zoroaster mythology is very close.

SCANDINAVIAN WORSHIP.

The Scandinavian worship was simple, and at first carried on in the groves, but later they worshiped in temples. They held three great festivals during the year. The first festival was in honor of the sun, and was held with sacrifices, feasting and great mirth. This was held in the winter solstice, on the longest night of the year, which was called the Mother Night, as that which produced the rest. This feast was called Yul, whence comes the English Yule, the old name of Christmas, which festivals took its place when the Scandinavians became christians. The second festival was held in the spring, in honor of the earth, to ask for fruitful crops. The third festival was also held in the spring, in honor of Odin. The sacrifices offered at these festivals were first, fruits; second, animals, and occasionally, in later times, human beings.

The people believed in, first, divine interposition: second, fixed destiny; third, in their own force and courage. The infidels among them laughed at the gods, some challenging them to fight with them. One warrior said Odin alone was worthy of his steel. It was considered lawful to fight the gods. The northern nations had their soothsayers as well as their priests. They believed in all kinds of absurd charms.

TEMPLE AT UPSAL.

In the great temple at Upsal, in Sweden, sacrifices were offered every ninth year. The King and all prominent persons were required to come with offerings. Great crowds came together on those occasions. Nine human beings, usually slaves or captives, were sacrificed. The bodies of the human sacrifices were buried in groves, which were ever afterward regarded as sacred groves.

There are the remains of but few temples in the north, but in the usages and languages of the descendants of those who worshiped him, there are to be found the most permanent remains of the religion of Odin. These descendants all retain in the names of Wednesday, Thursday and Friday the recollections of the chief gods of this mythology.

THEIR HISTORY.

The Scandinavians overran Gaul and Southern Germany, overthrowing four Roman armies, till the Roman General, Marines, met and defeated them. They subsequently reappeared under the name of Northmen, conquering England, as Saxons, in the fifth century, in the ninth as Danes, and in the eleventh as Normans, again overrunning England and France, thus furnishing to England most of its inhabitants, driving most of the original inhabitants back into the mountains.

In A. D. 860 they discovered and settled Ireland, and in 982 A. D. they discovered and settled Greenland, on the western coast of which churches were built, and so on.

Finally, in the year A. D. 1000, by sailing from Greenland, they discovered the American coast, and sailed down it to below where Boston now stands, and five hundred years before Columbus discovered

America they gathered grapes and built houses as far down as Rhode Island.

Having colonized themselves everywhere in northern Europe, and even in Italy and Greece, they have left the familiar stamp of their ideas and habits in all our modern civilization.

Reader, good bye to Scandinavia, and now we will go to the Holy Land.

CHAPTER II.
PALESTINE.

Palestine, or the Holy Land, as it is called by all Christians and Jews, is only one hundred and forty miles long, running north and south, and only forty miles wide, east and west. It is bordered on the east by a desert, or sea of sand, and on the west by the Mediterranean Sea. It has mountain ranges, running north and south only, between which are well watered, fertile valleys. From the top of some of her mountains can be seen all of Palestine and the sea of sand on her east and the beautiful sea of salt water on her west. This little historic land being the original home of the people whose history, laws and literature constitute the Jewish Bible, it is, in a historic sense, the most interesting spot on earth to all Jews and Christians. The mind of the Christian instinctively turns to Jerusalem, where Christ was crucified. The story of the enslavement of the Jews in Egypt, their escape from there, subsequent capture at Jerusalem, and bondage in Babylon, their final release from that and return to Jerusalem, made the history of the children of Israel more romantic than that of any other people on the earth. They belong to the Semitic race, that other great division of white people who have played about as great a part in the history of this world as has been enacted by the Aryan race. The Semitic race, like the Aryan race, was composed of different tribes. These tribes were the Assyrians, the Babylonians, the Phœnicians, the Hebrews, and other Syrian tribes, the Arabs and the Carthaginians. The great history of these different tribes will not be related here. That they all belonged to the same race is proven by the undisputable evidence of language.

RELIGION OF THE SEMITIC RACE.

The minds of the different tribes of the Semitic race, like the minds of the different tribes of Aryans, traveled from nature woship to the worship of the imaginary gods. They, too, had imaginations that created imaginary gods. They all, also, believed in a Supreme God, called in different tribes by the different names of Ilu, Bel, Set, Hadad, Moloch, Chemosh, Jaosh, El, Adon, Asshur. They all believed that the imaginary gods were emenations from the Supreme God, and were rulers of the planets. Like the Aryans, they would go wild over one subordinate god awhile and then over another. The Assyrians, like the Egyptians, often arranged their subordinate gods in triads, as that of Arm, Bel and Ao. Arm wore the head of a fish; Bel wore the horns of a bull; Ao was represented by a serpent. The Semitics, like the Aryans, look upon the gods as powers behind the objects of nature, as the Sun-God behind the sun and so on.

The Semitic worship of these imaginary gods combined cruelty and licentiousness, and was as debasing a superstition as has ever been in the world.

The Greeks, who were not puritans themselves, were shocked at the impure orgies of this worship, and horrified at the sacrifice (murder) of children by the Canaanites and the Carthaginians to appease the anger of imaginary gods.

THE ONE ONLY GOD OF THE JEWS.

Whence came the monotheism of the Jews? Undoubtedly from Abraham, who came about two thousand years before Christ. But where did Abraham get it, and what was back of him? Both Jewish and Mohamedan traditions describe his father, Terah, as an idolator and a maker of idols. That being true, and seeing so many idols about his father's tent all the time, no wonder Abraham became disgusted with the plural gods, knocked them out and left only the Supreme God for himself and his tribe to worship. Socrates did the same for the Greeks. In the book of Genesis Abraham is described as a great Arab Chief, whose government of his tribe was entirely paternal. According to the book of Genesis, only the family god of Abraham was the highest of all gods, the Almighty (Gen., xvii, 1), who was also the god of Isaac (Gen., xxviii, 3), and the god of Jacob (Gen., xxxv, 2). Abraham was chief in both politics and religion, as he was not only chief, but was also priest. But he was priest of the Most High God, not of the local gods of the separate tribes, but of the highest god, above all the rest. Clarke, in his Ten Great Religions, says, as he gathered it from Genesis, Abraham's faith in God was as a Supreme God, not as the only god, and that his monotheism was therefore of an imperfect kind, as it did not exclude a belief in other gods, although they were regarded as inferior to his own. These facts taken into connection with the fact that the Jews worshiped the golden calf at the foot of Mount Sinia, and that Moses, who came about a thousand years after Abraham, found it necessary to make a commandment forbidding them from worshiping any other god but the Supreme God, constitute sufficient proof that the Jews, like all the other Semitics and Aryans, did once worship the imaginary gods.

PROPHETS.

The Jewish prophets were their lawyers and politicians. The mere act of prophesying future events was a very small part of their duty.

CHRIST AND MAHOMET.

As offshoots from the Jewish religion came first the Christian religion, and then the Mohamedan religion. The followers of Christ claimed that he was the son of God. The Jews denied it and crucified him. To get the Roman authorities, who then held Jerusalem as conquerers, to authorize his crucifixion, they falsely accused him of having claimed that he was king of the Jews, and of blasphemy, in this, that he had claimed that he was the son of God. Pontius Pilate, the Roman Judge, before whom Christ was tried, after having heard all the evidence, acquitted him of both charges, taking a bowl of water and washing his hands said: "I wash my hands of this innocent man's blood." Here it was judicially established that Christ never claimed to be the son of God; but, nevertheless, his Jewish accusers and the Roman soldiers took him out and crucified him on Mount Calvary, an immense stone in the shape of a human skull, which was immediately along side of the north wall of the temple, which was at that point the north wall of the city. The temple was the last building in the extreme northeast corner of the city. Christ denied the existence of the plural gods, and his religion is now the prevailing religion in both Europe and America.

Mahomet, an Arab, came later, and denied the existence of the plural gods, and also denied that Christ was the son of God, and thought that there was but one God, but falsely represented him to be a monarchic God. He also falsely claimed to have received revelations from God, after every epileptic fit that he had, in which he fell down and frothed at the mouth. His fits must have caused his imagination to act abnormally and falsely. His followers are as numerous as those of Christ.

The religion of Christ was propagated by the sword, and the religion of Mahomet was also propagated by the sword. To the age of thirty Christ was a common house carpenter. He only preached three years, and was then crucified. In his early manhood, Mahomet was a common shepherd tending his flock. He died a natural death.

FREE MASONRY.

In all ages and countries mankind have attached more or less interest to both origin and antiquity.

Be it a nation or an institution that engages our attention, we instinctively ask as to its origin and the period of time it has existed among men.

If credit attaches to a good origin and to a great antiquity, we, as Free Masons, may feel a just pride in the precedence our order takes above any other in both.

ORIGIN OF FREE MASONRY.

We are taught as Masons that King Solomon organized the order of Free Masons during the building of his temple at Jerusalem. But its real origin dates back much further than that. In fact, it dates back to Nature

Worship, the first worship known to mankind, and the study of nature, the beginning of the great search after light, more light, even to the finding of God. Its real origin was, therefore, the beginning of intellectuality on this earth.

NATURE WORSHIP.

Nature Worship, the first worship known to man, consisted of the worship of the sun, the moon, the stars and the earth. The first generation of people having no parents to inform them, naturally looked off into space at the sun, the moon and the stars, and wondered what they were. Then seeing that the sun caused the grain to grow, in gratitude, worshiped the sun. As the moon gave them light when the sun was gone away, in gratitude, they worshiped the moon. As the stars gave them light and were a delight to their eyes they worshiped the stars. As the earth, under the influence of the sun, grew the grain, the fruit and the vegetables, in gratitude, they worshiped the earth, and called it "Mother Earth." The smartest men assumed the office of priest to the people, and organized the secret

ORDER OF SACRED MYSTERIES.

As this order was organized for the study of

nature, the sun, the moon, the stars and the earth, and through that study, finding out the origin of all things, they continued to study nature, gaining light and further light till they found out which was the true God. In this order in their study of nature they originated Chemistry, Geology, Arithmetic, Algebra, Geometry, Trigonometry, and Astronomy. This order was at first in only one degree, and when they gained more light they added a second degree, and when they found out which was the true God they added the third degree, in which they taught which the true God was. The secret rites and ceremonies of these degrees were called Sacred Mysteries. In the first degree the candidate was given some light; in the second degree he was given further light, and in the third degree he was told which was the true God, and that the plural gods were all imaginary gods.

WHO WERE ADMITTED.

At first nobody but the priests of the Nature Worship were allowed to enter the order of the Sacred Mysteries. Some of the priests only were allowed to enter the first degree; others were only allowed to take the second degree, while but few were ever allowed to take the third degree, that is, be introduced to God. The people were kept in profound ignorance of the secret ceremonies of the order of Sacred Mysteries and its great secret, who the true God was, and the priests only imparted very little of the knowledge they gained by the study of nature to the people. Their object seemed to be to get all the knowledge they possibly could for themselves, but at the same time to keep the people in ignorance that they might play on their superstition and control them to their own purposes. They let the people go on worshiping the sun, the moon, the stars and the earth, and subsequently the imaginary gods, Jupiter, Mars, Saturn, &c., who were supposed to preside over those objects in nature, while they, in the order of the Sacred Mysteries, concealed from the people and worshiped the true God, whom we now worship publicly.

LODGE ROOM OF SACRED MYSTERIES AND INITIATION.

In India the degrees in the Sacred Mysteries were at first conferred in dark caves in the earth. The cave was supposed to be divided into three rooms, first, second and third, the last being called the Holy of

Holies. The candidate, who was invested with a cable-tow, having long wandered in darkness in the cave, truly wanted light, and he was given light finally in the worship of the true God in the Holy of Holies. In the last degree he was admitted into the Holy Cavern, which blazed with light, called the Holy of Holies, where in costly robes sat, in the east, west and south, the chief officers of the lodge, called Hierphants, and who represented the Indian Triune Deity. The ceremonies in this degree began with an anthem to the great God of Nature. In this degree he was told the truth, who the true God was. He was then required to promise that he would be obedient to his superiors; that he would keep his body pure, govern his tongue, and observe a passive obedience in receiving the doctrines and traditions of the order, and the firmest secrecy in maintaining inviolable its hidden and abstruse mysteries. Then he was sprinkled with water (whence our baptism); certain words, now unknown, were whispered in his ear, and he was divested of his shoes and made to go three times around the cavern.

FREE MASONRY.

During the building of the temple at Jerusalem, Solomon organized the Order of Free Masonry.

Being the head of the church, and a member of the Order of Sacred Mysteries, Solomon knew just how to build his temple after the plan of the Lodge of Sacred Mysteries—first chamber, second chamber, third chamber, or outer chamber, middle chamber, and in-chamber, called Holy of Holies.

Being thoroughly conversant with the secret rites and ceremonies of the Sacred Mysteries, Solomon also knew just how to organize the Order of Free Masons, after the plan of the Order of Sacred Mysteries—first degree, second degree, third degree. The blue lodge room of Masonry he constructed on the same plan of the lodge room of the Sacred Mysteries—first chamber, second chamber, and third chamber, called Holy of Holies, in which the letter "G," standing for God, is always suspended from the ceiling.

DEGREES.

In prescribing the ceremonies of the different degrees in Free Masonry, he gave to the architects and operative Masons the secrets of the Sacred Mysteries with only a few variations. The object of the variations was to prevent a Mason from working his way into the Lodge of Sacred Mysteries. The similarity between them, however, is great.

SACRED MYSTERIES AND MASONIC MYSTERIES COMPARED.

The lodge rooms in both are the same. The three principal officers are seated the same in both, in the east, west and south. The cable-tow is in both. The circuits around the room are the same in both. In both a candidate is neither barefoot nor shod. There are other points of similarity not necessary to mention now.

In the Order of the Sacred Mysteries the sun, the moon and the stars are the three great lights. In the Masonic order Solomon substituted the Master of the Lodge for the stars, and called the sun, the moon and the Master, the three lesser lights of Masonry. *This was one of the variations.* In compliment to the operative Masons, Solomon made the tools of their trade, the square and the compass, two great lights of Masonry; and in compliment to his own religion he made the Jewish Bible the other great light in Masonry.

In every lodge room, in the first chamber, on top of the columns, Jachin and Boaz, are the earth, the sun, the moon in crescent, and the strars painted on the sun, to indicate to Masons that their order came from nature worship, as they were the first objects of nature worship.

OBJECT OF MASONRY.

Solomon intended that the order of Free Masonry should unite the operative Masons into an exclusive and fraternal order for the study of architecture, and the erection of magnificent buildings. That their knowledge thus acquired should be kept within the order, so as to prevent architects and operative Masons from becoming too numerous, and thereby placing them all on starvation wages.

At the completion of the temple, Solomon bade them go into all the nations, demand good wages and erect magnificent buildings. They spread all over Europe, organized lodges of Free Masons, demanded and received from Kings and Popes exemption from taxation and the other duties of the subject, as well as good wages for their work; and built the grand temples and magnificent cathedrals from Italy to Scotland.

The ancient Sacred Mysteries are still practiced in Persia by the Parsees. They were also practiced by the Mayas and the Quiches in Yucatan and Central America eleven thousand five hundred years ago, as is clearly proven in a recent work by M. Le Plongeon. The great similarity between the degrees of the Sacred Mysteries and the degrees of Free Masonry, and the lodge rooms of both, is proof positive that the real origin of Free Masonry was the Sacred Mysteries. So we may truthfully claim that Free Masonry came from a good origin and a great antiquity. That Sacred Mysteries and Masonic mysteries are almost synonymous terms.

SPECULATIVE MASONS.

Out of this, operative Masonry gradually grew by receiving into the lodges Kings, Popes and nobles, in return for their favors, the Masonry to which we belong—speculative Masonry.

As in the Sacred Mysteries, the poor, blind candidate started out in search of light, knowledge, so does the poor, blind candidate in Masonry start out in search of light, knowledge; and in both he finds light in the first degree.

In the second degree, in both, he finds more light; and in the third degree, in both, he finds still more light, the whole truth. He is then supposed to be a graduate in knowledge. He is supposed to have wisdom to be a wise man. Hence, the Mason will always pray for light, the light of wisdom to guide him right in this life. So the first great object of Masonry, like the great object of the Sacred Mysteries, is the acquisition of light, knowledge. The other great objects in Masonry are fraternity and charity.

FRATERNITY AND CHARITY.

Fraternity, because none are strong enough to stand alone; charity, because all will need it in some respect.

Let us cultivate Masonic charity in its highest and noblest sense, that of forgiveness. It is right to relieve the wants of a brother Mason in financial distress, but let us also carry our charity to a higher plane; let us forgive our brother Mason who has faults, but not his crimes against the laws of the State. Where a Mason has entered into a conspiracy with other Masons, or outsiders, to slander, poison and murder a Mason, or any one else, the honor of Masonry demands that no charity should be extended to him; on the contrary, that he should be dismissed from the order, and sent to the penitentiary. To retain him in the order would be to make a screen of Masonry to help bad men practice the foulest of crimes. To forgive him would be to make a crime of Masonic charity. Masonic charity is only for the worthy erring, not for criminals. The Governor of a State alone has the power to pardon criminals.

WILLIAM WIRT.

Masons may sometimes learn lessons in charity from those who are not Masons.

The young lady who, riding by, saw young William Wirt lying on the roadside dead drunk, dismounted and spread her handkerchief over his face to keep the burning sun from it, exhibited charity in the highest sense, that of forgiveness for his sad condition. Wirt awoke from his drunken slumbers and found that a human angel had stood guard over him, and on the handkerchief the initials of that sweet angel of charity. She had saved him. Moved to tears of gratitude, he reformed, sought out the young lady, courted her, and she became the wife of William Wirt, the most celebrated Attorney-General of the United States. In this case charity proved to be its own reward. Both as Masons and individuals, let us emulate her noble example.

TRIED BY ALL NATIONS.

Free Masonry has to commend it not only its good origin and great antiquity, but also the fact that it has stood the test of a trial by all nations and tongues. Lodges have existed and flourished among the most barbarous. Kings, Presidents, and Chiefs of Indian tribes have passed through the various degrees of Masonry. All these have been impressed and moulded in some measure by its teachings and associations.

WASHINGTON.

At Alexandria, Virginia, there sat as Master of the Lodge one of the purest and grandest characters the world has ever known—George Washington.

Every nation contributed a stone to help build his monument, which now stands at Washington City, the highest ever erected to any man. This noble character of our country's history took pride in presiding as Master of the Lodge in the ripe maturity of his serene old age.

He gave them light, taught them knowledge in the three degrees of the Blue Lodge, gave them the Masonic mysteries.

GENERAL PUTNAM.

In his younger days Israel Putnam became a prisoner in the hands of the Indians. He was tied to the stake, and the fagots were ready to be fired, when, as a last resort, he gave the proper Masonic sign of distress, which was recognized by the Indian Chief, and Israel Putnam was saved to be a hero of the revolutionary war.

TECUMSEH.

That illustrious Indian Chief, Tecumseh, even in his wild Indian wars bowed before the mysterious power of the Masonic signs, and mitigated the horrors of savage warfare. So, through his Masonic signs, a Mason can find a brother Mason in any land, even across the dividing lines of all languages.

So, let us become ourselves bright in Masonic knowledge, the first great object of Masonry, and always practice fraternity and charity, those other great objects of Masonry, toward all worthy Masons, and ever keep our eyes turned toward the East, on the letter "G," the Mason's star of promise, so that when we shall be called to the Great Lodge above, our great Master may be able to say to each of us: Brother, finding you worthy, I welcome you to this Grand Lodge of purified, immortal, worthy and accepted Masons.

CHAPTER 12.

EUROPE.

Every nation in Europe had its mythical religion, with its plural gods, as well as its Supreme God, when the Kings all agreed that they would allow but one religion in Europe, and that should be the Christian religion, which recognized only the Supreme God, and Christ as his son: that the Pope should be the head of that church, or King in religion throughout Europe: that they would enforce all his decrees as such by military power, in consideration that he should use his religious power over the people to keep them and their progeny in their places as Kings in politics, by telling the people that they were called to reign over them, and that they must obey them. The idea that Christ was the son of God, and authorized as such to deliver his commands to the people, suited the monarchic purposes of the Kings exactly, as the idea that the Kings themselves were the sons of God, and authorized to do so, had worn out with the people. It was judicially established in his trial before Pontius Pilate, as reported in the New Testament, that Christ never claimed that he was the son of God, in the meaning that God begat him by his mortal mother, the Virgin Mary, but it suited the monarchic purposes of the Kings to claim it for him, and to use his religion to keep them in their political places. Throughout Europe no person was allowed to entertain any opinion contrary to the Christian religion, as interpreted by the Pope. For daring to do so, or because they could not or did not believe as they were ordered to, the martyrs were burned at the stake, twenty thousand people murdered throughout France, in the St. Bartholomew massacre, and great numbers persecuted and murdered by the Spanish inquisition. This awful tyranny was continued till a revolt against it came, and sent into the world all the Protestants that are now here, those that have been, and will send those that are to be. It drove the Pilgrim Fathers from England to Massachusetts, and the Huguenot Fathers from France to South

Carolina. The religious monarchy, the church, tried the martyrs on a charge of heresy, because they did not or could not believe everything they were ordered to believe, and condemed them to be burned at the stake, and the political monarchy carried out the sentence. Subsequently the Protestants, both in parts of Europe and America, tyrannized over the people for differing with them in their religious beliefs. The two wrongs did not make a right. To prevent such awful wrongs, our constitutional forefathers placed in our Constitution a clause prohibiting our Republic from establishing any church, and another clause declaring that the right of free speech shall not be infringed, thus preventing it from going into any partnership with any religion to murder people because they have opinions of their own in religion. The political monarchy used to also murder them for having opinions of their own in politics, when those opinions happened to be republican, or in any way against the reigning King. Our Constitution also prevents any person from being murdered on account of his political opinions, or the expression of the same.

The priests and preachers of the Christian religion have always denounced all other religions as mythical, and the priests of the other religions have always denounced the Christian religion as mythical. That the religions of the plural gods were mythical, is now generally admitted. Is the Christian religion mythical? Its rivals in religion declare it to be so, charging that it is founded on the mythical idea that Christ was the son of God. It is universally admitted, say they, that God is a spirit, out in space somewhere, they know not where. As a spirit has neither blood nor flesh, they say it was an impossibility for the Spirit God to be the father of Christ, who had both blood and flesh. They say the idea that a spirit without blood and flesh could beget a being possessing both blood and flesh, by a mortal woman, is contrary to the laws of nature, and therefore an impossibility; and therefore the other religionists say, the Christian religion is also a mythical religion, as well as the religions of the plural gods. All the Jews in the world, all the Mohammedans, all the Unitarians, all the Chinese, Japanese, Hindoos or East Indians, and in fact, four-fifths of all the people in the world, do not believe that Christ was the son of God. Christ was undoubtedly a good man, and his religion has done much good, notwithstanding the many crimes that have been committed in its name.

As the plural gods, say the other religionists, have been knocked out as mythical, and in time Christ will also cease to be worshiped as the son of God, and will only be reverenced as a saint in the church, the Supreme God alone will be left to worship, and then we will have a true Monotheism. That is the case already with the Unitarians and the Jews, and in fact with all the world except the Christians. It was so with the priests in the Order of the Sacred Mysteries in ancient times. They had a true Monotheism. Is the Supreme God also mythical? No, a million times no! and the reasons of the author for this assertion will be given in the true story of the world, at the end of this book.

If Christ ever did claim to be the son of God, in the meaning that God begat him by his mortal mother, he was not the first to do so, and has not been the last. Those who followed him were not able to make others believe it. That monarchic trick the kings played on the people all around the earth, long before Christ was born into this world, the king claiming to be either the son of the Supreme God or the son of one of the plural gods. They played it against the people of China, India, Egypt, Greece, Central America, Peru, Japan, and in fact it became general in the ancient nations.

In Japan even the people have pretended to have descended from spiritual gods, the most stupendous lie of all, and produced two geneological tables to try and prove it.

Some are now asserting that Christ was not the son of God, but was God himself. That God begat himself by the Virgin Mary. As God had neither flesh nor blood, it was an impossibility for him to beget himself into a being of flesh and blood, or to beget himself in any way. The idea of Christ being the son of God was a heathen idea, borrowed from the heathen religions. And the idea of God begetting himself was also a heathen idea, as it was borrowed from one of the heathen religions, in which one of the heathen or plural gods was claimed to have begotten himself. It is evidently as much a myth in one case as in the other. Some have asserted that it might have been done by a miracle. As a miracle is a myth, it can not be done that way. Nothing can be done contrary to the laws of nature. As miracles are contrary to the laws of nature, they are necessarily myths.

The idea of God being born of a woman as himself, or as his son, is not only mythical, but a degraded and digusting idea of God. The idea that he is a spirit, out in space in heaven and never was on this earth, is a higher and holier idea of him, and is the true Monotheism.

That our nearest neighbor planets, Venus and Mars, are peopled worlds there can be no doubt. Would it·be reasonable to think that God had left heaven and gone to each of those worlds and been born there of a woman, and been murdered on the cross, either as his own son or as himself, to manifest himself to the people and save them?

All the fixed stars are larger suns than our own, and the centers of solar systems, the worlds of which are undoubtedly peopled. Would it be reasonable to think that God had left heaven, gone to each of those countless worlds and been born of a woman, and murdered on the cross on each of them to manifest himself to the people and save them? No, a million times no. The very idea is absurd; so, too, is the idea that he would leave heaven to come to this insignificant, little planet of ours, to the exclusion of all the other planets, to be born of a woman and be murdered on the cross, even if it were in his power to do so, which it is not. From all of which it is plain that there never were and never will be any persons but mortals on the earth.

In Rome the Pope in his power was king in both politics and religion, till some of the kings dethroned him in both, and put Victor Emmanuel on the throne of Italy, when Protestant churches were allowed to be established in Rome. The Pope was recently reported as having said that the future belongs to the people, meaning the kings would be dethroned and the people would again enjoy their natural right of self-government. Since they would not allow him to remain a king in Rome he should not allow them to use his religion to retain them as kings. It is high time that the people of Europe should resume their natural inalienable right of self-government, in both politics and religion.

In his late encyclical letter on the condition of labor, or laborers, the present Pope, Leo 13th, truthfully declares that the people had their natural rights before the existence of any state, which means any state in politics or religion, thus substantially sustaining the author and history in the position that originally the people had the natural right of self-government, in both politics and religion, and that they were subseqently deprived of both by the pretended revelation overthrowing Republican government and uniting both religion and politics in that fraud called devine right monarchy.

We now know why the great preacher, James Freeman Clark, declared that revelation wears out with intellectual people, because he believed that it was only a pretended revelation, but it is evident that he did not discover how it was started. Revelation was undoubtedly a manufactured story, incited by ambition, and only meant monarchy, in both politics and religion. In our country we have got rid of it in politics, and it is time we should get rid of it in religion, and allow religion to stand on the only true basis, the truths of nature and the reason and hope of man, just where it stood before the pretended story of revelation was started by the ambitious old chief to overthrow free government and create monarchy in both politics and religion. In other words, on an intellectual basis.

As the monarchic idea of God, as a king and a tyrant, of religion as a tyranny, and of hell as a place of eternal torment, has been hammered into the brains of the people by monarchic power for so many centuries, ever since the day ambition caused the old Chinese Chief to play the monarchic trick on the ignorant and superstitious people through his pretended revelations, with the few exceptions in republics where they have had religious liberty, it will require some time to get the previous Democratic or people's idea of God, of religion and of hell back into the minds of humanity. In the interest of the truth, true religion and human liberty, Democracy, and Republican government the world over, it is to be hoped that it will be done as soon as possible.

CHAPTER 13.
MODERN FRANCE.

Through the awful French Revolution of 1789, brought on by the French monarchists denying to their white slaves, the French people, equal rights before the law, self-government was recovered in modern France, and a people's republic was established, in which all had equal rights before the law. But the allied Kings of Europe sent their armies into France to sustain what they called the cause of all Kings, to suppress the Republic, but they were gallantly driven back by the Republican army.

And no sooner had the National Convention formed a Constitution for the Republic, and was about to submit it to the people for ratification, than the French monarchists made an effort to overthrow the convention and restore the monarchy. Napoleon Bonaparte, who had been dropped from the rolls of the army on account of his radical Republicanism, and wandered on the bank of the Seine, intending to suicide by drowning himself in that river, was then in Paris living in poverty. Barras, the head of the committee of safety, gave him command of the troops in Paris, and ordered him to protect the National Convention. The fighting was severe, but Bonaparte, with only five thousand men, suppressed the revolt of forty thousand armed monarchists, and saved the Republic, by sweeping the streets of Paris with his artillery. The Constitution was then ratified, and the Government of the Directory provided for by it was then organized, and lasted till 1799, when dissentions among the Republicans enabled the ambitious Bonaparte, through the use of the army, to overthrow the Directory, and have himself made First Consul for a term of ten years.

COUP D'ETAT.

Napoleon's scheme was to have all the members of the Directory resign, and thus leave the Republic without an executive head, so as to give his co-conspirators in the French Congress a chance to declare him First Consul, and place arbitrary power in his hands. Three of the Directory, among whom was Barras, resigned according to program, but two refused and were thrown into prison. The next morning Bonaparte had at his house to breakfast all the prominent milltary officers in Paris, who were required to give in their adhesion to his cause under penalty of immediate arrest. He then went into the Council of Ancients, accompanied by a few of his soldiers, and made a speech to that body, closing thus: "I am accompanied by the God of fortune and war," at the same time pointing significantly at his soldiers. They took the hint and submitted. He then hurried to the Council of Five Hundred, over which his brother Lucien presided. They refused to hear him, and cries of "Cæsar! Cæsar!" came from all parts of the house, and one member, Arena Corsican, tried to slay him with a dagger, but the soldiers rushed to his rescue, just in time to save him and take him out. A vote of outlawry was proposed, but Lucien refused to put the question to the house, and was being closed in on by members, when soldiers sent by Napoleon arrived, and rescued him also. Lucien, on horseback, made a

MODERN FRANCE. 131

speech to the soldiers, in which he told them that a majority of the members of his house were in favor of Napoleon, but were overawed by the daggers of the minority, all of which was false, but it had the desired effect on the soldiers. They charged into the Council of Five Hundred, and dispersed them at the point of the bayonet. The next day the subservient Upper House and about forty members of the Council of Five Hundred met together and declared Napoleon First Consul, and conferred on him despotic powers. He then dictated a Constitution, providing that the French Congress should consist of a Senate and a House of Tribunes, and that the chief executive of France should be called First Consul. Thus evidently trying to make himself and France a parallell of Cæsar and Rome, in names at least. Napoleon, while First Consul, on one occasion was hailed as King. He denied that he wanted to be King, and was indignant that any one should doubt the sincerity of his Republicanism. At the same time he was only waiting for the opportune moment to declare himself Emperor, which he did in 1804.

And thus ended the great French Republic.

From this career of France it is plain:

MODERN FRANCE.

1. That the French Revolution and all its horrors were brought about by the French monarchists denying to the French people equal rights before the law.

2. That dissentions among the Republicans gave Bonaparte a chance to overthrow the Republic, and make himself Emperor.

MORAL: Man should never deny to his fellowman equal rights before the law, and the people of a Republic should always avoid dissentions, lest an ambitious Napoleon overthrow the Republic.

So much for the careers of dead Republics, Greece, Rome, and the first French Republic, from which we have ascertained the political diseases that kill Republics, viz: Disintegration, patricianism, corruption at elections, and dissentions.

CHAPTER 14.

LOST CONTINENTS; OR, ATLANTIS AND LEMURIA.

Since the earth was first peopled, traditions of all people, except the blacks of Africa, tell us of a great flood, or deluge, in which many people were drowned. The Jewish Bible account of the great flood from which Noah and his three sons, Shem, Ham and Japhet, and their families, and the animals and fowls, two of each kind, male and female, were saved in the ark, is too well known to be repeated here. It is now well known to learned men that the deluge was only a partial drowning of the people of the globe. It only drowned the people of Noah. The then aborigines of Central Asia, Aryans, the aborigines of China, of Africa, of Japan, of the American continents, and the

Finns, or Lapps, the Australians, were all untouched by the deluge. It is now conceded by scholars that the geneological table given in the Bible (Gen., ch. x.) does not include any of them. That it only refers to the Semitic races. That the sons of Ham were not negroes, but the dark brown races. The Bible does not satisfactorily locate the scene of the deluge. Scholars, however, are trying to do so. Some of them claim that the deluge was simply the closing of a continent, or island, called Atlantis, about one thousand miles wide, and about two thousand miles long, in the center of the Atlantic ocean. That the people on that continent were highly civilized, and when it sunk some of them escaped in ships to the eastern continents, Europe and Africa, and some of them escaped in ships to the American continents, and found aborigines on both sides of the Atlantic. The earth has had many local deluges, in which many people have been drowned, but this sinking of Atlantis has been called the greatest deluge of all. Plato, the Greek philosopher, so called it. Plato received his accounts of it from the books of his ancestor, Solon. Solon got his information from the Egyptian priests, who told him that Atlantis had sunk in one day and night, nine thousand years before, now making it eleven thousand five hundred years ago.

M. Le Plongeon says that there are inscriptions on the ruins of ancient temples in Yucatan exactly corroborating Solon's account of the sinking of Atlantis. This ought to settle the matter. Atlantis is now an immense ridge in the Atlantic ocean, running from opposite the English channel to below St. Helena. The Azores Islands are simply the tops of mountains on that ridge. The earth below Atlantis burned out by volcanic action and let it down, and the ocean flowed over it. All along on the top of that ridge can be found the evidence of volcanic action. The Bible account of the deluge was doubtless founded on the tradition concerning the sinking of Atlantis, and written up as we find it in our Bible.

SIMILARITY OF NAMES.

They try to prove that Atlantis did exist by similarity of names on the opposite sides of the Atlantic. As a mountain called Atlas on the shore of Africa; a town called Atlan on the shore of America; a people called the Atlantes living on the north and west coast of Africa; an Aztec people from Aztlan, in Central

America; an ocean between the two continents called the Atlantic; a mythological deity called Atlas, whom they imagined held the world on his shoulders; and an ancient tradition of an island called Atlantis. This would indicate that all these names came from Atlantis. They also try to prove it by similarities of languages and architecture that are found on the opposite sides of the Atlantic.

As an apple tree bears apples, whether it grows on one side of the globe or the other side of it, so the human brain thinks the same thoughts, no matter where it is on the earth. The brain being fundamentally the same in all races, and the objects of nature, on which the brain has to act being fundamentally the same all around the earth, the thoughts are necessarily the same or similar. As the vocal organs are also the same or very similar everywhere, it follows that languages and architecture would very naturally bear similarities everywhere. So similarities of languages and architecture will not positively prove sameness of origin, that is, that they all came from the same locality. We also know that different nations have borrowed from each other's literature, which may account for similarities to some extent. The weight of evidence is in favor of the idea that Atlantis once existed as a continent in the middle of the Atlantic, but not that all the civilizations of the earth came from there.

The Atlantes who escaped to either shore doubtless mixed with the people on either shore, and added their contributions to their civilizations. The civilizations of Mexico, Central America and Yucatan are undoubtedly as old as any in any other part of the world.

MYTHOLOGY OF ATLANTIS.

Plato tells us that the Greeks had a mythology, and that it declared that the gods divided the earth among themselves. That Atlantis fell to an imaginary god called Poseidon; that he begot children by a mortal woman called Cleito; that his oldest son he named Atlas, and made him King of Atlantis, and the rest of his children he made Princes. Here again comes the idea of that fraud called divine right monarchy. In Homer's Iliad Poseidon appears as ruler of the sea.

LEMURIA.

Science declares that series of islands reaching about half way across the Pacific ocean, and then that great island between them and the coast of South

America, simply the mountain peaks or table lands of a drowned continent that once reached across the Pacific ocean from India to South America, called Lemuria.

Reader, farewell to the Lost Continents, and now we will go to America, that glorious land of the free and home of the brave.

CHAPTER 15.
AMERICA.

America began her career, as a Republic, the Fourth of July, 1776, under the *style* of the *United States of America*, given to her by the Declaration of Independence. In that Declaration the issue between Republicanism and Monarchy was squarely made, in these immortal words: "*We hold these truths to be self-evident, that all men are created equal; that they are endowed by their Creator with certain inalienable rights; that among these are Life, Liberty and the pursuit of Happiness.*" Thus did our forefathers declare, in unmistakable language, that no man has any right to be born into this world the ruler or king of another. Thus did they declare the doctrine of *equal rights before the law*, and that Monarchy was a usurpation of the rights of man. That even the people have no right to establish Monarchy, on the principle that the dead have no right to rule the living, or that one generation has no right to force on succeeding generations hereditary rulers. Each generation, undoubtedly, has the right to choose its own rulers, or public servants.

In the seven years' war that confirmed that declaration the Americans proved themselves equals, in valor, of the Greeks at Thermopolie, the Romans at Pharsalia, the French at Austerlitz, or the English at Waterloo.

But during that great struggle all was not sunshine with the Americans, as some of their own people, called Tories, sympathized with Monarchy, and they were divided among themselves, to some extent, as to what kind of government they should set up over the new Nation they had brought into existence. Some wanted a Confederate Government, and others wanted a National Government. The Nation existed under the Revolutionary Government, and by *common consent*, and by virtue of the *Declaration of Independence*, till 1781, when a Confederate Government was officially established by the Articles of Confederation which had been framed by the Continental Congress, and ratified by the Legislature of all the States. This Government consisted, like the Revolutionary Government it superseded, of only one branch, the *Continental Congress*. Under this Government the votes of *nine States*, in the Continental Congress, were necessary to pass a law, and when it was passed there was no President to enforce it, nor Supreme Court to pass on its constitutionality, but it was sent to the Governor of a State, who laid it before his Legislature, and if the Legislature ratified it, he enforced it in his State, and if the Legislature failed to ratify it, it remained a dead letter in that State, and the Nation was powerless to enforce it.

By the Articles of Confederation, the Union was declared to be *perpetual*, but those Articles, at the same time, left the Continental Congress utterly powerless to enforce that declaration.

The State Governments neglected to enforce the terms of the Treaty of 1783, in which Great Britain acknowledged our independence, in consequence of which neglect Great Britain *indignantly* remonstrated with the Continental Congress, and for some time *refused* to surrender to us our western forts. It being the duty of the State Governments to enforce the national laws, their neglecting or refusing to do so, and the fact that the doctrine of secession had been whispered about, gave rise to the establishment of the National or General Government under the Constitution, with full power to enforce its own laws.

The Convention that framed the Constitution convened at Philadelphia, Pa., on the 14th day of May, 1787, in the same hall where the Declaration of Independence had been made. Owing to the absence of members, nothing was done till the following Friday, when the Convention was organized, George Washington being elected President of that body by a unanimous vote.

In that Convention there were two distinct parties, a Confederate party and a National party. Outside of these two parties there were some extremists in that Convention, monarchists on the one hand and secessionists on the other, but they were so few in numbers as to be powerless in the Convention.*

The Confederates and Nationals had stood side by side during the Revolutionary war against Monarchy,

---

* Luther Martin's Report to the Maryland Legislature, p. 13, as published by Alston Mygatt at Louisville, Ky., in 1844, in Secret Proceedings, and Debates of the Convention of 1787. Ibid. p. 83. Elliott's Edition of Madison's Debates, vol. 5, p. 244.

and the debates in the Convention prove that they were equally patriotic, and both sincere lovers of human liberty. As they were both aiming to attain the same objects, why did they differ so widely as to the means of securing those objects?

The explanation is easy.

The Confederates had inherited from their European ancestors the idea that the words Nation and Nationality were synonymous with Despotism. As a matter of fact, such had been the case in the different European monarchies. Prior to that time all efforts and all successes at gaining human liberty in those despotisms had been made in localities, as by a city or small district, and therefore *localism* and *liberty* came to be regarded by the Confederates as identical, while Nationality was regarded by them as despotism.

The Confederates, therefore, feared that *any* National Government would eventually run into despotism and monarchy. Hence, they opposed the National principle.

The Nationals, on the contrary, had before them the fact that European *Confederacies* had disintegrated and the parts run into monarchic despotisms, as well as the fact that their own Confederate Government had signally failed to secure the objects for which it had been framed. The Nationals, therefore, feared that any kind of a *Confederate* Government would result in *disintegration* and anarchy, and eventually run into Monarchy. Hence, they opposed the Confederate system.

With these respective ideas and fears in their minds the Confederates and Nationals met in the Constitutional Convention. Both sought to perpetuate Republican liberty, but differed as to the best means of attaining that result.

The Confederate party proposed to continue the old Confederate Government in existence, but was willing to make such amendments to the Articles of Confederation as to give the Confederate Government the power to execute its laws; requiring, however, that it should still continue to *act on States*, instead of *on individuals*, in the enforcement of those laws. This party proposed that the Continental Congress should pass laws and send them to the States, to be enforced by the State authorities, and when the State authorities failed or refused to enforce the laws of Congress, then Congress was to declare war on that State: call out the militia; march on that State and treat all the people therein as enemies to the Nation—punishing the innocent as well as the guilty.

Under such a rule a bad Governor, if not alone, still with the aid of bad men in the Legislature, could cause the entire people in his State to be treated as enemies to the Government of their Nation, when perhaps nine-tenths of them would have gladly seen the laws of Congress enforced in their State. The injustice of punishing the innocent for the acts of the guilty, because they happen to reside in the same State with the guilty, was too manifest to be tolerated by the National party in the convention.

That party, having a majority in the convention, resolved to substitute, in the place of the old Confederate Government, a National Government, with full power to create its own laws, and to act *on individuals* in the execution of its laws, and to punish only the guilty who might resist the enforcement of those laws, and it was in pursuance of that resolution that the Constitution was framed,* providing for a National Government of unlimited powers, and making it the duty of that Government to guarantee to each State local self-government. The old Confederate name of the country was continued by the Constitution.

When the Constitution was sent to the people for ratification, the Confederate party, wishing to remain under the old Confederate Government, tried to defeat its ratification, denouncing it in the bitterest terms, declaring that its adoption would entirely destroy the *federal principle* of Government, and establish a Government purely *National*. The friends of the Constitution, on the contrary, claimed that it would establish a Government that would be partly National and partly Federal, and took upon themselves the name of Federalists. The Confederates declared that the Nationals took that position thinking they would thereby the more certainly secure the ratification of the Constitution.

* The resolution in favor of a National Government was in the following language: "That a National Government ought to be established, consisting of a Supreme Legislative, Executive and Judiciary." This resolution was subsequently amended so as to make it read: "That a Government of the United States ought to be established, consisting of a Supreme Legislative, Executive and Judiciary," which evidently only changed the phraseology of the resolution, so as to continue the old name of the country.

See Elliott's Debates on Federal Constitution, vol. 5, pp. 132, 133, 134; also, Luther Martin's Report to the Maryland Legislature, p. 39, as published in Secret Proceedings and Debates, of the Convention of 1787, by Alston Myatt, at Louisville, Ky., in 1844. Also, Elliott's Debates on Federal Constitution, vol. 5, p. 214.

These notes refer to page 145.

Whether this be so or not, the fact still remains that the Constitution was *thoroughly discussed* before the people, and in the various conventions that ratified it as the act of the people. It is not at all unreasonable to suppose that the friends of the Constitution and its opponents took such steps and used such arguments as they thought would carry their respective points; and we should make due allowance, therefore, and always remember that arguments made to gain a point during a political campaign are not reliable as interpretations of constitutional law.

After a bitter contest the Constitution was adopted, or, as its preamble tells us, was ordained and established by the people of the United States for the United States of America.

The Government created by it is, therefore, appropriately called a Government of the people, by the people, and for the people.

After the adoption of the Constitution, some of its dissatisfied opponents claimed that it was only binding on a State so long as the people of that State saw fit to obey it; and, in support of that declaration, resorted to certain theories of construction for the Constitution, which will now be stated.

The first may be appropriately called the *No Common Arbiter Theory*.

NO COMMON ARBITER THEORY.

The upholders of this theory asserted that each State had the right to judge for itself as to what was the proper remedy for it, in case a dispute arose, between it and one or more other States, and that if it deemed secession the proper remedy, it had the right to peaceably secede, and thus release the people within its lines from the operation of the Constitution, on the ground that the Constitution provided no common arbiter in case of disputes between the States.

This theory of construction fails, as the Constitution does provide that the Supreme Court of the Nation shall be a *common arbiter* between them, by giving to that court "original jurisdiction in all controversies between two or more States." Hence this theory failed.

Art. 3, Sec. 2, Constitution United States.

State New Jersey vs. State New York, 5 Pet., 283.

State of Rhode Island vs. State of Massachusetts, 12 Pet., 657.

POWER OF ATTORNEY THEORY.

Under this theory it is claimed that the Constitution is merely a power of attorney from the State to the General Government, conferring upon it certain powers, and, as such, may be revoked by the State at will.

This theory, like the last, is based upon the assumption that the States were separate Nations prior to the Constitution, and as Nations separately ratified the Constitution, thus making it a power of attorney from the State to the Nation.

By express provision of the Constitution, it is made the *supreme* law of the land (the entire American people), and thus the asserted maker of the Constitution (a State) is prohibited from revoking the same.

By the Constitution the General Government was created to enforce that supremacy, and punish any one who resists the enforcement of the Constitution as the supreme law of the land. All of which utterly precludes the possibility of the Constitution being a power of attorney.

Further, as by express provision of the Constitution, it was to have no legal effect till nine States ratified it, it follows conclusively that it could not have been made a power of attorney or anything else by *one* State. Hence this theory fails. See U. S. Con., Art.VII.

RESERVED RIGHT THEORY.

It was asserted by these theorists that a right to secede, and thus release the people within its lines from the operation of the Constitution, was one of the reserved rights of a State.

This assertion was, also, based upon the assumption that the States were, prior to the Constitution, separate Nations, and, as separate Nations, had delegated to the General Government all the National powers it possesses. And as each State had delegated those powers for itself separately, it, therefore, had the reserved right to separately withdraw those powers and resume its separate existence as a Nation.

1. The States were never separate Nations.

2. It is evident that a delegated right is not a reserved right. Hence a righht to National existence which is delegated by the Constitution to the General Government can not possibly be a reserved right of a State.

3. Had the States beeen separate Nations prior to the Constitution, which they never were, it is plain that their right to a separate existence as Nations is just what they would, in that case, have delegated away to

the General Government, and therefore did not reserve, as they, under the Constitution, constitute but one Nation, and the Constitution makes it the duty of the General Government to enforce those National powers as the Supreme Law of the Land. Hence, this theory fails.

CONTRACT THEORY.

Under this theory its advocates, also, went outside and back of the Constitution, and asserted that, prior to the Constitution, the States were independent Nations, and that, as Nations, they separately agreed to the Constitution, thereby making it a contract of partnership between the States, and that, as each State gave its consent voluntarily to the Constitution, as an independent Nation, it had the right to withdraw that consent at any time. and set itself up as an independent Nation, and in that way release the people within its limits from their allegiance to the Government and the operation of the Constitution.

In reply, it is said that there is not now, and never was, at any time, a law of contracts that would permit a party to a contract to withdraw from the same at will, or that gave a party any right to withdraw from a contract because another party to it had violated the same, unless such power was reserved to the party by express language of the contract. No such power has been reserved to a State by express or implied language of the Constitution.

This question as to whether the States had ever been separate Nations, and on that ground held a right to pass any law contravening the supremacy clause of the Constitution, was several times carried up to the Supreme Court of the United States, long years before our late war. In all of such cases, that court of last resort, on that question, decided that the States had never been different Nations, but had always constituted but one Nation, and that a State had no right to contravene the supremacy of the Constitution.

The Supreme Court of the Nation thus decided against secession.*

These theorists based their assertion, that the States were originally separate Nations, on that clause of the Declaration of Independence which declares the colonies to be free and independent States.

In reply it is said that the word State did not necessarily mean Nation, in its European sense, and *never*

---

* Chisholm vs. Georgia, 2 Dall., 419.
McCullough vs. Maryland, 12, Wh., 419.
Barron vs. The Mayor and City Council of Baltimore, 7 Pet., 243.

had, in its American sense, and that the same clause of the Declaration that declares the colonies to be free and independent States, also first speaks of them as the United States of America, thus proving that while they were to be free and independent States, they were to be so in their *united* condition, and were to constitute but one Nation, under the style of the United States of America.

Prior to the Constitution, no one of the States ever claimed or performed the functions of a Nation. On the contrary, all such functions were performed by the United States of America as one Nation.

It is also said that contracts and powers of attorney never were, at any period of the world's history, called laws, or known as laws, and laws were never known as contracts in the ordinary meaning of the term, nor as powers of attorney; but, on the contrary, that they have always been known as separate and distinct things; that they differ in form, differ in language, and differ in meaning.

When the American people or States agreed to the Constitution, what did they agree to make? A contract, a power of attorney, or what?

The express language of the Constitution answers

the question, and tells us they agreed that it should not only be a *law*, but that it should be the *supreme law of the land*, and the Supreme Court has always so held it.

If, on the contrary, we view it in the light of a contract or power of attorney we will still find that by its express provisions, it is declared to be the supreme law of the land, and creates a government, places the sword and purse in its hands, and makes it the duty of that government to enforce the Constitution, (contract or power of attorney or whatever it may be called,) as the supreme law of the land, and to punish any inhabitant who resists the government in the enforcement of that law. To call such an instrument a contract or power of attorney is simply absurd.

SOVEREIGNTY THEORY.

The upholders of this theory claimed that the States were, prior to the Constitution, separate Nations, and as such were incapable of permanently delegating away their sovereignty so as to unite into one permanent Nation.

Consequently, said they, a State by virtue of its sovereignty which it was incapable of permanently delegating away, has the right to peaceably secede.

That sovereignty was indivisible, once lodged in a Nation it could never be divided or parted with so as to prevent that Nation from peaceably seceding and setting up as an independent Nation whenever in its own judgment it saw fit to do so.

1. As in a Republic there is neither sovereign nor subjects, it follows conclusively there can be no sovereignty in a Republic.

2. Since that old political trick, Divine Right Monarchic idea, sprang from the brain of a man in the interest of separate Monarchs or Chieftainships and the perpetuation of their separate sovereignties, hereditary blood rule, it cannot be used in Republics to prevent the people from ruling themselves, permanently uniting into one Nation, for their common defense and general welfare.

That so-called Divine Right sovereignty trick falsely claimed that God had placed the allegiance of the people in a certain Chief, and his progeny forever, and as God had so fixed it, it could not be divided or transferred by the people. As the Chief by his arbitrary will prescribed the laws as well as enforced them, he claimed to be the State and his sovereignty was therefore sometimes called State Sovereignty. Cunning politicians played that old monarchic trick which did not come from God, but sprang from the brain of cunning man on a part of our people, under the name of State Sovereignty and made them believe they had a right to secede their States, telling them that their States were, before the Constitution, separate sovereignties, monarchs, and therefore the people of a State, or the people of the different States, could not by ratifying the Constitution deny to any one State the right to peaceably resume the sovereignty at any time by secession. Thus was the old political tricks of so-called Divine Right monarchy, under the name of State Sovereignty, played on the people of some of our States to induce them to secede.

These theorists claim that the doctrine of State Sovereignty, as they call it, is all-powerful for purposes of disintegration, but powerless for purposes of consolidation and protection to life and property; in fact, that it is of such a nature as to prevent this from ever being permanently done.

To deny the people of different Nations the right to form themselves into one permanent Nation, is to deny the people the right to rule themselves, the foundation principle of Republican Government.

The right to fix their own supreme duty and that of their posterity, to obey the supreme law made by themselves, subject alone to changes made in accordance with the Constitution of their new Nation, the right of emigration, and the right of armed revolution against unbearable oppression, is necessary to protect them against both anarchy and alien dangers.

The doctrine of secession in denying to different Nations the right to permanently unite into one Nation, denies to the majority in a Nation the right to determine to what National Government they, as well as the minority, shall owe their supreme duty, and thus gives to the minority the absolute right to rule the majority in the matter, the most important to them, viz.: To what Government they shall owe their supreme duty of obedience, which only shows how absurd is the doctrine of secession.

The rule of the minority on any question is monarchic in principle and cannot be admitted in a Republic for one moment.

Had the States not constituted one Nation prior to the Constitution, but, on the contrary, had existed as separate independent Nations for a thousand years before, and, as different nations of people, had deemed it their interest, as against the rest of the world, to cease to be many Nations and become one, it would undoubtedly have been their right to do so according to the principles of free Government, the right of the majority to rule in each Nation, under any Constitution they might have seen fit to ordain and establish, for the one Nation they proposed to create. And they would be bound by the provisions of that Constitution, after organizing under it, the same as though they had previously constituted but one Nation. And if they had adopted a Constitution reserving to themselves the rights of local self-government, and providing for the organization of a National or General Government over all, and still further providing that the said Constitution should be the supreme law of the land or new Nation, no one of the former Nations, now integral parts of one Nation, would have any right to do anything contravening that declaration.

The people of Texas constituted an independent Nation prior to the time they became a part of our Nation, and it was by their voluntary consent that they became a part of this Nation. When they gave their assent to the same they agreed to be amenable to the supreme law of the land in all its parts. And when they subsequently passed an act of secession, endeavoring to release themselves from their obligation to obey the National Constitution as the supreme law of the land, their ordinance of secession was null and void, as it was in contravention of the supremacy of the Constitution.

This view of the subject is sustained by a decision of the Supreme Court of the Nation, in which that Court decided that the people of Texas had no right to secede, thus sustaining the supremacy of the Constitution, although Texas had previously been a separate Nation.

Texas vs. White, 7 Wal. 700.

In a case from Tennessee, since the late war, the Supreme Court also decided that Tennessee had no right to secede, and thus again sustained the supremacy of the Constitution.

The only way power delegated to the Nation can be withdrawn is laid down in the Constitution itself, and is declared by that instrument to be the supreme law of the land on that subject. That way is by an amendment to the Constitution ratified by the Legislatures of at least three-fourths of the States. Any other way is consequently null and void. *Hence the Sovereignty theory of secession also fails.*

Some have asserted that the word law, in the last sentence of the supremacy clause, only meant statute when the Constitution was framed, and therefore a State could secede, through an ordinance of secession, claiming that an ordinance of secession is not a law. The framers of the Constitution used the word law because it was a broader term than the word statute, and covered laws of all kinds, and was not confined to statutes. Blackstone defined a law to be a rule of action long prior to the Constitution.

The city of London and other cities ruled themselves under ordinances for many years prior to our Constitution, and the members of the National Convention, as well as those of the different State Conventions, were familiar with the word ordinance.

An ordinance of secession was intended to be a rule of action, and is therefore covered by the word law in the supremacy clause of the Constitution.

The first sentence of the supremacy clause of the Constitution is a general command to everybody to obey the Constitution as the supreme law of the land, and the second sentence is a special command to the judges to so hold it on the bench.

Some asserted that the Constitution was only to

be the supreme law of the land unto any State, so long as the State saw fit to remain in the Union.

If that was so it would not be the supreme law at all, when the Constitution says it shall be the supreme law.

The language, so long as a State sees fit to remain in the Union, is not in the Constitution, and it would require an amendment, ratified by the Legislatures of three-fourths of the States, to place it there. It can not be placed there by word of mouth, and the supremacy clause of the Constitution be thus destroyed by the trick of construction.

The trick of trying to evade, or abolish law, by construction was well known and practiced long before our Constitution had an existence, and it, like all other laws, had to run that gauntlet, and has done so triumphantly.

UNDERSTANDINGS OUTSIDE THE CONSTITUTION.

Some, also, asserted that the Constitution was framed by the National Convention with the understanding that a State should have the right to secede, notwithstanding the language of that instrument.

1. The appeal to an understanding outside the

language of the Constitution is an indirect admission that the language of that instrument is against secession.

2. The assertion attributes to the convention either a lack of understanding or insincerity, and either charge against that body is utterly unjust.

Luther Martin reported to the Legislature of Maryland that he, while a member of the National Convention from that State, offered an amendment to the treason clause of the Constitution, providing for secession, or that in case of war between a State and the United States, that those who adhered to the State should not be deemed guilty of treason to the United States, which proposition was voted down. In consequence of which Mr. Martin seceded from the Convention, and advised the people of Maryland to refuse to ratify the Constitution. This utterly excludes the idea that the Convention could possibly have framed the Constitution with the understanding that a State should have a right to secede, or that one who levies war against the United States in obedience to the order of his State should not be deemed guilty of treason to the United States. It was urged by the advocates of secession that in case of a conflict between the Nation and a State, an inhabitant of that State would be placed in a dilemma. If he stood by his State the Nation would punish him, and if he stood by the Nation his State would punish him. If *forced* by either power to levy war against the other, that fact would be a valid defense against a charge of treason in the Courts of either the State or Nation. If he *voluntarily* levies war against either power he ought to be willing to stand the consequences.

Some, also, asserted that the Conventions elected in the different States by the people had *ratified* the Constitution with the understanding that a State should have the right to secede, notwithstanding the language of the Constitution. In support of that declaration they asserted that the States of New York and Virginia reserved the right to secede in their ratifications of the Constitution, and that therefore the right to secede would belong to any other State also. The assertion is untrue, as no such declaration is to be found in those ratifications. On the contrary, the declaration on that subject, made in those ratifications, is this: "That whenever the powers granted to the United States are turned to the oppression of the people, they may be withdrawn by the people of the

United States," *not* by the people of *one* State. The way in which the people of the *United States* have a right to withdraw the powers delegated to a Nation is by an amendment to the Constitution, ratified by the Legislatures of at least three-fourths of the States.

In all the debates that took place in all the ratifying conventions, not a single member in any of them ever claimed that a State would have the right to secede. On the contrary, the debates prove that they thought justh the reverse.

It is further urged that: The Constitution is declared to be the supreme law of the land; this is, the supreme law of the *entire* American people. That it can not be the supreme law of the *entire* American people, if a State can, at its pleasure, destroy that supremacy. An ordinance of secession is intended to destroy that supremacy, and is, therefore, in contravention to the supremacy clause of the Constitution, and is consequently prohibited by that clause.

It is, also, urged that the preamble to the Constitution expressly states, that the Constitution was ordained and established by the people of the United States, not only for themselves—*the people of the Nation*—but for their *posterity*. The word posterity

AMERICA.   165

being used without words of limitation, it means the same as though the preamble had said the *Union shall be perpetual*.

With all the foregoing considerations and declarations of the Constitution staring the *ratifying State Conventions* in the face, it is plain that, in the very nature of things, they could not possibly have ratified the Constitution with any other understanding than that the Union should be perpetual; particularly as by the Articles of Confederation it was declared to be perpetual; and by the Preamble of the Constitution, it was declared to be the object to form a more *perfect* Union for the people of that day and their posterity, without limit. All of which destroys all idea of a State having any right to secede, and thus releases the people within its borders from the operation of the supremacy clause of the Constitution.

CIVIL WAR.

Excited on the slavery question in 1861, eleven of our then slave States resorted to this old doctrine of secession, passed ordinances of secession, some declaring their former ratification of the Constitution of the United States repealed, and all declaring their inhabitants released from any further obligation to obey that Constitution. They then organized themselves into what they called the Confederate States of America, and claimed to be one of the Nations of the earth. The events of the four years' war that followed are too well known to you to require repetition here. It is sufficient to say that the war resulted in maintaining the Constitution as the supreme law of the land, the abolition of slavery, and the securing for all equal rights before the law, a denial of which, although the principle had been enunciated in the Declaration of Independence, finally led to civil war here, as it had in Greece, Rome and France.

The Monarchists, the world over, had prophesied that whenever civil war came upon us, that our Government would not be able to stand the shock, but would fall into anarchy, and we would have to resort to Monarchy to protect life and property. The prophesy was false. Our Government grandly stood the shock of the greatest civil war that ever occurred on the earth, and the assassination of our Martyr President, the immortal Lincoln, who was killed as the war was ending, and lived on, protecting life and property more fully than had ever been done by any Monarchy.

AMERICA. 167

No civil war ever occurred on the earth in which was displayed so much valor, chivalry, humanity and magnanimity. Prisoners of war were not murdered, and the leaders of the vanquished were not put to death as in Greece, Rome and France. When our Government came, triumphant, through that war, suppressing the Rebellion and maintaining the Supremacy of the Constitution, the first great danger to the Republic, disintegration, was safely passed. And in overcoming it we Americans proved ourselves a greater people than the Greeks, in all their glory, for they failed to overcome it.

Of our war, death to its prejudices, but immortality to its patriotic memories.

From our past it is evident that our late war was inherited from our forefathers.

Some of our forefathers seriously doubted that a Government such as ours could permanently stand. Some believed that either the General Government would destroy the States, or that the States would destroy the General Government; that they could not work in harmony together. They congratulated themselves that they got the Government organized and started without having to resort to the sword, but the sword had to come in at last. It was a problem in government that had to be solved, and it required two sides to solve it, and in its solution both sides did their parts gallantly and gloriously. And the auther has no fault to find with either side.

Of our dead heroes on both sides it may be truly said:

> "On fame's eternal camping ground
> Their silent tents are spread,
> And glory guards with solemn round
> The bivouac of the dead."

Since our war, statues of the great heroes and other great men of the Union cause have been erected in Washington City and the Northern cities. In the same way the South has honored her heroes and great statesmen.

While traveling in Europe in 1890 I noticed that in Paris the statues erected to the heroes of the monarchy are allowed to stand there in the Republic, because they represent parts of the history and glory of France. The statues erected to the horoes of the Republic were allowed to stand during the Empires, because they also represent parts of the history and glory of France. I noticed the same state of affairs in Rome. In one of the halls of the vatican, devoted to statuary, I saw, side by side, busts of Cæsar, Pompey, Brutus and Cassius, who had fought on opposite sides of their civil war two thousand years ago. The busts of the heroes of the monarchy were also there. All were there because they represent parts of the history and glory of Rome. The French guide and the Roman guide seemed to point with equal pride to the glories of the monarchy and the glories of the Republic, because they all represent parts of the history of France and Rome. So in the future will the American guide point with equal pride to the statues of Grant and Lee, McClellan and Beauregard, Hancock and Stonewall Jackson, Custar and Jeb Stewart, because they all represent parts of the history and glory of our common country.

BUT WHAT OF OUR FUTURE?

To the wise it is evident that the Roman evils, Patricianism and corruption at elections, are the great dangers that now threaten the future of this Republic, and that we are, therefore, in danger of repeating the career of the Roman Republic. It is true that our Constitution does not classify us into Patricians and Plebeians, but, in spite of that fact, we are drifting into those conditions.

When our country was new, and none were wealthy, these dangers were absent. But millionaires have sprung into existence, and while some of them are true to human rights, others are not, and with these have come corrupt and aristocratic tendencies.

The mere fact that some are wealthy and others are not does not constitute the *political* distinction of Patricians and Plebeians, and will not cause a civil war between them; but if the wealthy manipulate the Government in their own interest, to the detriment of the people, that distinction is thereby raised, in reality, if not by names, and if persisted in will cause civil war between them.

That some millionaires have united their fortunes and used their consolidated wealth to manipulate the Government in their own interest, to the detriment of the people, is charged and generally believed.

PATRICIANIZING PROCESS.

This Patricianizing process is greatly accelerated by the fact that all political parties now prefer rich men for their candidates, and practice corruption at elections, rendering it almost impossible for any poor man, however cultured, worthy, and well qualified, to obtain high office.

In Athens and Rome, at the zeninth of Patricianism, the great offices were reserved to the rich by the Constitution.

Corruption at elections has almost brought around the same state of affairs in this country, in spite of our Constitution. Particularly in our great cities.

When our purest and greatest intellects, simply because they are not wealthy, find themselves barred from the honors of the Republic by corruption at elections, and the bad practice of all parties running after rich men for their candidates, and the people find out that money, and not their will, *rules*, how many will feel like risking their lives to save the Republic, when run by the millionaires and for millionaires, from a Coup d'Etat, by an ambitious Napoleon in the Presidential chair? This is a question worthy our serious consideration.

DEVICES OF THE MONARCHISTS.

Trouble between our political Patricians and the people may be accelerated by our would-be Monarchists, taking their ideas from monarchic writers across the Atlantic, trying to frighten our wealthy into favoring Monarchy, by suggesting that when our country becomes densely populated, Republican Government will not be strong enough to protect property, and pretending to fear that the people will then take advantage of universal sufferage to vote the wealthy out of their property.

Their fears are unfounded. Our system of government can be as readily applied to five hundred millions as to sixty-five millions. And the result of our late civil war has proved that our Government is strong enough for any emergency, when maintained by the will of the people. And if it were a question of numbers, the people are now sufficiently numerous to vote the wealthy out of their property, and have been from the foundation of our Republic.

In Athens, Rome and France, when universal suffrage prevailed, the people made no effort to vote the wealthy out of their property; on the contrary, they protected their property rights, and stood between them and the alien enemy on the battle-field. Which proves that the property rights of the rich are as safe in a People's Republic as in a Patrician Republic, or even in a Monarchy. No, there is no danger from the people; on the contrary, the fate of dead Republics proves that the danger lies in the opposite direction.

Great students of history have declared that a People's Republic is only possible in a country where none are possessed of great wealth. That as soon as a part of the people become millionaires, in their greed for more, they manipulate the Government, in their own interest, to the detriment of the people. And thus, in time, in all Republics, a contest is brought on between the millionaires, of the ambitious, scheming kind, who always want partiality from the Government, and the people, who only ask equal rights, or impartiality from the Government.

If the present drift of our affairs is allowed to go on that contest will soon come upon us. And, thus, political Patricianism will have arisen in our Republic.

It is a bitter cup that all true patriots, rich or poor, high and low, will pray may be allowed to pass our country.

But, however much we may regret its approach, current events warn us that the great question of our *Future* will be: Shall this remain a People's Republic, as our fathers made it, or shall it be allowed to drift into a Patrician Republic, and bring on us the civil wars of the Patricians and the Plebeians of Rome, with the possibility of eventual Monarchy?

WHAT ARE THE PREVENTATIVES?

Neither absolute centralization, nor the opposite extreme, disintegration, can ever prevent the civil wars, or save Republicanism in America. For if the States were abolished, and all power centered in the National Government, the great dangers, Patricianism and Corruption at Elections, would still threaten the Republic. And if the National Government was abolished, the same dangers would threaten each State.

Whether a Republic is great or small, the four great dangers, Disintegration, Patricianism, Corruption at Elections, and Dissensions, will attack it. For they are the political diseases of which Republics have died.

GENERAL EDUCATION.

Some have suggested that general education will save Republicanism in this country. We cannot rely upon this, highly important as it is; for the Greek and Roman Republicans were as generally and as highly educated as we Americans can ever hope to become; and their education and splendid literature, which have served as models for the world, failed to save Republicanism.

PURITY OF THE BALLOT.

The purity of the ballot is the sure remedy, *true preventative*. 1. Because it will always express the *will* of the *people* and keep the people in love with Republican Government. 2. Because it will give a worthy, poor man an equal chance with a millionaire for the honors of the Republic. And will thus prevent the Patricianizing of the Republic, and, therefore, all danger of Monarchy.

Strike down Corruption at Elections, the root of the corrupt tree, by a vigorous enforcement of the law against it, and an indignant, honest refusal to support any candidate who trifles with it, and you will destroy it everywhere. For men who obtain office purely will make honest officials. To carry out these purposes, I would propose an Amendment to our National Constitution, making it the duty, under penalty, of all voters to go to the polls and vote. This would put an end to bummer rule, run by money, in our large cities, and help to perpetuate our Republic, by bringing out the class of voters who are most interested in pure government. I would, also, suggest that corrupt acts in primaries and nominating conventions be punished by law, as the same offenses are when committed at elections. The corrupt now evade the object of the law against Corruption at Elections, in some cases, by buying and selling nominations. It should also be made a felony and severely punished for any man, or editor of a newspaper, or reporter, or writer on the paper, to either oppose or advocate the nomination, the election, or appointment, of any person to any office for money. This is necessary to prevent money from ruling in many cases.

Republicanism lasted among the Greeks for nearly seven hundred years, and with the Romans five hundred. And so great was their confidence in its perpetuity, they indignantly refused to believe there was any possibility of it ever perishing. But now, after the dark waves of monarchy have rolled over them for twenty centuries, Greece and Rome cry out to us from the tomb of the past: Build up no Patrician class, for the doctrine of *equal rights* is a law of nature, and cannot be violated without the certainty of punishment, in awful civil war.

In these remarks it is no purpose of mine to array the people against our millionaires, nor to array our millionaires against the people; on the contrary, it is my purpose to prevent such a conflict, by pointing out to both the great calamity that *will* come upon all, if they fail to treat each other with justice and due forbearance.

Neither is it my purpose to be the bearer of bad news, but I cannot forget that just before our late war but few of even our leading statesmen believed it possible, but it came nevertheless, and slaughtered and maimed a million of men. That made me a thinking man. And I say to you, by thinking ahead for our Republic, we may prevent the necessity of fighting for it.

We have seen that the denial of *equal rights* caused civil war in Greece, Rome, France and America. And that the Romans, digusted with the fact that their elections did not express the will of the people, but had been, for many years, shamelessly carried by the power of money, yielded to Monarchy, at the hands of an ambitious Cæsar. Now, as human nature is the same in all generations, like causes will produce like results in all generations, unless special care is taken to prevent. Therefore, if we would be free from civil wars in the future, and prevent history from repeating itself in the death of our Republic, we must avoid *dissensions*, and always take care,

1. That we are not drifted by class legislation into Patrician and Plebeian classes.

2. That our elections express the will of the people, and not the power of money; and that our Government is run as a Government of the people, by the people, and for the people, with favoritism to none, with equal and exact justice for all.

Failing to do so, we will repeat the civil wars of the Patricians and Plebeians of Rome, and end as they did—in Monarchy. And, thus, history will again have repeated itself in the death of a Republic.

I believe there are enough lovers of liberty and purity in elections left in this country to prevent such an awful calamity. And when we do prevent it, we will prove ourselves a greater people than the mighty Romans, for they failed to prevent it.

But this can only be done by eternal vigilance against the great political diseases that kill Republics, as explained from the careers of the dead Republics of Greece and Rome, and the first French Republic, viz.: Disintegration, Patricianism, Corruption in Elections, and Dissensions.

Come what may, let us solemnly swear by the Old Flag of our Fathers: This Government of the people, by the people, and for the people, shall live on Forever.

Having full faith in the American people, I predict that it will live on, and through all time, lead the grand march of Nations, a purified, immortal People's Republic.

RELIGION.

The Christian and Jewish religions were brought to America by the white races, the descendants of the Aryans and the Jews. They found primitive religion among the native inhabitants, the many tribes of Indians, who were red or copper-colored people. In the great American bottom, on the Mississippi River, opposite the City of St. Louis, and elsewhere, were found evidences, that at some previous period, the original inhabitants had worshiped the sun. Thus proving that Nature worship came first on this Continent, as it did everywhere else on the face of the earth. Which proves that the brain of man is essentially the same in all races, in its primitive state.

In the City of Mexico they found great temples in pyramidal form, on the tops of which the native priests sacrificed human beings, slaves, to their God of War. They were a civilized and cultured Indian people.

In Yucatan excavations have been made disclosing inscriptions which were made more than eleven thousand years ago, proving that man has been on this earth longer than the Jewish Bible, is understood by some people, to assert.

In ancient times Central America, including Yucatan, was called the Kingdom of Mayax, and the people were called Mayas. They were a very ancient civilized people. Between their country and Africa, Atlantis reached across the ocean almost from shore to shore. The Egyptian priests told Solon that Atlantis had sunk beneath the ocean in one day and night, owing to earthquakes and volcanoes, nine thousand years before. Since which time all communications between the Mayas and Egyptians had been cut off by the ocean.

The priests of the Mayas also had an account of the sinking of Atlantis, which agreed exactly with the Egyptian account of it, thus proving the truth of it. The ruins of the ancient cities of the Mayas proved that they had the same kind of architecture that the Egyptians had.

When the Spaniards asked the Mayas how long since their ancient temples and palaces had been built, they answered: "They were built by giants before the sun was placed in the heavens." That was undoubtedly an exaggeration, but it gave an idea of what an immense antiquity they had. M. LePlongeon tells us in his writings that the alphabet of the Mayas was very similar to that of the Egyptians. The ancient pyramids of Mexico are larger than those of Egypt.

Nature worship, the worship of the Plural Gods and the Order of the Sacred Mysteries, were also practiced by the Mayas.

All the rest of the Western Hemisphere was covered with uncivilized tribes of Indians. Ancient statues of white people, the negro and red people, were found on this hemisphere in Yucatan and Central America. And plenty of white people have come to other parts of this hemisphere since and built up the great American Republic, as a forerunner of liberty, religious and political, and culture for the people of the entire world.

Religion, like politics, is either Republican or Monarchic. In religion, as in politics, the people were evoluted into existence with the natural right of self-government. And this is the grand idea, religious, as well as political liberty, on which our free Republic is founded. It is not only a Republic in politics, but is also a Republic in religion, all human beings having the right to think and choose for themselves in religion as well as in politics. They have to be free in both or they can not be free in either permanently. As a rule, all the crimes committed in the name of religion, the world over, have been committed in monarchies, and with the aid of the monarchies, or have flowed from the practices of some monarchic idea in a Republic. People had to believe in religion, as in politics, just what the monarchic ursupers of the rights of the people ordered them to believe, or be sent to the stake to be burned, or put on the rack to be pulled to pieces, joint by joint. But our glorious Declaration of Independence, that all men are born free and equal and endowed by their Creator, nature, with certain inalienable rights, among which are life, liberty and the pursuit of happiness, carried out by our laws, has prevented such tyrannical murders in our free land. The author of the Declaration of Independence, Thomas Jefferson, believed that Nature was the

Creator. And this perfect religious liberty has at last led to the discovery of the entire truth concerning creation, life and salvation, or the true story of the world. The American who made that discovery was born in Moscow, Rush County, Indiana, the 29th day of January, 1835. His parents were Asa Gooding and his wife, Matilda Gooding. About seventy-one years ago Asa Gooding and Matilda Hunt eloped and were married. Matilda's father, Lemuel Hunt, of Fleming County, Kentucky, objected to the marriage on account of the youth of both of them. Asa being but eighteen years of age and Matilda only fourteen. According to prearrangement, Asa came one midnight, accompanied by a young gentleman friend, and the two hitched their horses a short distance from the residence of Mr. Hunt, who was at that time a slaveholder, and waited for Matilda to meet them there. In every slave-holding family there was a negro woman who took care of the children and who was called the mamma. This character in the family of Mr. Hunt helped Matilda to elope. She occupied a room immediately above that of the old folks. At midnight Matilda gently raised her window and threw out a bundle of her clothing, which was caught by the mamma. Then gently descending the stairway, as the old folks snored, she lightly slipped through their room out into the yard, where the mamma awaited her, and carried her bundle for her to the horsemen. The young gentlemen mounted. Asa's friend carrying the bundle and Matilda mounted behind Asa, they started on their night ride to Maysville, fifty miles away. There they took a boat down the Ohio River, and on the Indiana shore, below Cincinnati, were married by a Justice of the Peace in the presence of all the officers and passengers of the boat, who went out to the residence of the Justice to see the young runaway couple married. After visiting Cincinnati, they returned to Kentucky, and were forgiven by Matilda's father, in whose home they lived for some time before they went to housekeeping and finally moved to Indiana. When Matilda's father discovered that she had fled from home during the night, he at once suspected that she had eloped with Asa and talked of pursuing them, but being unable to find out in what direction they had gone, gave up the idea of pursuit. Asa Gooding's father was Captain David Gooding, of Fleming County, Kentucky, a slaveholder, for whom my brother, David, was named. He was a Captain in the Kentucky Regiment of Col. Richard M. Johnson, in the war of 1812.

In the battle of the Thames Capt. Gooding killed the famous Indian chief, Tecumseh. He was very proud of his son, Asa, and frequently visited him. He used to take pleasure in telling his grandchildren about the war of 1812. On those occasions he would take my sister, Vira, who was then a little girl, on his knee, and with the rest of us, his grandchildren clustered around him, he would tell how he killed Tecumseh. He said it was a battle man to man. White man to Indian, and Indian to white man. That he saw a plume rising up from behind a log; that he watched it closely, and soon saw that it was on the head of an Indian: that he fired with a rifle and the Indian fell dead; that he then ran and jumped over the log and scalped the Indian, who proved to be the great chief, Tecumseh. That scalp was in his house for many years, and was seen by my parents, and was finally torn up by his dogs, after he had moved to Indiana. Tecumseh had gotten a plume from some white man. My mother once said to my grandfather: As you killed Tecumseh, how did it pen that Col. Johnson got the credit for it? He said that Col. Johnson came to him and asked him if he ever expected to become a public man, and he told him that he did not; that he was satisfied with what he was, a planter. Whereupon Col. Johnson told him that, as he was a public man, it would help him very much if he could be given the credit of having killed Tecumseh, and asked him not to deny it if his, Johnson's friends, started a report that he had killed Tecumseh. Capt. Gooding too generously promised him that he would not deny it publicly. Col. Johnson's friends soon after started the report that he had killed Tecumseh, and he ran into the Vice-Presidency of the United States on the strength of it. Col. Johnson, when asked about it, never claimed the credit of it for himself, but simply allowed his friends to circulate the report that it might benefit him politically.

Judge Delaney R. Eccles, of Greencastle, Indiana, told the author that Capt. Gooding's company always claimed that he killed Tecumseh. The Judge lived in the same neighborhood with Capt. Gooding, in Kentucky, and knew him personally. Soldiers of the war of 1812 buried the old hero with the honors of the war in 1853, in Indiana, in the presence of a large concourse of people. Two of the great grandfathers of the author fought under General George Washington in the Revolutionary War. At the early age of two years the discoverer of the true story of a world removed with his parents to Greenfield, the county-seat of Hancock County, Indiana, east of Indianapolis, only twenty miles away. Here he passed his youth in a community of people from the South, mostly from Kentucky. His own parents being from that State. His father was during his life a farmer, school teacher, dry goods merchant and hotel keeper, doing business in his own property, a prominent citizen and a county officer; and his house was the political and social headquarters of the town. For fifty years past his family has been the most prominent family in the county, both politically and socially; in fact, the most prominent family that has ever lived in the county.

They were Whigs, as were nearly everybody else in town. At that time Democrats were few and far between in Greenfield, but the county was nearly equally divided between the two parties. His father died when he was not quite eight years old. For some time he grieved greatly for his father, whom he dearly loved. His mother nobly continued the struggle of life for their children, educating and bringing them up honorably. All the children in town went to school together in the County Seminary. There the discoverer of the true story of a world got his start in education. And there when a little boy he fell in love for the first time. The object of his love was a little girl, only two years younger than himself. She was the daughter of a prominent physician, who had a beautiful home in the west end of the town. They were familiarly known as Ol. and Dos. All the school children were in one room in the Old Seminary, seated behind desks. The older and larger children being seated behind the rear desks, while the smaller children were seated at the last row of desks in front. He on the boy's side of the room, and she on the girl's side. So they could be seen by all the children in the school. They were so much in love that they could not keep their eyes off each other. So everybody in the school soon discovered that Ol. and Dos. were desperately in love with each other, and determined to get all the amusement out of it they could. At first she tried to hide her love from him while he was looking at her, and had the girl who sat at the desk immediately behind her watch him and tell her when he was not looking at her so she could then feast her eyes on him. Once he suddenly looked around and caught her at that. Seeing she was caught she smiled sweetly at him and then kissed at him across the school room. He looked bashful and all the school laughed. Her brother, who was of the same age as Ol., reported that to her parents when they went home from school. Her father forbade her from acting so any more, and threatened to take her out of school if she repeated that conduct. The other girls, seeing Ol's. bashfulness, for their own amusement tried to get Dos. to go and kiss him on the play-ground one day. But she had been forbidden to do that and refrained. School ended and they had no more school in that town for several winters. Dos. told her sister Lou how much she loved Ol. and how much the girls all said Ol. loved her. And Lou told his sisters all about it. His sister, Mary Delilah Gooding, said: "What! are those little children thinking about love?" Ol. went to Dos'. father and asked his permission to call on her at her home. The Doctor thought they were too young and would not give his consent.

About this time Ol's. oldest brother changed from Whig to Democrat. He was a very bright and promising young lawyer. He had been a member of the

Legislature and the Whigs were very proud of him and wanted him to be their leader. So when he changed it made them so mad that one night they burned a tar barrel in the street and pretended to rejoice over his departure from the Whig party. A very powerful Whig and a Democrat had a fight over it and the Whig gained the victcry, notwithstanding Ol. held his little hands over the face of the prostrate Democrat to prevent the Whig from beating it. Ol's. brother and the same Whig were about to fight over it, when he, a twelve-year-old boy, looked so fiercely at him that he broke down completely and started home, and his Whig friends could not stop him. That broke up the crowd and everybody went home and went to bed. He was asked by some of his Whig friends why he broke down as he did. He explained to them that Ol. looked at him so fiercely that he was afraid he would shoot him; that he had heard that Ol. owned a pistol, and that he had gone home that night and laid awake all night thinking how near he had come to losing his life, and that he had resolved never to have anything more to do with politics as long as he should live. Ol. did own a pistol and would have used it had his brother been attacked. He changed his politics and stood by his brother and went to associating with Democrats. Dos'. father sent word to him not to let politics make any difference between him and Dos. Several other prominent Whigs became afraid that the boy would shoot them and demanded that he should be disarmed. To allay their fears his mother disarmed him.

Several winters passed before another teacher was employed by subscription, as was then the custom before days of public schools, and the school was again started in the old Seminary. Ol. and Dos. were again in the school room and gazing at each other. He was now a pretty good-sized boy, and she was a pretty good-sized girl. He was sixteen years old and she fourteen.

SPELLING CLASS.

The teacher placed in the spelling class those he thought were the four finest boys and the four finest girls in the school, standing them up out in front of the desks where all the scholars could see them side by side. One end of the class he called "head" and the other end "foot" of the class. When called out to take his place in the class, Ol. started to take his place alongside of Dos., when the teacher ordered him to the foot of the class. So Dos. started at the head of the class and Ol. at the foot of it. The teacher made a rule that whenever any member of the class missed spelling a word and it was spelled by any member standing lower in the class, the latter might move up and take the place of the first that misspelled it, and the misspeller would be left just that much nearer the foot of the class. For the pleasure of standing by Dos., Ol. resolved to study his spelling lessons hard and tried to spell his way up to her at the head of the class. It was the first time he had ever had ambition to study anything. Whenever that spelling class took its place out in the room all the scholars at their desks quit studying their lessons to watch that class and see how long it would take Ol. to spell his way up to Dos. Finally he spelled his way up till he stood along side of her at the head of the class. When he took his stand there all the school smiled, for they knew that was the object of his ambition and the reason why he had studied those spelling lessons so hard. A few days thereafter he spelled her down from head, when everybody smiled again. Not long thereafter she spelled him down from head and the teacher sent him all the way down to the foot of the class, and everybody laughed aloud, much to his mortification. To relieve his feelings the teacher announced that thereafter any person allowing himself or herself to be spelled down from head should go foot. That discouraged Ol., and for a while he neglected to study his spelling lesson, but the desire to stand by Dos. again caused him to study and spell his way up to her at the head of the class, when the teacher discontinued the class. Feeling deeply hurt, Ol. went home and said to his mother: "I don't want to go to that school any more." She tried to get out of him the reason why he did not want to go to that school any more, but he would give no reason. Believing her son had been wronged in school, she was very indignant, and declared that she would see if her child could not be treated right in that school. She went to the trustees and demanded of them that the trouble in school should be investigated and that her child should be treated right in school. The trustees called the teacher before them and required him to explain. He did so by stating that Ol. and Dos. were in love with each other and everybody in school knew it, and relating the foregoing story, and said that when spelling class was spelling all the rest of the school would stop studying their lessons to watch Ol. and Dos. That it was interfering with the rest of the school, and that he did not believe that school children ought to be in love with each other. So he discontinued the class. Others confirmed the teacher's statement and the trustees reported accordingly to Ol.'s mother, who laughed heartily at the story. She thought it was entirely too good to keep away from Dos.'s folks, so stepping into her father's drug store, she related to the Doctor the story of Ol. and Dos., as above related. The Doctor and Ol.'s mother had a hearty laugh over it together, and agreed that when the youngsters became of proper age they should marry. That evening at the supper table the Doctor told Dos. what he had heard and how he and Ol.'s mother had engaged them. Dos. told all the girls that she and Ol. were engaged. That their parents engaged them. His mother intended to tell him that she and Dos.'s father had engaged them. She began by asking, " Oliver, do you love that little girl?" He blushed and looked so bashful she desisted, and concluded to tell him some other time. At a party at her home she again tried to tell him about it in the presence of Dos., but owing to his bashfulness, she again desisted. But a gentleman told him. Envious grown people now conspired to break the engagement by lies and tricks. And through a misunderstanding coming home from school one day he thought she deserted him for another boy. Her father concluded that they had better be married, and she told their neighbors so. A Whig lawyer, who lived next door to her home, told her that the Whigs were not going to let her marry Ol., because he was a Democrat, and they were going to make her marry a Whig. On Back street, just opposite her home, lived a Democratic family, the only one in that part of the town. She, the Whig girl, went out through their garden, climbed the fence, crossed Back street and entered the home of that Democratic family for the first time and introduced herself. She then told them how the Whigs were going to prevent her from marrying Ol., because he was a Democrat, and make her marry a Whig. They inquired if her parents were willing that she should marry him. She told them they were. They then assured her that the Democrats would see that she married him. She then went home very happy.

CHAPTER 16.

AT WEST POINT.

Oliver then received an appointment to a cadetship at West Point from that distinguished statesman and polished gentleman, his life-long personal friend, Thomas A. Hendricks, who died as Vice-President of America under Cleveland's Administration, and who was fortunate in having a wife who has always been eminent in all the good qualities, and was an intellectual and congenial companion for him.

Cadet Gooding went to West Point at the age of eighteen years, leaving behind Dos., a sixteen-year-old girl, believing she had deserted him for another. The day before he left she sent word to him to be sure to call and see her before his departure, but as the young man by whom she sent the message wanted to marry her, he treacherously failed to deliver it. She told all the young folks she was going to wait for Ol. till he graduated, then marry him and go into the army with him. She said that in two years he would come home from West Point on forlough, highly educated, and she was determined to study hard while he was gone and be his equal when he came home. She said she had been his equal at school, if not his superior, and she intended to remain so and be worthy of him. He had studied hard to get to stand by her in the spelling class, and now she was studying hard to get to stand by him in marriage when he should graduate at West Point. It was a noble ambition for a sixteen-year-old girl. Her father employed a private tutor for her, who taught her the higher branches. She soon become a thoroughly educated and polished lady. It was June, 1853, when he entered West Point. The great Robert E. Lee was then Superintendent of the Academy, Jefferson Davis was Secretary of War, and Gen. Winfield Scott was Commander-in-Chief of the Army. These three great men reviewed the corps of cadets together. Scott walked in front of the line between Lee and Davis. Scott was dressed in full uniform, and was the grandest looking man that ever appeared in uniform, and he towered head and shoulders above Lee and Davis, who were themselves men full six feet tall. Lee was at that time the handsomest man in the world, and had as fine a presence as history accords to Washington. Davis was not handsome, but presented a tall and very dignified presence. One year passed by, and the corps of cadets went into camp on the north-east corner of the plain there at the Point, where they did every summer.

While Ol. was in Camp, Dos was at her home in what was then considered the West. She was at that time the most beautiful brunette in the world. From the crown of her head to the sole of her foot she was the perfection of beauty. Her large, glorious black eyes were never equalled, her features were classic perfection and her form was more perfect than that of the Venus de Medici. A finer suit of luxuriant black hair never adorned a woman's head. Her young lady friend having an illustrated New York paper, in which a grand fashionable dress party was represented, immediately insisted on Dos. making herself a full party dress, now called a party dress decollette. No such dress had ever been in Greenfield. There was nobody in that town that had ever made such a dress, so she had to make it herself. When it was done her particular friends among the girls went up to her house to see her dressed in it. They were so delighted with her beauty as shown by that dress that they insisted on her going down to the picture gallery and having her picture taken in that dress. They all repaired to the gallery and the picture was taken. When her mother saw the picture she did not recognize it as her daughter's photograph. To prove that it was her picture she put on that dress again and had her hair done up a la Pompadour for her mother to look at her. Then the old lady acknowledged it was a good picture of her, but told her to pull off that dress and never dress that way again as long as she lived. She said that she never would but once more and that would be for Ol. when he came home on furlough. Her mother told her not to do so then and not to have any more pictures of that kind taken. She went to the photographer and ordered him to destroy the negative and not to take any more pictures from it. He agreed to do so, but did not do it at once. Some men in town who knew that Ol. was under the full impression that Dos. had gone back on him for another, got the photographer to take one more picture from that negative and let them have it to send to him, expecting he would think Dos. had sent it to him, and would write to her thanking her for it, and that would bring matters all right between them. They sent it alone in an envelope without explanation. The post office at West Point was kept by a woman who had a younger sister, who, seeing that it was not a letter, through curiosity coaxed her older sister to let her open it and see what was in it. She found nothing there but the photograph, and was completely carried away with its beauty. She herself was engaged to be married to a cadet, and got her sister to let her show it to her intended before it should be delivered to Cadet Gooding. He was so carried away with its beauty he insisted on being allowed to take it up to the camp and show it to some of his cronies, promising he would return it. He and some of his cronies asked a cadet, William Proctor Smith, of Virginia, who was chief engineer to Gen. Robert E. Lee for a time during the war, to take it to Gooding and tell him how they had come into possession of it, and ask him to let them keep it if it was not the picture of any particular friend of his. Smith came into Gooding's tent while he was seated at his locker, busily engaged in writing, and laughing heartily as though he had a big joke to play, came up behind him, and, pushing the picture over his head held it in front of his eyes, and said as though he meant it: "That is fancy, do you know it?" Looking up at it suddenly, Gooding answered "No," and Smith said: "Somebody sent it to you from Greenfield; you had better take it and keep it," and immediately walked out of the tent with it. Ol. thought that the eyes looked like Dos'., but believing that he knew that she had never been dressed that way in her life, he concluded that it must be what Smith said it was, a fancy picture, sent to some other cadet, and they were trying to play off a joke on him with it. A cadet from Indiana, two classes ahead of his, was written to from Indiana and requested to explain to him that Dos. had not gone back on him. Instead of doing so, as was his duty, he went to two of Gooding's classmates and requested them to explain to him. They promised to do so, but did not. They explained to Gooding's roommate and requested him to explain to him. And from the description given to them of Dos. they knew that picture was Dos'. So they requested him to tell Gooding to come and get the picture. Gooding's roommate was so envious of him that he would not deliver the information, but falsely reported that he had. Not till thirty-five years afterwards did Gooding receive those explanations. During this encampment, as is the custom every summer, cadet hops were given three times a week in the Hall of the Academy. Ol. had the right to send away a certain number of invitations to ladies to attend the hops. He sent several to the young ladies of Greenfield. He sent one to Dos. for the express purpose of commencing a correspondence with her, which he hoped would lead to their marriage. But the meanest man in Greenfield, by the name of Moses W. Hamilton, instigated by great envy and the fact that Dos'. sister Lou had refused to marry him, corrupted the postmaster at Greenfield to intercept Ol's. invitation to Dos. and let his invitations to the other girls go to them. Dos. felt deeply hurt on learning that the other girls had received invitations from Ol, as she had not, not knowing that the postmaster had destroyed her invitation. She told the girls who received the invitations she felt like quitting her studies and giving up in despair. They told her to do nothing of the kind, and assured her they knew that Ol. did not care for them and did care for her. That some day or other her failure to receive an invitation from him would be satisfactorily explained. Ol. felt deeply hurt at receiving no thanks from Dos., not knowing his invitation to her had been intercepted. He gave up, believing that she had treated his invitation with silent contempt. Another year passed by and he went home on a furlough. He arrived at 10 o'clock A. M. Somebody who had seen him on the street had the news conveyed to Dos. All day he was nervous and longed for evening to come, when he intended to call on her. Finally evening came and he called on her. Her mother met him at the door. He asked if Miss Dos. was in. She answered sharply: "No, she has gone down to Mr. Hart's." He did not announce himself and her mother did not recognize him in the dark. He believed that she had gone away from home that evening to avoid him. The way one misunderstanding after another happened between them, and a regularly organized band of conspirators, professed friends to them, played tricks and lied to make trouble for them, is too disgusting to relate. Sufficient to say he returned to West Point at the end of his furlough a sad and disappointed lover. She was equally sad and disappointed, but he did not know that.

THE WEST POINT CONSPIRACY.

Cadet Gooding's envious roommate and another narrow-minded, mean classmate by the name of Marmaduke organized a secret conspiracy to try to dismiss him from the Point. The first went to his instructor in Chemistry, by the name of Shunk, and told him that Gooding was a very bitter enemy of his, and had called him "Skunk." That was an unmitigated lie, manufactured by the base and perfidious conspirator, but he insisted upon it so often with Shunk that he believed it, and entered into the conspiracy. The second went to Professor Bailey and told him that Gooding was a great enemy of his, and had abused him and all the other professors and instructors at the Point, and that he ought to be dismissed for it, and suggested that he have him declared deficient in Chemistry and sent away from the school. The professor agreed to it. Finally examination day came around. There were two subjects in Chemistry Gooding had entirely neglected, having never even looked at them. He had marked them, to be studied before examination day, but neglected to do that. All this was known to the treacherous roommate, and he went to Shunk and told him which the subjects were, and he selected them as the subjects he would give to Gooding to be examined on. Gooding went to the examination unconscious of the conspiracy, and faced the academic board with a clean black-board, and, in the language of the cadets, "fessed frigid," that is, confessed his entire ignorance of the subjects, and was declared not up to the standard in Chemistry required by the board. This was done, notwithstanding his marks received from his hostile instructor showed that he was proficient and more than up to the standard required. At that time the maximum was three, and an average mark of two was regarded as proving that the cadet was proficient in his study and up to the standard required. Gooding had an average of two and a half in Chemistry, thus proving that he was undoubtedly proficient in that study. But he was, nevertheless, turned back into the next class, and graduated one year after his own class. At times he exhibited great talent, even doing better than the book. In Trigonometry he originated a very simple, new way of solving a problem, which, as solved in the book, was very difficult. He was the only man in the class that ever did such a thing. Whenever he could get his mind away from his love affair he did well in his studies. In a mathematical work, entitled

"Stone Cutting," in the course of architecture, the most difficult study in the mathematical course, he stood head of his class.

The late General Robert H. Anderson, of Savannah, Georgia, was a classmate of his, and made the mean liar go with him to Professor Bailey and take back the lies he had told him, and ask him to retain Gooding at the Point. Bailey ordered the liar out of his house and ordered him never to show his face to him again. This was not the only time that Gooding was saved by the noble Anderson at the Point. Once they, with other classmates, went swimming in the Hudson River, at Gee's Point, which ends West Point in the river, opposite Constitution Island. Gooding took the cramp in one of his arms, and was about to drown, when Anderson swam out and brought him in to shore.

Gooding will never forget the clear, star-light night, after he was turned back, when Bob Anderson brought his sweet-heart, Sallie Clitz, who afterward became his wife, to serenade him with her glorious voice, singing a song, the chorus of which was "Hard Times, Hard Times, Will Come No More," with a few appropriate verses composed by her for the occasion.

That voice will sweetly sound in Gooding's ears as long as he lives, and Bob will always be in his heart. Anderson was the very soul of truth, honor and bravery. During the war he was a dashing cavalry General in the Southern Army. May God bless him, may God bless him, will ever be the prayer of my heart. In his efforts to save me Anderson had the assistance of his roommate, who was our classmate, Tom Berry, of Georgia, a noble character. He was a Colonel in the Southern Army during the war, and, like Anderson, is now dead. May God bless him, also. Gen. Joseph Wheeler, the great cavalry leader of the South, was, also, then a cadet, and was my friend. General George C. Strong, of Massachusetts, who was killed while leading a charge against Fort Wagner, in Charleston Harbor, was, also, then a cadet and was my friend.

Dos. was very much mortified by her lover being turned back, as she did not know the secret of it, but continued to wait for him. He could have mastered those two subjects inside of two hours, and saved himself being turned back that year, but neglected to do so, though he had more than ample time. Marmaduke's motive for his meanness was that I had, when we were plebes, once made a remark to him that he did not like. It was simply an innocent remark, which I forgot the moment it was made and could not now tell what it was to save my life.

Shunk died in the army, and Tom Lee, the base and treacherous roommate, whose motive was that he wanted the honor of being the only graduate in the class from Indiana, was a year thereafter found deficient, but on begging for it, was granted a re-examination, and passed by the skin of his teeth, but subsequently left the army under disgraceful circumstances to avoid dismissal, and now fills a dishonored grave.

Gooding's friends should have asked for a re-examination for him, in which case he would have passed it and graduated in his own class. One more year rolled by, and then, in less than a year more, Gooding was to graduate, and, unless something was done to prevent, he and Dos. would then marry. The envious Hamilton could not stand that, so he organized a conspiracy to prevent it. He sent women to Dos. to underestimate Gooding and praise up a certain man in Greenfield, who had been for years trying to get Dos. to marry him, and to continue to urge her to marry him. Hamilton also sent his own wife to her to do that dirty work. The rascally, cunning Hamilton manufactured what should be said to Dos. and the others delivered it. But Dos. gave them all the same answer: "That she did not want that man and that she did want Ol." Nevertheless, they boasted that they intended to beat Ol. out of Dos. The cunning Hamilton was not satisfied with his defeat, so he sent a woman to Ol's. sister, Vira, to say to her that they were boasting that they intended to beat Ol. out of Dos. On the impulse, Vira, through pride for her brother, indignantly replied: "I do not suppose Ol. will care if they do beat him out of Dos. I wrote telling him they were boasting that they were going to do so and he has written me no answer. So I do not suppose he will care." Vira told her mother what she had said about it, and her mother told Vira she was sorry that she had made such a reply, as Oliver might have been afraid to write about it for fear if he did Dos. might yet be pressed into marrying that man, and then everybody would say he had been cut out; and, besides that, Dos., when she should hear of her reply, might get mad and marry that man through pique. Dos. did that very thing. As soon as the conspirators reported to Dos. what Vira had said, she became very angry and declared that she would show Ol. whether he would care or not, and immediately told the conspirators she was ready to marry their man. She also told her father, mother and brother that she intended to marry that man. They asked her if she wanted that man and she said she did. They advised her to wait till Ol. graduated and see him before she thought of marrying anybody else. They told her that all her life she had told them she wanted him. She declared that she wanted the other man. The conspirators urged her to marry him at once. She did so, in the Methodist Church, only a few being present. The people would not go to the wedding, as they knew how it had been brought about. Dos. regretted the step she had taken, and soon resolved to see Ol. when he came home and try to get his consent that she should yet get a divorce and marry him. This was in the fall. The following year he graduated and came home.

Feeling that Dos. had not acted right in allowing the conspirators to press her into that marriage he never even looked toward her home as he passed by on his evening walks out the west end. Peeping out through the window blinds, Dos. saw that he never even looked toward the house and appeared so utterly indifferent to her, she concluded not to try with him that summer. She never appeared on the street, nor went to church that whole summer, but remained housed up till he had left for the army. This was not as it should have been. Dos. should have been allowed to wait for him till he graduated, been allowed to marry him, and when they started for the army all the people of that town should have turned out and made the welkin ring, cheering them as the train dashed away, and as long as it remained in sight. That is what it should have been. Years rolled by. The great civil war came, passed, and I was out of the army and living in Greenfield. Dos., as good and noble a woman as ever lived, appealed to my mother and sisters, and sister-in-law, and others, to get my consent that she should get a divorce and marry me yet, and suicided because I would not give my consent. As she had lived with her husband so many years I thought it was too late for her and me.

CHAPTER 17.
IN THE ARMY.

I was first stationed at Governor's Island, in New York harbor, where I remained for nearly ten months. Here I was introduced into the first society of New York City by the family of my friend, Cadet Samuel N. Benjamin, who was still at West Point. The Benjamins resided in a splendid brown stone front on Fifth avenue, near Twenty-first street, the then fashionable part of the city.

The following summer I went with recruits to Utah, and joined the Tenth United States Infantry at Fort Bridger. The army of Gen. Albert Sidney Johnston, who fell at Shiloh in command of the Southern army during our late civil war, was then occupying Utah, having marched out there against the then hostile

THE AUTHOR.

Mormons. The following spring I went over to Camp Floyd and Salt Lake City on leave of absence. I then returned to Fort Bridger, and soon afterwards marched with two companies of the Tenth Infantry to Fort Laramie, near the junction of the rivers Laramie and the North Platte. Here I was stationed when the troubles began after the election of Abraham Lincoln in 1860.

PRESIDENTIAL CANVASS OF 1860.

In 1860 Lincoln was the Republican candidate for the Presidency on a platform that expressly declared in favor of Congress passing a law prohibiting slavery in the Territories.

The Democratic party was opposed to that, and was divided as to whether the people of the Territories should have the right to abolish slavery within their borders. The Southern Democrats claimed that slaveholders had the same right to take their slaves into the Territories that the Northern farmer had to take his horse there, and that the slaveholder should enjoy the same protection for his slave property from the Territorial laws that the Northern farmer in the Territory had for his horse. And that neither Congress nor the Territorial Legislature should abolish slavery in the

Territories. That the people of the Territory alone, when they became a State, should have power to abolish slavery within their borders.

The Northern Democrats claimed that the slaveholder had the right to take his slaves into the Territory, but that the Territorial Legislature could abolish slavery at any time. This was called Squatter Soveriegnty.

This difference between the Northern Democrats and the Southern Democrats divided the Democratic party, which resulted in the Northern Democrats running Douglas for the Presidency and the Southern Democrats running Breckinridge for the same office.

The division in the Democratic party caused Lincoln's election by a strictly Northern vote, he carrying every Northern State. Douglas, although receiving the Northern Democratic vote, with the exception of a few who voted for Lincoln, and an occasional voter who voted for Breckinridge, failed to carry a single Northern State. He, however, carried Missouri. Breckinridge carried all the slave States except Missouri and Maryland.

John Bell, of Tennessee, running for the Presidency on a platform of "The Union, the Constitution and the Enforcement of the Laws," carried Maryland.

It was not safe for any one to vote for Lincoln in the South, so intense was the feeling against him in that section. Because Lincoln was elected, eleven of the slave States seceded and formed the "Southern Confederacy," and defied the National authority.

Jefferson Davis was elected President of the Southern Confederacy by the Confederate Congress and inaugurated as such at Montgomery, Ala. The Capitol of the Confederacy was afterward removed to Richmond, Va., and there it was when Lincoln was inaugurated at Washington, at which point he had been compelled to arrive in disguise, to avoid assassination, owing to the great hostility of the pro-slavery people of Baltimore and Washington.

A Peace Conference had been held in Washington by delegates appointed by the Governors of the States, the object of which was to arrive at a compromise that would prevent an armed conflict. The effort was a failure.

The leading Union men in Congress from the North, Republicans and Democrats, offered to put an amendment in the Constitution making slavery eternal in the States, where it was at that time, unless each State saw fit of its own volition to abolish it in its own borders, but prohibiting its extension into the Territories. The Southerners refused this offer of compromise. The Southerners had already taken possession of some of our forts and custom houses in the South. Lincoln, in his inaugural, declared that he would hold, occupy and possess our forts and public property in the South.

WAR.

Jefferson Davis, as President of the Confederacy, demanded the surrender for Fort Sumter. The issue of war was thus presented to the Government. Lincoln called a meeting of his Cabinet to consider it. At that meeting, all of the Cabinet except one member, a West Pointer, voted in favor of surrendering Fort Sumter. Lincoln, although overruled by his Cabinet, refused to surrender the fort. To Lincoln's firmness on that occasion we owe the Union of to-day.

Davis ordered Beauregard to fire on Fort Sumter. At the end of three days' bombardment by the Confederate batteries around Charleston Harbor, Sumter was surrendered by Maj. Anderson, who was in command of it. And thus the war began. No one disputed that Lincoln had been legally elected President, but the South made an appeal from the ballot-box to the bayonet. Lincoln called for seventy-five thousand volunteers. The fires of patriotism glowed throughout the North. The call was more than filled. Lincoln called a special meeting of Congress for the Fourth of July. Congress met and legalized Lincoln's acts and declared that the Government would only continue the war for the purpose of preserving the Union, and when that object was accomplished the war should cease, and expressly declared that it was not the purpose of the Government to abolish slavery. And Lincoln, as President, repeatedly warned the Southerners to lay down their arms and submit to the National authority, and if they did not, slavery would be abolished in the States, and if they did, slavery would not be interfered with. They indignantly refused to do so and defied the Government. In revolutions men's minds travel rapidly. The repeated refusals of the South to submit to the National authority, although assured that slavery in the States would not be interfered with, soon satisfied the wise men to close the war without abolishing slavery would simply be to leave the bone of contention in existence to breed a subsequent civil war. But notwithstanding that fact, Lincoln notified them if they did not submit to the National authority by the 1st of January, 1863, he would issue the Emancipation Proclamation at that time. And in the Proclamation there were exceptions in favor of certain parts of the South where they were supposed to be submitting to the National authority. Subsequently an amendment was offered to the Constitution abolishing slavery throughout the country. And, thus, the war on the part of the loyal people became not only a war to compel the Southerners to submit to the National authority, but, also, one for universal freedom. On these issues the Presidential canvass of 1864 was made and the war fought to a conclusion.

PRESIDENTIAL CANVASS OF 1864.

In the Presidential canvass of 1864 Lincoln and Andrew Johnson were the successful candidates, for President and Vice-President, of the Union party, composed of Republicans and war Democrats.

At the beginning of the war, Douglas, the great leader of the Northern Democracy, called on the people of the North to lay down party and support Lincoln as long as the war lasted, telling them it would be time to go back to their parties when the war was over.

Such was high patriotic ground and a great honor to Douglas. But some men loved office too much to follow that patriotic advice and returned to their parties during the war.

General George B. McClellan, running for the Presidency as the candidate of the Democratic party, that party having a Peace Platform demanding a cessation of hostilities, that a Convention of the States might be held, to the view that the Union might be restored by compromise, they declaring four years of war had failed to restore the Union.

The true war men of the country believed the time for compromise had passed, and while four years of war had failed to restore the Union, five or more years of war would accomplish that result, and, therefore, opposed a cessation of hostilities, and favored fighting it out. The glorious result proved the wisdom of their judgment. McClellan was a true war man, and his letter of acceptance repudiated the platform of his party by declaring, if elected President, he would prosecute hostilities till the Union was restored by war.

For the organization and discipline of the Army of the Potomac and the great victories of South

Mountain and Antietam, won by that army under McClellan, the country is under everlasting obligation to that gallant and accomplished General. In the matters leading to the removal of McClellan from the command of the army, I neither condemn Lincoln nor McClellan. It is sufficient for me to know they were both patriotic and did the best they could for their country in the light before them.

THE WAR FROM A MILITARY STANDPOINT.

The South had to be compelled to obey the Constitution as the supreme law of the land. The topography of the country at once suggested to the military mind the campaigns necessary to accomplish that result, which were finally made, and resulted in the submission of the South.

These were campaigns by the Army of the Potomac down the Atlantic slope to Richmond. By the Army of the Shenandoah from Harper's Ferry up the Shenandoah Valley toward Lynchburg. By the Army of the Ohio from Louisville, Ky., across Kentucky and Tennessee. By the Army of the Mississippi, at Cairo, Ill., to open the Mississippi river, in conjunction with our army from New Orleans coming up the river. By the Armies of the Tennessee and Cumberland to open those rivers. In a military sense, the opening of these rivers meant the dividing of the enemy's forces, and then dstroying them in detail. By an army from St. Louis operating west of the Mississippi river in Missouri and Arkansas, while our army in New Orleans operated in Louisiana. The naval and army movement against New Orleans, under Farragut and Butler, which resulted in the fall of that city, was an attack in the enemy's rear. The army and naval movements against Wilmington, N. C., and Port Royal and Charleston, S. C., were attacks in the enemy's flank. The western army and the naval squadron under Admiral Farragut, moving down the Mississippi, taking all the fortified places, including Vicksburg, and our army from New Orleans moving up the river with Farragut's squadron, taking Baton Rouge and Port Hudson, opened the Mississippi, thus dividing the South. The South was again divided by the movements up the Tennessee and Cumberland rivers, in a south-east direction from Cairo, Ill., toward Savannah, Ga., the line of Sherman's grand march to the sea, on which was captured Fort Donaldson, Fort Henry, Nashville, Shiloh, Atlanta and Savannah. From Savannah Sherman's army marched up the Atlantic slope through Richmond to Washington City, capturing Joe Johnston's army on the way at Goldsboro, N. C.

The Army of the Potomac and Sherman's army passed in review by the Capital and up Pennsylvania avenue in front of President Johnson and Cabinet, making the grandest military scene ever witnessed on earth, President Lincoln having been assassinated on the 14th of April, 1865.

At Fort Laramie, where I was stationed when the war came on, the North and South were about equally represented by officers. Among the Southern officers were Generals Bee and Dunovant, of South Carolina, both of whom, I am proud to say, were my closest friends. John Dunovant had killed Legree in a duel at Charleston in 1852, and was first to start for the South. Barnard E. Bee was also a Captain in my regiment. One day Bee came to my quarters and said: "Gooding, come, Dunovant is going to start for home, and wants to bid you good bye before he goes." I went with Bee across the Laramie river, and there in the bottom was Dunovant alone with his steed. He wanted to coax me to go South. Bee would not allow him to say anything to me about it. There we bade Dunovant farewell, and, as he rode away toward the States, we longingly looked after him, and wondered if we would ever see him again.

It was destined to be the last time I should ever see him on the earth. He fell gallantly fighting in one of the cavalry engagements near Petersburg, near the close of the war, as a Brigadier-General in the Southern army. Bee was the next man to leave for the South. He was a Brigadier-General, and in command of a brigade of South Carolina troops at the first battle of Manassas. In the hottest of the fight his men were wavering a little. Pointing with his sword toward Jackson's brigade, he said to them: "Look yonder at Jackson and his men; they stand there like a stone wall," and thus caused Jackson to become known as "Stonewall Jackson" forever. But no sooner had he done that than he fell from his horse, slain by the enemy's bullets. Thus perished those two Southern friends of mine. No nobler nor braver men ever died on the battle-field.

When the regular troops from Utah, under the command of Col. Philip St. George Cook, passed by Fort Laramie on their way to the defense of Washington City, I joined the column and went with it to that city, arriving there in September, 1861. With that column were officers who afterwards became prominent in the Union army, Gen. John Buford, Gen. W. P. Sanders and Gen. Wesley Merritt. Dr. John Moore, since the war Surgeon-General of the army, now on the retired list, was also with the column. I remained on duty in that city with the regulars till the following February. While there I was introduced to President Lincoln, and made the acquaintance of many of the then leading men of the nation, both in civil and military life. Governor John A. Andrew, of Massachusetts, then asked the War Department to send him a good regular officer to command a volunteer regiment. The War Department selected and sent me to the Governor. I reported to him at the State House in Boston. He immediately commissioned me Colonel of the Thirty-first Massachusetts volunteers. I assumed command of that regiment at Lowell, where I reported to, and was the guest of Gen. Benj. F. Butler.

CHAPTER 18.

EXPEDITION AGAINST NEW ORLEANS.

The 21st day of February, 1862, I sailed on a new ship, called the Mississippi, with the regiment from Boston, for Ship Island, in the Gulf of Mexico, to join the Farragut-Butler expedition against New Orleans. On board were Colonel Neal Dow, and a part of his regiment from Maine. At Fortress Monroe, Virginia, we took on board Gen. Butler and his staff, and Mrs. Gen. Butler.

At Cape Hatteras the vessel ran on Frying Pan Shoal and knocked a hole in its bow, and the water ran into the forward compartment of the hull seventeen feet deep. The vessel had four air-tight compartments. If she had had only one, the entire hull would have filled with water, and the ship would have sunk.

We went into Port Royal, South Carolina, which was in possession of the Union troops, to have the vessel repaired. We arrived at Ship Island about thirty days from the time we left Boston. About five weeks thereafter we started on the expedition against New Orleans.

FARRAGUT RAN BY THE FORTS.

The troops had no fighting to do, as the forts surrendered after Farragut's fleet had run by them. This was the first time in naval warfare that feat had ever been performed. I had the pleasure of witnessing that grand sight from the hurricane deck of a naval magazine boat, in company with Gen. Butler and his staff. It was a clear, starlight night, when, leaving our troops on transports below, we steamed up the center of the river toward the forts. As we passed up, first was Porter's mortar fleet, on the left, and then, on either side, close up to the shore, were the two sections of gunboats. Not a light was in sight in either or fleet on shore, and all was silent as death. Impatiently we looked back to see the gunboats start up the river to run by the forts. The signal for that movement was to be the running up of a light on Farragut's flagship, which headed the section on the right hand shore going up the river.

At exactly three o'clock in the night we saw that signal run up on the flagship, and held up our boat till both sections of the gunboats passed by us. The guns of Fort Jackson, on the left bank, were the first to open fire on the gunboats. As they went up the river, and as they ran by the forts, the right section of the fleet replied to the guns of Fort St. Philip and the batteries outside on that shore, while the left section of the fleet replied to the guns of Fort Jackson and the batteries outside on that shore. The leading gunboats also replied to the Confederate gunboats, which were firing down the river at them. At the same time Porter's mortar fleet was throwing shells from below into Fort Jackson and the batteries outside on that bank. The flashes from all the guns on both sides, and the burning raft that came down the river into the faces of the Union fleet, along with the roar of all the guns, made the grandest display of warfare that ever was seen on earth.

Farragut, lashed on high to the mast, the better to view the fight, started to run by the forts with seventeen vessels. All but one got by, and went on up to the city, after destroying the Confederate gunboats. Gen. Lovell retired from the city with his Confederate troops, thinking the army was following the fleet. Farragut sent some sailors on shore to run up the American flag over the custom house and the mint. After they retired to the boats, a mob tore down the flag from the mint, trailed it in the dust of the streets, and then tore it up, each taking a piece of it home with him. In a few days the forts surrendered, and we went up in transports to the city. We made our dispositions to attack the forts, but they surrendered before we could do so. We arrived before the city the first day of May, 1862. I led the advanced regiment in taking possession of the city. We landed at the foot of St. Joseph street, marched up that street to St. Charles, and down that street to Canal, and down Canal to the custom house, and took possession of it. We quartered in the custom house for some time. Gen. Butler made his quarters in the St. Charles Hotel temporarily. He then ordered a military commission to try the leader of the mob that had torn the flag from the mint and trailed it in the dust. The commission sentenced him to be hung. Butler accordingly had him hung. Soon after, Butler gave me command of all the country below New Orleans, with headquarters in Fort Jackson. My command also included Fort Pike, on Lake Pontrochaine. In December following, Gen. N. P. Banks relieved Gen. Butler of the command of the Department of the Gulf, and I was then assigned to the command of the Third Brigade, Third Division, Nineteenth Army Corps. This brigade consisted of the Thirty-first Massachusetts Volunteers, the Thirty-eighth Massachusetts Volunteers, the Fifty-third Massachusetts Volunteers, the One Hundred and Fifty-sixth New York Volunteers, and the One Hundred and Seventy-fifth New York Volunteers. This brigade I commanded on the Teche and Port Hudson campaigns. At the battle of the Teche, on Bayou Teche, near Pattersonville, Louisiana, this brigade carried off the highest honors of the battle. I was in command of all the troops on the north side of the bayou, and made my own dispositions for the battle. The enemy were behind breastworks. My loss in killed and wounded was heavy.

We pursued the enemy, Gen. Dick Taylor's army, up the Teche and beyond Alexandria on the Red river. We then marched down the Red river to the Mississippi, and down that river to Morganza, where we took boats to the village of Bayou Sara, on the east side of the river, about twelve miles above Port Hudson, which was on the same side of the river.

PORT HUDSON.

From there Gen. Banks marched out and invested Port Hudson on the north and east, Gen. Augur at the same time having come up from Baton Rouge on the east bank, twenty-two miles below, and invested it on the south and east. Our army, making an investing force in the shape of a semi-circle, eight miles long, reached from the river above around to the river below. Farragut came up the river at the same time and bombarded the river front. He subsequently ran some of his gunboats by the works to patrol the river above, Admiral Porter, at Vicksburg, having run some of his gunboats by the works at that point to patrol the river below. We arrived in front of the enemy's works the 26th of May, and drove the enemy into his works by night-fall.

FIRST ASSAULT.

The next morning we assaulted the works, and were repulsed, with heavy loss. Early in the day one of my officers, Captain, afterwards Lieutenant-Colonel, William S. B. Hopkins, came to me and asked me to go with him to the extreme right of the white troops, from which point he pointed out to me a place where the enemy had not thrown up any works. I immediately went to Gen. Weitzel and asked his permission to take my brigade and charge in at that point and down in front of his position, thus to double up the enemy and enable him to charge over the works and take Port Hudson. Weitzel gave his consent, but just then Gen. Grover came to that part of the line and assumed command. Weitzel said: Grover, Gooding wants to take his brigade and go to a point where the enemy have not yet thrown up their parapet and charge in. Grover immediately said: The troops will all remain just as they are, and thus prevented Port Hudson from being captured that day by assault, which would have been led by Gooding, and put us all to the trouble of another assault and a siege.

Then we began the siege. My brigade was assigned a position in a mignificent magnolia grove, which was in bloom. At first we pitched no headquarter tents, but the members of my staff slept around the root of a great tree, while I slept alongside of a small log near by. Inside of the enemy's works was a forty-two-pound gun, which the Confederate soldiers called the "Lady Davis," after the wife of the Confederate President. Lady Davis used to throw her great shells into our magnolia grove, of nights, just to keep us awake and wear us out. One night she threw a shell into my headquarters, which struck on the other side of the log I slept with, about opposite my waist, and burst, covering me with splinters from the top of the log. Hearing the noise of the coming shell, I involuntarily contracted into a knot and pulled the blanket over my head and held it tight. Had the shell lit on my side of the log the blanket would not have protected me, but that action only showed how a man in great danger will act when he has no time to think what to do. That was an extremely dark night. The headquarters of Gen. Godfrey Weitzel were not far from mine. Shortly after the shell exploded I heard a voice coming through the darkness calling my name. I answered to let him know where I was. He then said Gen. Weitzel sends his compliments, and wants to know if that shell hurt any of you, as he thinks it must have fallen in your headquarters. He was Weitzel's Orderly. I sent my compliments to Gen. Weitzel, with the information that none of us were hurt. My staff officers then built a very pleasant arbor, in which they built a stationary table. Around that table we used to sit after dinner and smoke and listen to Capt. Russell read Pickwick Papers. After the surrender I marched away, but looked back at that arbor with genuine regret.

THE SECOND ASSAULT.

Saturday afternoon Gen. Halbert E. Paine, who was at that time in command of our division, came to my brigade headquarters and took me alone with him, on foot, around to the left of our position, and showed me that part of the enemy's works he had been ordered to assault with his division. He asked me what I thought of it. I told him it was a very rough place to assault; that we would have a bloody time of it there. Yes, but we must go in, said the General. Yes, said I, we must go in, but we will have a bloody time getting in. We then went back to his tent, where we sat and talked for some time. While there I happened to notice what a beautiful foot he had in a patent leather boot, and mentally said to myself, if a man could have a cork foot as beautiful as that, it would not make much difference if he did lose a foot. The next morning, the 14th day of June, 1863, in the assault, which was repulsed, Paine lost a foot. He was shot below the knee. He fell and laid in a small furrow, which hid him from the sight of the enemy when his Chasseur cap was off. When he put it over his face to protect it from the sun the enemy would shoot at it, so he had to lie there most of the day with the sun burning in his face.

Several men tried to get to him during the day to carry him back to the surgeon, but all of them were killed by the enemy. Finally Lieutenant-Colonel John A. Foster, of the One Hundred and Seventy-fifth New York volunteers, came to me with a canteen full of wine, and told me that he was going to send Woods, a cool and determined man, who was in command of the stretcher corps, whose duty it was to carry the wounded back to the surgeons, to Gen. Paine. Capt. Hollister, the Captain of the company to which Woods belonged, came at the same time, and protested against Woods being allowed to go to Paine, saying that it would be certain death to Woods, and that he was not willing to lose Woods, as he was the best man in his company. I was placed in a tight place. There was one officer wanting to send him to a wounded General, and another, his Captain, protesting against it as certain death to him. I determined to let Woods decide the question for himself. I asked Woods if he was willing to go. He said he was. I then told him he could go. He went, and before he got near him he got down on his hands and knees and crawled till he got near him, and told him he had a canteen of wine for him. Paine told him not to come any nearer, but to throw the wine to him. Woods did as Paine directed, and he got the wine. Woods then crawled off for some distance and rose to walk away, when he was shot dead. There died as brave a soldier as was ever killed on the battlefield. When night came I ordered a member of my staff to take some men and carry Paine back to the surgeon. I never saw him again till I met him after the war in Washington City, where he was a member of Congress. He had a cork foot, and on it a beautiful patent leather boot, just like the pair he had on that Saturday afternoon before the second assault. I told Paine the thoughts I had that afternoon concerning his beautiful boot. He immediately said he remembered the boots, and that they did not belong to him; that he had borrowed them from Captain Pierce, of the Fourth Wisconsin. I then told him the story of the gallant Woods. He was deeply moved by it. He remembered how he got the wine, but never had before known who the man was that threw it to him, and that he had been killed in trying to get away from the spot. Paine said that the wine had braced him up and saved his life, otherwise he thinks he would have died with exhaustion lying there in the sun.

We then resumed the siege. After having been

there forty days and forty nights, Port Hudson surrendered. My loss in the second assault was very heavy. When the assault was repulsed in the morning, our orders were to screen ourselves from the enemy's fire the best we could till night, and then withdraw and resume our original position in line around the works. My men were immediately in front of the enemy's works, where we had charged, with the exception of the One Hundred and Seventy-sixth New York Volunteers, which I had ordered to remain in reserve behind the hedge. A cannon ball fired at us as we charged the works in front of the hedge passed over our heads and killed Col. Bryan behind the hedge, who was there in reserve with his regiment. During the day I went from one regiment to the other to let them know I was with them, as they laid on the ground trying to screen themselves from the enemy's fire. Every time I passed from one regiment to another, I was shot at by sharpshooters behind the enemy's works, but their bad firing saved me.

Col. Dudley came by and asked me to go a short distance to the rear with him, where his cook had brought his dinner. I dined with him, and was refreshed by his food and his claret wine. We then returned to our commands. Col. Birge and I sat behind a solitary bale of cotton for a little while in the afternoon, and then went around visiting our regiments, and were shot at every time we moved. It was as dangerous behind the hedge as it was in front of it. A party of us sitting in rear of it at one time had four bullets fall among us that had been fired at men in front of it, but fortunately none of them hit either of us. Banks' entire army charged the works, and were all repulsed in both assaults.

General Frank Gardner commanded the enemy on the inside of the works. On the outside of the works, Gen. Cuvier Grover, who commanded a division, Col. N. A. M. Dudley, who commanded a brigade, and myself, who also commanded a brigade, were all, as well as Gen. Gardner, from the Tenth United States Infantry, and then we were fighting each other in the civil war. In command of my brigade I participated in both assaults on the works, and in the siege of forty days and forty nights. My loss in killed and wounded was heavy in both assaults, and in the first assault I was slightly wounded in the left hand, but on account of its being so slight a wound I did not report it. We were besieging Port Hudson at the same time Grant was besieging Vicksburg. Vicksburg surrendered on the Fourth of July. When the news reached us by way of the navy down the river, our men went to cheering all along the lines. Across the works, only a few feet away, the enemy wanted to know what we were cheering about, and were told the news. Gardner sent a flag of truce to Banks to inquire if it was true that Vicksburg had fallen. General Banks convinced him that it was true, and he surrendered Port Hudson on the 8th of July, and the Mississippi river was open and flowed unvexed to the sea; and when we heard of the great victory of Gettysburg, that had been won on the third of July, we all then knew that the Union would be preserved, and great was the rejoicing by the loyal people, in the army and out of the army, throughout the land. Port Hudson would have fallen in a few days, had Vicksburg never fallen, as its provisions were all out.

The day of the surrender Gen. Banks had Gen. Gardner and his staff dine with him at his headquarters in rear of our line around the enemy's works, where I met them. One of his staff proved to be an old friend of mine, Col. John A. Jaques, who was a nephew of my brother-in-law, Dr. N. P. Howard, Sr., who is a prominent physician of Central Indiana, and was an assistant surgeon in the Union army during the war. I asked Gen. Banks to let me take Col. Jaques to pass the night with me at my headquarters. He gave permission, and Jaques and I talked over old times at Greenfield that night. He had married in Louisiana, and had gone with the State of his wife. Gen. Gardner was too proud to tell Gen. Banks that the rations were out at his headquarters, but Jaques told me so. The next morning, when Jaques returned to Gardner, I sent my Commissary along with him, with a wagon load of provisions and good things for Gardner and his staff. I afterward dined with them in their prison in New Orleans. The last time I saw them was in Fort Lafayette, New York Harbor, where all that was left of the Tenth United States Infantry, which had been almost decimated in the Army of the Potomac, less than one hundred men, were guarding Gardner and his staff. I was then on my way to go on the Red river campaign.

Gen. Gardner made a gallant defense of Port Hudson, not only against us, but against Farragut's fleet on the river side, and Banks made two gallant assaults on the works. After the repulse of the second assault, Banks organized a forlorn hope. I went to him and volunteered to lead it. He thanked me very kindly, but told me he had already selected Col. Birge for that. The enemy surrendered before we had any use for it. By his position at port Hudson, Gen. Banks not only held Gardner's forces there, but also held Dick Taylor's army in Western Louisiana, and detached forces of the enemy east of the river, and kept all of them from uniting and marching against Grant at Vicksburg.

After the fall of Port Hudson I marched my brigade to Baton Rouge, and took all the light artillery that had been captured at Port Hudson along with me, by a night march. I then went home to Indiana on a short leave of absence. I went up the river as far as Vicksburg on an ocean steamer with Gen. Banks, where I first met both Generals Grant and Sherman. I had not been at home for five years, nor had I seen the face of a relation during all that time. I was only there about twelve days. During that time I took the Blue Lodge Degrees of Free Masonry, under special dispensation. Returning to Baton Rouge, I found myself the ranking officer, and assumed command in that district. I was there in command till December, when I was sent via the ocean to Washington, D. C., as bearer of dispatches to the General-in-Chief, Henry W. Halleck, and the Secretary of State, Wm. H. Seward. Having delivered the dispatches, I went to the Adjutant-General of the United States Army, E. D. Townsend, and told him that I would like to remain in Washington for a while, as Congress would soon be in session. He told me that would suit him, as they were trying to find officers enough to organize a military commission to try some offenders. He told me that the Secretary of War, Edwin M. Stanton, required him to report each officer to him for his approval. He told me that he would not tell Stanton that I was a regular, for if he did Stanton would not select me as one of the commission, as he thought regulars were too lenient toward the Southern offenders ; that he would only tell him that I was Col. Gooding, of the Thirty-first Massachusetts Volunteers, and, as I hailed from Massachusetts, he would think I was all right.

CHAPTER 19.
DOUBLEDAY COMMISSION.

I was then put on the commission, which is known in history as the "Doubleday Military Commission," General Doubleday being President of the same. That commission subsequently tried some of the assassins of Abraham Lincoln. I had been recommended by my superior officers, who served with me, for promotion to a Brigadier-Generalship. When Congress met, Senators Sumner and Wilson, of Massachusetts, and Gov. John A. Andrew, of the same State, and the delegation in the House from that State, as well as the delegation in Congress from Indiana, asked for my promotion. There were only seven vacancies in the number of Brigadier-Generalships allowed by law. When President Lincoln, Secretary Stanton and Gen.

Halleck met to consult as to what Colonels they would place in those vacancies, Lincoln and Stanton were both in favor of promoting me. Gen. Halleck argued them out of it by saying that while I had earned the right to promotion, the department in which I served was not entitled to it, as the troops in other departments had done more fighting than the troops in the Department of the Gulf, and that I was a young officer and could afford to wait for promotion. In that way I was cheated out of my promotion. This much I was told at the time, but all I never knew till many years after. Col. John C. Kelton was Adjutant-General on the staff of Gen. Halleck. General Halleck was very anxious to get regular officers to take rank in the colored troops. Kelton told Halleck if he could defeat my promotion to a white Brigadier-Generalship, he could get me to take a Brigadier-Generalship in the colored troops. Halleck accordingly defeated my promotion, as already related. Kelton then informed me that I could have a Brigadier-Generalship in the colored troops if I would accept it. I explained to him that the disinclination officers had to entering the Corps D'Afrique was simply a prejudice, and that while I had no prejudice against any race of men on earth, I felt that I had won my right to a white Brigadier-Generalship. Soon after I learned that the Red river campaign would be made in the spring. I went to Col. Townsend and told him I wanted to go on that campaign, and asked him to have me relieved from duty on the military commission that I might do so, a thing that few officers would have done. They selected one of Halleck's staff to relieve me. I returned to New Orleans, and commanded a cavalry brigade on the Red river campaign, which consisted of the Second New York Veteran Cavalry, Col. Chrysler; the Eighteenth New York Cavalry, Col. Byrne, and the Third Rhode Island Cavalry, Col. George R. Davis.

RED RIVER CAMPAIGN.

Going up Bayou Teche and the Red river my brigade was rear guard to the army. When we reached Grand Ecore I was sent across the Red river to drive Gen. Liddell's brigade of Confederate cavalry and some artillery he had away from the river bank, where they were annoying our transports and our gunboats.

BATTLE OF CAMPTI.

This battle was at the town of Campti, on the north bank of the river, about five miles above Grand

Ecore. Fearing that the enemy would escape, I personally led the charge through the little village of Campti and up the hill back of it into the immediate presence of the enemy. Looking around I saw that my troops had not kept up with me; that Lieut. Payne, of my staff, was the only man with me. I ordered him to go back and hurry up the command, and sat on my horse there and saw the enemy ride off down toward the bayou, west of town. Before they rode off I heard one of them say, that is their commander; let us kill him or capture him. No, said another, that is not their commander, for he has no insignia of rank about him. He is nothing but a private soldier. Let him alone. At the time I had no insignia of rank about me, and that is what saved me. I had already ordered Lieut. Payne to go back and hurry up the command. When the command came up, but a few moments after, we pursued them to the bayou, where they took position on the west side of the bayou, tearing up the center of a bridge that crossed it, according to his previous arrangements, and there had our fight, which was as desperate a cavalry engagement as was fought during the war. The gallant Chrysler charged with his men onto that bridge, and, finding it torn up, had to return under a galling fire. All my officers and men displayed great bravery in that engagement, which resulted in a glorious victory for us. Having gained this victory over Harrison's cavalry, which precipitately retreated to the west, I then marched out the road to the north of the town to fight Gen. Liddell, who retreated rapidly before me.

BATTLE OF PLEASANT HILL.

A few days later, on the 9th of April, 1864, the battle of Pleasant Hill was fought. The day before that battle I received my orders early in the day from Gen. William B. Franklin to go into position to fight a battle at Pleasant Hill, facing the south near the large brick seminary building there. At the same time he informed me that Gen. Green's Texas Confederate cavalry was expected to come in there to attack our army in the rear. Gen. Franklin ordered Col. Dickie's colored brigade to support me. I placed it in line of battle, and waited all that afternoon for Gen. Green to come, but he came not. Near evening we heard heavy cannonading off to the west, in front, which ceased very suddenly. That night, about twelve o'clock, one of Gen. A. J. Smith's staff came to my tent and woke me up and said: Gen. Smith sends his compliments to you, and wants to know if you have heard anything of the disaster in front. I sent him back to the General with the information that I had not heard anything of the disaster in front, and did not believe that any had occurred. No sooner had he left my tent than a cavalry officer from the disaster came to my tent and told me all about it. In a few moments more came, and I set my cook to cooking food for all that came. There was no more sleep for me that night. A little after daylight Gen. Franklin sent for me and said: "Gooding, you have the only organized cavalry in our army; all the rest of it was scattered yesterday. Get your brigade into the saddle, go to the front, and hold the enemy in check till we can get our army into position to fight a battle. We will have to fight a battle here to-day, and the enemy will be here on us soon. Drive in our stragglers as you go out." We were soon in our saddles and on our way toward the front. We met Gen. Emory coming back with his infantry. He asked me: "Where are you going, Gooding?" I answered: I am going in front to hold the enemy in check till our army can get into position to fight a battle, and to drive in our stragglers. When I said drive in our stragglers, the old General exclaimed:

"God! the enemy will do that for us." In an open space, just west of Pleasant Hill, I placed my brigade in line of battle, and, taking a platoon of cavalry, I went to the front to reconnoiter for the enemy. An ordinary country road, lined on both sides by dense woods, lead out to the front. Out that road I went in advance of the platoon. About a mile out that road made a sudden turn. Just before we reached that turn, I could not see, but heard what appeared to me to be a cavalry force charging down the road toward us, firing their pistols at what I supposed were the last of our stragglers. Believing the enemy might be coming down on us in force, I ordered the platoon to wheel about and gallop back to the brigade. They insisted that I should get in front of the platoon and let them keep between me and the enemy on the retreat. I refused to do that, but ordered them to get back as quick as they could. Hearing no more firing in my rear, I looked back, and as I could not see any enemy in sight, concluded to bring my horse down to a walk, and go back to my command in a dignified way. The platoon had already gotten back, as well as my orderly. The enemy had scattered in the woods, and that was the reason I did not see them when I looked back up the road. They saw the mistake I had made, and concluded to play a joke on me; that they would slip up behind me, capture me, escort me back near my command, turn me loose and let me go back to my brigade. They did that. Having no idea that the enemy was near, all at once one of them dashed up alongside of me, and, looking fiercely at me, bowed. I returned the same kind of a bow to him. Looking back over my left shoulder I saw about twenty-five or thirty, and realized that I was in the hands of the enemy. One of them, more nervous than the rest, made a motion to draw his pistol and shoot me. Don't do that, said two of them; he can't hurt any of us while we are all here. Although they had on blue overcoats they had captured from our forces the day before, I knew they were the enemy, and realized that I was in the hands of the enemy, and at his mercy. As they made no demand for me to surrender, I concluded to ride alone in silence with them and watch for a chance to escape from them. None of them ever spoke to me nor I them. When we came near the open space, where my brigade was in line of battle, I heard one of those in the rear of me say: "We had better halt now and let him go back alone. If his troops see him with us they will doubt him." They halted for a few moments, and halloed to me as I rode off: "Get out of the way as soon as possible or we will kill you." I rode slowly along, notwithstanding their threat, and they dashed by me and entered the open space where my command was, and lined themselves on either side of the road, close up against the woods, facing my line.

As I rode into the open space, one of them said: "He is not with us now, and there are his troops; let us kill him now." Two of them drew their pistols and leveled them at me to shoot me when I was still in their immediate presence. A third promptly and firmly said: "Let him go now, we will kill him after while, anyhow. Only a few yards from them, Col. Chrysler met me, and asked: "Who are those fellows there that came out of the woods with you?" Thinking he knew they were the enemy from their leveling their revolvers at me as they did, I answered: "I don't know who they are." He started to ride toward them, when one of them, Chas. R. Gregory, now a prominent wholesale merchant in St. Louis, who had leveled his pistol at me, fired on him. With a look, I ordered the Confederate to put up his pistol. He at first partially raised it to fire at me, but when I placed my hand toward my pistol holster, and looked firmly at him, he lowered his pistol and put it in his holster. I did this because there were not enough of the enemy there to fight us, and as they had not made me a prisoner nor killed me when it was in their power to do so, I concluded to give them a fair fight, and ordered my troops not to fire on them till their troops came up and formed a line. Gregory seemed to understand the reason for the look I gave him, and that is the reason he put up his pistol. I remained in front of my line till several of my officers rode out to me and insisted that I should go to my position in rear of my command. When I did that the members of my staff came to me, and then the enemy discovered that they had let go an officer of rank. They halloed out to my men: "Was that a Brigadier-General we let go?" They answered: "He is our brigade commander." "Well," said they, "If we had known that we would not have let him gone back to you." I had no insignia of rank about me, and that is what saved me on that occasion. It was not long, however, till they had a line, and I ordered my troops to fire on them. Thus I opened the battle of Pleasant Hill, Louisiana, one of the most hotly contested battles of the war. Col. Dickie's colored brigade was sent to reinforce me. I placed them in the woods on the left of my line. I fought the enemy until about eleven in the day, when I was relieved by the infantry. My loss was heavy. One member of my staff was killed, and another wounded. My hat was shot off my head, the Minnie ball grazing my scalp. They came that near killing me "after awhile," as the Confederate said they would. My orderly dismounted, picked up my hat, and handed it to me, and when I placed it back on my head, the Eighteenth New York Cavalry cheered me loudly. Col. Chrysler galloped over to me and asked: "What is that cheering about?" One of my staff pointed to my hat, which was badly torn, and explained. "God! I would give a thousand dollars for that," said Chrysler. Having learned that Chrysler wanted to win some glory on the battle-field, and then go home and run for Congress on the strength of it, I coolly said to him: "Colonel, buy me a new hat, and you may have the glory."

I was then ordered to guard the trains back to Grand Ecore, and heard the heavy fighting done by the infantry and artillery of Banks' army in the afternoon, as I was on my way to Grand Ecore with our train.

The battle of Pleasant Hill was a decided victory for the Union troops, the enemy retreating for eight miles westward that night. The loss on both sides was heavy.

BATTLE OF MONETTE'S FERRY.

Fearing that the enemy might get in our front, and take possession of the heights on the east and south of that crossing of Kane river, and cut off our further retreat, Gen. Banks ordered me to make a night march of thirty miles and take possession of those heights, and hold them till our army could come up and cross. I made the night march, but at daylight found the enemy already in possession of those heights. I developed the enemy's position thoroughly, and prevented our army from marching into a disaster. I sent word back to Gen. Emory, who commanded the advanced infantry, to halt his command and cross over Kane river, and attack the enemy in the flank and rear, while I engaged them in front. This was done, and the victory was ours, the enemy driven from the heights, and our army crossed in safety. On the field I received the very highest praise from Gen. Emory for the generalship I displayed. Gen. Fessenden, son of the great Senator Fessenden, of Maine, lost a leg in that battle. We reached Alexandria, where we camped for about two weeks. When the army continued its retreat to the Mississippi, I was left behind at Alexandria with my cavalry, to keep up the picket line around the city, and make the appearance that our army had not left, so as to give it a day's march in advance of the enemy on the retreat. The next morning at daylight I had drawn all my pickets in, and marched out of Alexandria, to try and overtake our army. I had not gone far, however, when the enemy's cavalry attacked me. I turned and fought them off, which I had to do all day long. The next morning I caught up with our army. A severe battle was fought not far from the Mississippi river, at Yellow Bayou, which ended the Red river campaign. At the Atchefalaya river, Gen. Canby relieved Gen. Banks of the command of the army. Gen. Banks spoke to Gen. Canby in the very highest terms of praise of the gallantry and generalship displayed by myself on the Red river campaign, and advised him to place me in command of the cavalry division, which he did, and ordered me to march it to New Orleans. Banks also advised him to have me promoted, and keep me in command of the cavalry.

Just before we started on the campaign my regiment's time of enlistment expired. Nearly all of them re-enlisted under a law of Congress, which provided that if the number re-enlisting fell below a certain number, the Colonel and Major should be mustered out of the service. This was a mean act of economy on the part of the Government. My regiment fell a few men short of the number that would entitle it to a Colonel and Major. Some of the officers came to me and told me that they could get enough more of the men to enlist to save me my Colonelcy if they would make them drunk. I asked them what objection the men had to re-enlisting. They answered that the men said they wanted to go home to their families. I then said, they have been good soldiers. If you can not get them to re-enlist while they are sober, strictly so, let them go home to their families. I forbid that they shall be made drunk and re-enlisted while in that condition to save my Colonelcy.

CHAPTER 20.

VETERAN FURLOUGH.

At the end of the Red River campaign the regiment went home on veteran furlough via the Mississippi river, Cairo, Chicago, Cleveland, Albany and Pittsfield back to Boston, whence they had sailed via the ocean for New Orleans. I accompanied the regiment.

FANUEL HALL.

We were received in Fanuel Hall by the Mayor of Boston and the Adjutant-General of Massachusetts, Governor Andrew being out of the city, in the presence of a large audience. In response to addresses of welcome from those two gentlemen I made my first public speech, which was entirely impromptu. It was well received by the audience and the regiment.

I then went home to see my mother and the rest of my relations who were there. Two brothers were absent in the Union army, and a third, my brother David, was lying there at home wounded, fresh from the field. My brother William Harrison Gooding, a braver soldier than whom never lived, was in the hospital, wounded, at Covington, Ky. On one occasion he captured two soldiers of the enemy, one immediately after the other, by leveling his revolver on each as he appeared in sight, and demanding his surrender, and took them both to his regiment as prisoners of war, a feat not often performed by one soldier. For this he was promoted to a Corporalcy. He ought to have been promoted to a Captaincy. I took my sister Vira, and my niece, Flora Howard, now Mrs. Dr. Martin, of Greenfield, down there to see him, and brought him up home to Greenfield. He was both Postmaster of Greenfield and a clerk in the Postoffice Department at Washington during the administration of President Johnson.

My brother Lemuel, a lawyer of the finest legal mind, who was named for our maternal grandfather, who had also been after the Morgan raiders, was also at home. He was Recorder of the county, Circuit Attorney, and a candidate for Circuit Judge. The few days I was there I received the Chapter Degrees of Masonry, over at Knightstown, under special dispensation. Canby sent word, through Indianapolis friends of his, that he would have me promoted if I would come back to the department. I returned to New Orleans, down the Mississippi river. I was then assigned to the command of a cavalry brigade at Baton Rouge. In November following I was mustered out of my Colonelcy, along with the Major, because my regiment had not re-enlisted enough men to entitle it to a Colonel and a Major. As a Captain of the regular army, I was assigned to duty inspecting troops. At Fort Bridger, in Utah, before the war, Gen. Canby disgraced himself inside of his own household in such a way that the officers and ladies of the post quit visiting his family. Captain Shunk, who wronged me so greatly at West Point, brought to that department a report of Canby's disgrace at Fort Bridger. Canby heard of it, and jumped at the conclusion that I must have brought it there, as I was stationed with him at Fort Bridger before the war, he not knowing that Shunk brought it to that department. Canby sent one of his staff officers to me to tell me if I did not come to him and deny that I had brought that report down there he would not recommend me for promotion. Believing that Canby would have too much sense to send such a message to me by one of his staff, I paid no attention to it, and Canby denied me my right to promotion, at which the officers of the department were indignant. Captain Shunk feeling that I had been greatly wronged by his indiscretion in speaking of that matter down there, did not go to Canby and acknowledge that he was the man that brought it there, but resolved to accompany me to Washington City and tell the authorities there why Canby had not recommended me for promotion, and thus see himself that I was promoted. The first of March, 1865, I asked to be ordered to report to the Adjutant-General of the United States Army at Washington, D. C. The order was given me, and on the seventh day of that month I left New Orleans and proceeded up the river for Washington. Captain Shunk accompanied me up the river as far as Morganza, where an order from Gen. Canby intercepted him and forced him to return to New Orleans to prevent him from accompanying me to Washington and doing what he had intended there. Having arrived there, I called on Col. John C. Kelton at Gen. Halleck's headquarters, intending, after some preliminary talk, to tell him that

I was then ready to accept a Brigadier-Generalship in the Corps d'Afrique in order to get back into the field with a command, so I could do more fighting for my country. But before I reached that point, Kelton provoked and tantalized me into writing out my resignation, placing a pen, ink and paper in front of me. Taking it in the next room, in a few moments he returned and handed me a certificate, which stated that my resignation had been accepted by the President of the United States. He told me that Gen. Halleck had accepted my resignation, and abused him for doing so, saying that Hallcek would never accept the resignation of a worthless officer, but when a good officer, like myself, tendered his resignation he would accept it. He seemed very indignant toward Halleck. Knowing that the authorities had for nearly two years prior to that time refused to accept resignations from regular officers, I had no idea that my resignation, written out in a mement of anger, would ever be accepted. The next morning I went back to withdraw my resignation, but Kelton tantalized me about it and caused me to leave the room in anger without doing it. Kelton told Halleck that I had gone away without waiting to learn whether my resignation was accepted or not, and finally had me dropped from the rolls the first of January, 1867, on the idea that I had wilfully absented myself from the army without leave, but did not assign that or any other reason, but simply dropped my name from the army register, and subsequently had false records made in the War Department to try and hide Kelton's dishonorable trick. Kelton's motive for his trick and dishonarable conduct in depriving the army of a good officer was inexpressibly small and contemptible. While I was a cadet at West Point Kelton had a very stiff way of walking. One day I made an innocent reference to his stiffness, which was reported to him. Being very narrow-minded and pig-headed, he ever afterwards hated me, while I felt most kindly towards him, and did me that great wrong. Had officers who knew of the facts done their duty, Kelton would have been dismissed from the army on a charge of conduct unbecoming an officer and a gentleman. I then went home a sadly disappointed man. I arrived at home just in time to join with the people in rejoicing over the surrender of Gen. Robert E. Lee and his army, which occurred on the 9th of April, and which was practically the end of the war. All the other surrenders soon followed as a natural consequence of Lee's surrender. Only five days thereafter, the 14th, President Lincoln was assassinated by John Wilkes Booth, and our rejoicing was changed to grief. Sunday, the 30th of April, Lincoln lay in state under the dome of the old State House in Indianapolis. Trains on all the roads carried people to view his corpse. The people went in at the south entrance of the State House, viewed the corpse, and then passed out at the north entrance. It was said at the time that not less than one hundred thousand people viewed the corpse. I passed through and took a good look at it, and still remember how it appeared. It was embalmed, and death had made but little change. His nose was slightly pinched by death, and his lips were parted just enough to show a very beautiful set of regular teeth. He had a magnificent suit of black hair. I passed the summer in Indiana and went back to Washington in November.

CHAPTER 21.
IN CIVIL LIFE.

In the Presidential canvass of 1864, on account of his great ability as an orator and a canvasser, and the fact that he was a war Democrat, the Union party, which consisted of Republicans and war Democrats, placed my brother, David S. Gooding, at the head of its electoral ticket. In company with Andrew Johnson, who was also a war Democrat, and the candidate of the Union party for Vice-President, he and Johnson, as war Democrats, canvassed Indiana, calling on all Democrats, and everybody else, to stand by the Union, and vote the Union ticket. Accordingly, soon after Johnson was sworn in as President, after the assassination of President Lincoln, he appointed him United States Marshal for the District of Columbia. This office, from Washington down, was always given to a close personal as well as political friend of the President. At that time this office was regarded as a more desirable one than a place in the Cabinet. The Marshal was regarded as on the personal staff of the President. He stood by the President at all receptions, and introduced the people to him, and when the President traveled, he traveled with him. He was often consulted by the President on great political questions. The official duties of his office, with the exception of signing his official reports, etc., were performed by his deputies. One of his deputies had charge of the Supreme Court of the United States. That position my brother asked me to accept. I refused, but on being urged by him, and thinking that it would give me a good chance to hear legal questions argued by the greatest lawyers of the land, I finally accepted. I had taken Blackstone's commentaries to the frontier with me before the war, and commenced the study of law. Sitting at the Marshal's desk, and hearing legal questions argued by the ablest lawyers of the Republic, was a pretty good law school, and on that, and with what reading I did, I applied for and was admitted to the bar of the Supreme Court of the District of Columbia. I then practiced law in Washington. I got just enough practice, civil and criminal, to give me an idea of what the practice was. While there I was made a full Brigadier-General, and confirmed as such by the United States Senate, but was swindled out of it by my enemies in the War Department issuing to me a commission for a Brigadier-Generalship by brevet only. Kelton is supposed to have set up the trick. On the recommendation of General Grant, I was made a Major-General by brevet of United States Volunteers, "For gallant conduct in the assaults on the enemy's works at Port Hudson, in 1863, and gallant and distinguished conduct throughout the Red river campaign in 1864."

A young lawyer by the name of Stewart, from Rushville, Indiana, one day came to me and proposed that we, and some others, hold a meeting in Indianapolis and start a Presidential boom for Gen. Grant. This was before the politicians had begun to boom him for that office. Stewart proposed that I should make the speech on the occasion, and wind it up by placing Grant in nomination for the Presidency. I agreed to do so. Stewart then went to Grant, and told him what we were going to do. Grant agreed to it, but suggested that Stewart had better get my brother David to make the speech, as he was a good speaker and a politician, and I had never been anything but an army man, and probably could not make the speech. Stewart insisted that he wanted an army man to make the speech, and that I would be able to make it. So Grant agreed that I should make it. Stewart then suggested that he and Grant call on me and talk with me about it. Grant told him that he was going to attend the trial of John H. Surratt, charged with having been in conspiracy to assassinate Lincoln, one day, and that they would then call on me at my office in the City Hall, but would say nothing about it then, and when I should subsequently call on him he would talk to me about it. Grant and Stewart did call on me during the Surratt trial, but found me in front of the City Hall, where we had some talk, but nothing relating to his boom. Stewart came to me afterward and told me that it was all right with the General, and for me to go up to his headquarters and talk to him about it. I told my brother David what I was going to do, and he promptly informed me that I could not make good enough speech to do that, and, besides, that he was afraid President Johnson would get after him about it, as I was his brother and

Johnson and Grant were unfriendly at that time. Fearing that I would make a failure in trying to make the speech, I concluded to wait for Stewart to come to see me again, as I did not know where he was stopping, and then tell him that I doubted my ability to make the speech, and for him to explain it to the General, and tell him that I would help the boom quietly. As Stewart never called on me any more, I concluded that he and Grant had given up the idea, so I never went to see the General about it. I have since learned that Grant expected me, and, as I did not come, told Stewart that they would drop that, and he would put him in the army, which he did soon after. Later the politicians in both parties began to want Grant to run as their candidate. Before the war he was a Democrat, and during the war was supposed to be what was called a war Democrat. Some of the Indiana Republican politicians feared that they would not be able to carry that close State even for Grant, if he ran as their candidate, without the assistance of David S. Gooding, who was the greatest war Democrat of the State. Whether the war Democrats were going back to their old party, now that the war was over, or were going to continue to act with the Republicans was a very important matter to the latter. Some of the Indiana Republican politicians were anxious to learn whether Judge Gooding would help them to carry Indiana for Grant. Instead of asking him, they hit on the plan of sounding me, thinking that I, being his younger brother, would reflect his opinions. So some of them got me in the room of Gen. John A. Logan at Willard's Hotel one evening. Logan laid down on the sofa, and began to talk about Grant, saying that if he did not declare himself pretty soon and tell whether he was a Republican or not, little Phil. Sheridan would beat him with them, and so on, while the others watched my countenance to see how I took it. They concluded from the expression of my countenance that I was for Grant, although I said nothing, and therefore concluded that Judge Gooding would help them, but were very much surprised when the campaign came around and I supported Grant and my brother supported his Democratic competitor, Horatio Seymour.

Feeling that I would like to participate in the canvass, if I could make a good enough speech, I studied what I supposed would be the proper thing to say, but did not reduce it to writing, but got it well fixed in my memory without it. I told a man at Greenfield that I wanted to go to an out township, and find out by trial if I could make a good enough speech to be delivered in the Court-house in Greenfield; and I wanted him to go with me, and listen to me, and tell me whether it was good enough to be delivered there. He took me out to the little village of Cleveland, and there in the school-house I made my first political speech. As we rode home in a buggy that night, he remained silent, and from that I thought he was going to condemn my speech. I finally asked him what he thought of it. He quietly said to me: "You will do to speak in the Court-house." The next Thursday night I spoke in the Court-house, and my friends told me that I would do to speak anywhere. So I went to New York, and the National Republican Committee sent me to canvass California for Grant and Colfax. In that canvass, the first of my life, I made a very fine reputation as a political speaker. I was accorded that by Hon. Henry Egerton, California's greatest orator. I spoke along with him. I came by it honestly, for in Indiana my father's family had been called a family of orators. I went to California by way of the ocean, crossing the Isthmus of Panama, and returned overland to Washington. I stopped two days in Salt Lake City, and had an interview with Brigham Young, the head of the Mormon Church. I stopped in Indiana, and took my mother and sister Vira on to see the capital of our country. We all went to Grant's Inaugural Ball. My mother was said to have been the finest looking old lady at the ball. Gen. Grant sent word to me to bring my mother and introduce her to him, and be of his party there. I left that to my brother David, and went to looking after Minnie, the good and noble daughter of a rich and very distinguished Senator from a Western State. How she and I were prevented from marrying by the jealousy and the tricks of the daughter of another Senator, and others, need not be related here.

President Grant requested a Senator to say to me that he would place me back in the army if I would go. The Senator entrusted that to another, who betrayed his trust. Grant subsequently directed one of his Secretaries to go to my residence in Washington, and tell me that he wanted to put me back in the army, that I could select my place, and when the vacancy occurred he would place me in it, and in the meantime he would place me on duty with him in the White House. The Secretary entrusted it to an army officer, who betrayed his trust, because I gave him an unwelcome look when he came to my room. I gave him that look because I thought he had not treated me right previously. In August following, I went back to my old home in Indiana. There I lived for four years.

There I became engaged to Rosalind English. She is the only daugnter of the famous Congressman, Wm. H. English. He was author of the English bill, relating to the Kansas troubles, or the bitter agitation of the slavery question, which immediately preceded and brought on our great civil war. His object was to prevent the civil war. He is a man of great wealth, and was President of the First National Bank of Indianapolis for many years. He ran for the Vice-Presidency on the Democratic ticket in 1880. How misunderstandings, and the tricks of others, prevented her and me from marrying, will not be related here. Rose, at that time, was the popular belle of Indianapolis. Mr. English's only son, Hon. Wm. E. English, a bright and cultured young man, has represented the Indianapolis District in Congress since the war.

In 1870 my brother David ran for Congress in a District having more than two thousand Republican majority, he being a Democrat. My brother Clay, a cultured and accomplished orator, who distinguished himself for coolness and gallantry as an officer in an Illinois regiment, at the battle of Parker's Cross Roads, during our late civil war, at the same time was running for Congress in another District containing two thousand Democratic majority, he being a Republican. They were both State Senators. My mother said if the boys could only change districts, they could both go to Congress. Clay was defeated, but David was elected by about thirty majority, but was counted out by four majority. He contested the right to the seat, but was unjustly refused it by a strict party vote in the House.

In 1872, dissatisfied Republicans organized the Liberal Republican party, and nominated Horace Greeley for the Presidency. The Democratic party endorsed that nomination, but Grant was re-elected. I supported Greeley, and thus found myself back in my old Democratic party. I thought of going back to California to locate, but my brother Clay urged me to locate in St. Louis, as it was sure to be the future great city of the continent, and as I felt that I wanted to be near my mother, who was growing old, I located here instead of going to California.

Among my old friends in Indiana, I am proud to

number President Benjamin Harrison, ex-Governor Albert G. Porter, and the great Senator and famous orator, Daniel W. Voorhees, the famous Congressman, George W. Julian, Gen. Henry D. Washburn, also a Congressman, United States Senator Henry S. Lane, Schuyler Colfax, Vice-President of the United States, and those distinguished and noble-hearted Congressmen, Gen. John Coburn, Col. C. C. Matson, Hon. John E. Lamb, Lon Sexton and Godlove S. Orth; also, ex-Gov. Isaac P. Gray, and the noble Hollis B. Thayer. I also desire to particularly mention my friend, Gen. Milton S. Robinson, a gallant officer in the Union army during our late civil war, an ex-Congressman, and now a Judge of the Court of Appeals in Indiana, as a gentleman of great ability, and the very highest sense of honor; also, my venerable friend, Dr. Edward Howard, of Indianapolis. Daniel W. Voorhees and my brother David were regarded as the greatest Democratic orators in the State. Gen. James Shields, who was a hero of two wars, and a United States Senator from three different States, told me that he had never seen my brother David's equal before a popular audience but once, and that man was the great Stephen A. Douglas. A prominent member of Lincoln's cabinet told me that he had spoken with the finest public speakers in the country, and that none of them were equal to my brother David, that he could bear them all on the stump.

CHAPTER 22.

IN ST. LOUIS.

In this city, where I knew but few people, I hung out my sign as an attorney at law, and was here some time before I met any one with whom I had ever had any particular acquaintance. One day, however, by chance, in front of the post-office, I met Gen. John S. Marmaduke, late of the Southern army, who had been my class-mate at West Point, and treated me so meanly there. At his invitation we went and lunched together. A few days after he called at my hotel, and asked me to come and take a room in connection with his own, so we could be together. This I did, forgiving him for his meanness to me at West Point, and we lived together as bachelors for four years. At that time the prejudices engendered by the civil war were still fresh, and many wondered how two officers who had fought on different sides during the war could live together so harmoniously. On changing our location, we drew cuts for who should have the front room. The choice was against him, and he had to take the back room. In a day or two he noticed that a plaster cast of Abraham Lincoln was on the mantel piece in his room, and a plaster bust of Jefferson Davis was on the mantel piece in my room. He called to me, and told me that I had better bring Davis into his room, and take Lincoln into my room. On doing so, I discovered a decided resemblance between Lincoln and Davis in the upper part of their faces, and called his attention to it. He looked at them carefully, and agreed that there was a decided resemblance between them in the upper part of their faces.

JEFFERSON DAVIS.

While Marmaduke and I were living together, an invitation to attend a county fair in Illinois was extended to Jefferson Davis, ex-President of the Confederacy, by the manager of the fair. The war prejudice of the people there caused the managers to withdraw the invitation. This caused great excitement and severe criticism in the newspapers, resulting in a duel between two St. Louis editors, who had served in opposite armies during the war—Major Emory Foster, of the Federal army, and Major John N. Edwards, of the Confederate army. Mr. Davis was then invited to attend the connty fair at De Soto, Missouri. I went with Marmaduke to De Soto, where we heard Mr. Davis make a speech to the people, which pleased me very much. From there Marmaduke and I escorted Mr. Davis to St. Louis. I saw Davis in his room at the Southern Hotel, and talked with him, or, rather, listened to his talk. When Mr. Davis left for the South, I was the last man to bid him good-bye, Mr. Davis grasped my hand firmly, and said to me most cordially: "God bless you, God bless you, God bless you." When Jefferson Davis held on to my hand with a cordial grasp, and earnestly called on God to bless me, a Federal officer, I felt that the Union was restored in heart as well as in law, notwithstanding the duel between the two editors, and under the inspiration of that glorious idea, I wrote the following patriotic song:

GOODING'S AMERICA.

America! home of the free;
  Treads thy soil no slave!
Dear land of liberty,
  Thy sons are all brave.

Wave on! Wave on!
The old Flag forever.

No foe shall tread thy soil,
  Nor alien thee slave;
No tyrant thee shall spoil,
  For thy sons are brave.
    Wave on! Wave on!
    The old Flag forever.

Happy land of the free,
  Thy stars are all bright;
My heart I give to thee,
  Guard thy sons the right.
    Wave on! Wave on!
    The old Flag forever.

These words were set to strong martial music by Prof. Alfred G. Robyn, of this city, and a few copies printed for circulation among my personal friends. It was sung before the reunion of the Army of the Tennessee, in the People's Theater, and brought down the house, and was encored. It has never yet been placed on sale.

General Grant, on his way to Mexico, stopped over in this city, one of his reasons for doing so being to see me, and, if I was not doing well in civil life, to urge me to go back into the army, and to offer to help me get back into it. Some suspicious people thought the

General wanted to take me away from St. Louis and use me against the Democratic party. So they sent a mean man to him to tell him if I remained here a rich woman would marry me; that he knew the woman wanted me. The General said he did not want to interfere with that, so he would delay saying anything to me about going back into the army till later.

PRESIDENTIAL VISIT.

In October, 1887, President Cleveland and his party visited this city. I had been on the committee that went on to Washington to invite him to come, and was placed on the committee to entertain him while here. He and his party were here the first two days of the fair week. We, the committee, went to the residence of Mayor Francis, in Vandeventer Place, where we were presented to the President, his wife and others of his party. From there we were all taken in carriages to the fair grounds. It was the first day of the fair, and the grand circular amphitheater was crowded with the school children and other people. As the party drove into the grand circular stand, fifty thousand people, standing, greeted the President and his wife with hearty cheers, and, as they drove around the circle, continued the cheer, presenting very much such a scene as was presented by a vast audience standing and cheering in the Coliseum at Rome. From there we drove through the streets to the Chamber of Commerce, where the President spoke to the merchants and the other people who crowded the hall. From there we drove to the Lindell Hotel, where the ladies dined in one room and we gentlemen dined in another room with the President. After dinner the President and his young and beautiful wife held a reception in the parlor. As the people passed through the President shook hands with them and his wife bowed gracefully to them. She looked the perfection of beauty, dignity and grace. He looked, every inch of him, just what he is, a statesman and a stalwart man. Monday evening the party witnessed the grand illumination of the city. Tuesday evening they witnessed the Veiled Phophets' procession and grand ball in the hall of the Chamber of Commerce. The Presidential party were seated on an elevated platform at the north end of the hall. Among them were the President and his wife, Mrs. Mayor Francis and that dashing leader of society, Mrs. Don Morrison; also Mrs. Rainwater, that great leader in all works of noble charity, and her husband, a prominent St. Louis merchant, Maj. C. C. Rainwater.

THE AUTHOR. 281

As a ball room scene no grander view was ever seen on earth.

> And when music arose with its voluptuous swell,
> Soft eyes looked love to eyes which spake again,
> And all went merry as a marriage bell.

But hark! the Presidential party must quit the festive scene, and on the train dash away for another point on their tour, and the gay revelers stop the dance awhile to cheer them as they go.

In the spring of 1884 Gen. John S. Marmaduke was an aspirant for the Democratic nomination for the Governorship. There were quite a number of aspirants in the field against him. I was also an aspirant, and hoped to be nominated as a compromise candidate. On taking a tour through the State I discovered that he was going to be nominated, but that there would be dissatisfaction with his nomination. Such was the case. The Republicans and dissatisfied Democrats held a State convention and nominated a fusion ticket. They also made a fusion platform, in which they denounced the Southern element in the Democratic party as having ignored, ostracised and persecuted Union men on account of their loyalty. The Fusionists made their fight entirely against the Southern element, and called on all Union men to support their ticket.

CANVASSED THE STATE.

I canvassed the State and defended the Southern element against the assertions that they had ignored, ostracised and persecuted Union men on account of their loyalty. I also advocated the election of Marmaduke to the Governorship and the return of Cockrell and Vest, two Southern men, to the United States Senate. Marmaduke was elected by the skin of his teeth, and many gave me the credit for having saved him from defeat, as I defended him against charges that were made against him of a personal nature and called on all Union Democrats to vote for him, and set a good many Confederate Democrats right for him. He wanted me to take the Coal Oil Inspectorship, a lucrative appointment, and save up for both, to that proposition I would not agree. He reappointed me on the Police Board, where the salary was only $1,000 a year, and where I expected to remain but a few months, when I expected something better, and had a right to expect it, from the Federal Government, but it never came.

THE GREAT CONSPIRACY
AGAINST
GOODING AND GOOD GOVERNMENT.

CHAPTER 23.

A short time before I was re-appointed on the Police Board I was in the office of Arthur Lee and talking to him confidentially. During the conversation I remarked that if a man was Vice President of the Board and given full power by the Governor, as was formerly the case, he would have an opportunity to make a reputation as an executive officer that could be used as an argument in favor of him for Governor. Lee at once unjustly jumped at the conclusion that I wanted it as a stepping stone to the Governorship; and that if I got the Governorship, he, Lee, could not beat me out of a certain widow who has a large fortune, and who Lee knew wanted to marry me. I told Lee that I had my eye on a different lady, but he was afraid that she would continue her efforts to get me after her till she would succeed in that which she finally did. So he went to work to prevent that. Acting on his false impression that I wanted the Vice Presidency of the Police Board, when in reality I neither wanted that nor the widow at that time, but on the contrary wanted and expected a lucrative Federal aopointment, he went to James L. Blair and told him that he must go on the Police Board; that he would get Governor Marmaduke to have him made Vice President of the Board, and give him full power ; that he could then make a reputation as an executive officer, on the credit of which they could make him Governor. The idea caught the little man. He was made a Commissioner and Vice President of the Board according to Lee's program.

Professing to be a friend of mine, Lee then asked me to help him make Blair Governor. I declined to do that. Blair and Lee then regarded Mayor Francis, ex-officio President of the Board, and myself as both standing in the way of Blair for the Governorship. So they in turn made war on him and me. Francis became Governor and they are still making war on me to prevent me from becoming Governor. They at first, while professing to be friends of mine, carried

THE CONSPIRACY. 285

on a secret conspiracy against me. As I refused to help make Blair Governor, he at once became my bitter, unrelenting enemy, and spitefully declared that he and Lee would kill me or have me killed before I should ever become Governor or marry the widow or any other rich lady.

For the purpose of trying to prevent me from either becoming Governor or marrying either of several rich ladies, who they knew had declared their desire to marry me and divide their fortunes with me, fearing that would help me to become Governor, they investigated me, hoping to find something they could use against me in politics and before the ladies. After the most thorough investigation to which any mortal was ever subjected, having found absolutely nothing to my discredit; on the contrary, having found my record not only perfectly clear in every respect, but highly creditable and brilliant, and having found all my kindred, living and dead, as well as myself all right in every particular, they spitefully started a lie factory in the city of St. Louis, for the manufacture of lies with which to try and prevent me from either becoming Governor or marrying either of the rich ladies. They manufactured lies and got women to write them to the widow, but she paid no attention to them. When she came home they got up a lying manufactured interview concerning the widow and myself. All the St. Louis newspapers but one treated it with the silent contempt it deserved. They then got a forged affidavit containing a lie and had that exhibited to the widow, hoping thereby to turn her against me. She indignantly declared that she would not believe it if fifty men swore to it, not knowing that it had never been sworn to but was simply a forgery. Thomas Thoroughman, who would be more appropriately named if he were called Thomas Thoroughliar, ran away to Montana and remained there during the war to keep out of both armies, returned when peace came and the danger was all over, stole the title of Colonel and tried to play the role of Confederate Colonel, to run for the United States Senate. Without my knowledge or consent, a man placed in a newspaper a suggestion that I ought to be sent to the United States Senate to fill out an unexpired term. Thoroughliar saw the suggestion, and at once concluded that I would be in his way for the Senate, and therefore took stock in the lie factory, lied and forged that he might lie. He first tried to bribe a poor man

THE CONSPIRACY. 287

to swear to his lie, offering to let him set his own price for the perjury, but the poor man indignantly spurned his offered bribe. He then forged the lying affidavit that the widow or her agent still has in her or his possession. They even put their lies in the form of a book, in which Lee styled himself Rotten Lee and Blair styled himself Satan Blair. But the ladies paid no attention to their lies and refused to read their libelous book, and they have many times confessed that they manufactured the lies for the purposes heretofore stated.

THEY COMMITTED FELONIES!!

With the view of preventing me from becoming Governor or marrying Grace, the widow, they also committed felonies by intercepting my letters to Grace and hers to me. And also made attempts to have me murdered by poison and by assassination. Becoming alarmed for fear they might be sent to the penitentiary, they offered to give me libels to protect me against the lies and each to pay me $5,000 as damages, provided I would promise not to have them prosecuted for the crimes they had committed. This promise I refused to give and they continued their war on me.

THEY FOUND RICH CRIMINALS TO HELP THEM.

Wherever they could find any men that had committed crimes they got them into the conspiracy by telling them that I was such a great man to enforce the criminal laws that it would be necessary to keep me out of the Governorship to save themselves from the penitentiary ; and as I was a bachelor it would be necessary to keep me from marrying a rich woman, as a rich wife might help me to become Governor. Grace's fortune was principally in Granite Mountain stock, a great silver mine. Rotten Lee and Satan Blair found out that the deceased husband of Grace and some other stock-holders had gotten most of their stock by swindling others out of it. That in obtaining their stock they had committed a crime. Among the others were John R. Lionberger, who held for himself, and Thomas E. Tutt, Auguste B. Ewing, Charles Clark, Captain Bobinger and others were of that number. The other stock-holders were supposed to have come into possession of their stock honestly. This gave the criminals, Lee and Blair, an opportunity to get some more criminals into their conspiracy against me. Blair communicated the information to me in an indirect way by talking it to Frank Gainnie, another member of the Police Board, at a meeting of that body. He then told them that I had found out about their crime, and if they did not join him and Lee in preventing me from marrying Grace, by killing me, I would marry her, become Governor and compel them to disgorge their ill-gotten gains and have them all sent to the penitentiary, for I was such a great man to see that the criminal laws were enforced. They joined the conspiracy at once.

Before the facts concerning the Granite Mountain property became known to me, Wilber F. Boyle, the agent of Grace, of his own volition, tried to get me to agree that I would not take possession of Grace's estate, and wanted me to give a written promise to that effect. I declined to give the written promise or any other promise. At that time I thought Boyle's only object was to hold the agency, which was very valuable to him, but I now know that Boyle was trying to conceal the crime through which the property came and thus prevent the estate from having to disgorge it, which would cause him to lose the agency. As I refused to give the written promise, Boyle joined the conspiracy at once. He went to Grace's mother and set her against me. I became ill with rheumatism and was compelled to remain away from Grace. The conspirators thereupon urged her to go to Paris, telling her that I was not going to come to see her because I did not want to. She went to Paris, wrote back several letters to me which were intercepted in the postoffice here in this city. Satan Blair got the postoffice authorities to intercept Grace's letters to me and my letters to her, by having them told that they would not be punished for it, as Federal Judge Thayer, who held his Court in the postoffice building, was a brother-in-law to Boyle and would protect them from prosecution; that the judge was in with them. In his conduct toward me the judge evidently proved that he was in with them to some extent at least. Blair corrupted the postoffice through detectives on the police force. He also used the detectives to spoil the proprietor of my boarding house, and through detectives he got him to agree to murder me. By turning the key with pincers he got into my room and stood over me while I slept, turned the light from a dark lantern on to my face and raised his carving knife to cut my throat from ear to ear. At the last moment his heart failed him and he struck not the fatal blow. He told them if they wanted

THE CONSPIRACY. 291

that done they would have to get some one else to do it, for I was so kind to his children that he could not do that. Satan Blair first spoiled three detectives and the chief, and the Secretary of the Board, and then the other members of the Board. He finally got the consent of all of them that the detectives might murder me or have me murdered. One of the detectives tried to murder me in the rotunda of the Lindell Hotel, and was prevented from doing so by Colonel David W. Caruth.

Grace returned to St. Louis in the fall. The criminal, Lee, and the criminal, Blair, had the Lindell Hotel set up against me through their co-conspirator, Vincent Marmaduke, whose wife owned the building. I heard of it, but did not believe it, and stopped at the hotel. Vincent Marmaduke had confessed to me that he had been guilty of an infamous crime in his early manhood, and had always been afraid that I would publish it on him. Lee and Blair made him believe they would help him get Grace to marry his brother Henry if he would help them to put me out of the way, not intending to do so however. So he had these two motives for joining the conspiracy. Grace and I were treated very badly by the hotel people at the Lindell. I was poisoned by slow poison put in my coffee and left the hotel a mere skeleton. About this time I went off the Police Board by expiration of my term of service, and soon after Satan Blair was removed from the Board by Governor Francis, because he refused to surrender the office of Vice President of the Board to a new member who had been appointed. Charles H. Turner then went on the Board for the purpose of protecting his own wife, Mrs Satan Blair, Satan Blair and Rotten Lee from prosecution.

Grace went East to her cottage at Bar Harbor for the summer. In the fall she returned to still more troubles brought about by Rotten Lee and Satan Blair, which caused the death of her mother. And this time I was poisoned by slow poison put in my coffee at the Merchants' Hotel. On her death bed Grace's mother requested to have me brought to her that she might apologize to me for her conduct toward me, and ask me to forgive her and to marry her daughter Grace. Her request was kept away from me and she died and was buried without having her wish gratified, much to the regret of Grace. While she was on her death bed she

THE CONSPIRACY. 293

told Grace to have nothing more to do with she devil Turner and Mrs. Satan Blair, and go ahead and marry me, if she had to give me every dollar she had in the world, she and Grace having heard that a young lady worth a million dollars had offered to divide her fortune with me in consideration of marriage. That was true; the young lady had told she was going to make that offer to me. So Grace sent a prominent preacher, the president of a bank and the president of the Merchants' Exchange to me to offer me all her entire fortune if I would come and marry her. They came to my hotel to do so and approached me for that purpose, but having decided to wait for the noble Miss Allen, I turned to one side and walked away. Grace sent message after message to me, by both ladies and gentlemen, who betrayed their trust by failing to deliver them or pretending to deliver them by coming up behind me and whispering them to themselves so I could not hear them, then going away and reporting to Grace that they had delivered her message and if I did not come to see her it would be because I did not want to come.

DEATH OF MY MOTHER.

My mother was eighty-one years old, and the Satanic Blair and the Rotten Lee thinking she might die soon, determined to have my eye-sight put out so I could not see her corpse. Soon after, she had a fall that caused her death, after a lingering illness of three weeks. While she was lying ill they had me poisoned through my coffee at the Planters' House, to blind me. My eye-sight was so affected that it was all I˙ could do to see the corpse of my mother. Her death was a terrible blow to me, for I felt that in her death I had lost the best, if not the only, friend I had on earth. Just before her death she spoke the name, Asa, of her deceased husband who had been dead more than forty-seven years, in such a way as to indicate that she thought he had come to escort her home to heaven. There died as good and noble a woman as ever lived on this earth. She lived and died true to virtue, true to her husband, true to her children, true to her country and true to her God. Oh! that there were more such women on the earth. Her husband was a very strong character. He was an honest, gallant man and thorough gentleman, in the true sense of that term. She was a good and noble

THE CONSPIRACY.

woman and thorough lady, in the true sense of that term. They were both endowed with great strength, mentally and physically. They were both handsome in life and were both handsome in death. For the good lives they lived and the struggle they made in life, in behalf of their children, they deserve immortality. I am proud of the fact that I am the son of such noble parents. My mother was respected, honored and beloved by all who knew her. The last act of her aged father was to pay her a visit in Indiana during the last year of the civil war. He died in Kentucky, just before he reached his home from that visit. My father was also very popular with all who knew him. Among his friends were John D. Defrees, editor and proprietor of the Indianapolis Journal, the then organ of the Whig party of the State of Indiana; William J. Brown, editor and proprietor of the Indiana State Sentinel, the then organ of the Democratic party of that State; and at Greenfield, Captain John Rardin, a hero of the war of 1812; Isaac Stevens, Morris Pierson, Andrew T. Hart and William Sebastian, whose daughter, Francis, my brother David married. My sister Delilah married and died at an early age, respected and beloved by all who knew her. My sisters,

Cindrella and Vira still live, honored and respected by all who know them. They have both developed great ability as artists, and covered the walls of their residences with fine oil paintings of their own painting, making them homes of culture and refinement.

On my return from my mother's funeral, I determined to go and see both Grace and Anna, believing them both to be at the Southern Hotel. Knowing that the conspirators would try to prevent me from seeing them, I called on the preacher that Grace had sent to me to go and make an engagement with her and also one with Anna, for me to call and see them in company with him. The preacher declared that he was very busy, but would comply with my request the latter part of the week. Before that time, however, Grace was caused to believe that I would not come to see her and induced to go back to Europe. By going to the hotel and inquiring, I ascertained that Grace had gone and that Anna had not been there, but had two months before been sent to Europe to keep her from coming to St. Louis and away from me.

ATTEMPT TO MURDER.

In the month of January efforts were made to murder me at the Planters' House. The criminals, Lee and Blair, along with Mayo and Gitchell, tried to get into my room through a partition door after midnight at the Planters' House to murder me, and were only deterred from it by their noise made at the door waking me, and my covering the door with my revolver. Neither one of them was willing to be the first to come through. Early in the spring attempts to murder me were also made at the St. James Hotel. Satan Blair, having rented the second room from mine, under the assumed name of Maginnis, while disguised, kept his door slightly open and watched for chances to shoot me in the back as I was passing through the hall to and from my room. He, Lee, Mayo and Gitchell, also got permission to occupy the room next to me so as to break through the partition door and murder me while I slept, but as I always woke up and covered the door with my revolver in time, they finally concluded to all rush out of that room and attack me at the same time. Accordingly they met in that room early one evening, intending all to rush out and murder me in the hall, and then rush into the Maginnis room and lock themselves in before anybody could see who had committed the crime. I saw a light in the room adjoining mine early that evening, and knew instinctively that it meant what has just been described. I sat in front of the Southern Hotel and waited until after midnight, hoping they would get tired waiting for me to come and quit watching for me and leave. Finally I sent Policeman Grass, who was on duty at the Southern Hotel, to reconnoiter and report to me. He went over, came back and reported that it was simply a card party, and advised me that I should go over and go to bed, and urged me to do so. Having been told and feeling that Grass was treacherous, I sat in front of the Southern till daylight, when the party of would-be murderers put out the light, dispersed and Blair, alias McGinnis, went into his room and retired. I then went over to my room and retired, sleeping until about noon. Grass subsequently confessed his treachery to me, and that it was the intention of those parties to murder me that night. An attempt was also made to murder me in the rotunda of the Southern Hotel.

PLANS TO MURDER ME IN EUROPE.

Finally, the criminal band made out a programme to have me murdered in Europe; and had Grace informed that her great fortune did not belong to her and she and the others would be compelled to disgorge if I was not put out of the way, as I had learned the secret and was so honest I would compel them all to disgorge. So Boyle sent his law partner, Adams, all the way down to Rome, where Grace had gone temporarily, to inform her as to the condition of her estate and urge on her the necessity of my being put out of the way. She indignantly refused to talk with Adams about it. She returned to Paris, and Lionberger sent his gray-haired sister over there to urge on her the necessity of my being put out of the way, in order to avoid being compelled to disgorge their ill-gotten fortunes.

CHAPTER 24.

AT THE GRAND OPERA HOUSE.

In the meantime, about the first of May, 1890, one evening I went to a performance at the Grand Opera House. I was seated in the parquet, and Governor Francis and his party were seated very near me in the dress circle. Mrs. Francis saw me and became very talkative. She was not aware that I could overhear every word she said, so she talked freely to the lady who sat by her side. She told the lady all about the trouble I was in, and gave her a very correct account of the war on me. She told how the Governor had said that I would not only make a good Governor, but that I would make a good President—as good a President as Washington—and, notwithstanding that, said she, how badly he has been treated, both politically and socially; how he has been slaughtered politically for being right, and because he would not yield to the wrong; and now, said she, how he is going to be slaughtered when he goes over to Europe!—he is going to be murdered; they say Grace is going to poison him. She lowered her voice while saying that, and the other woman promptly said: "You want him murdered yourself; why did you not say that loud enough for him to hear it?" She then said, "Grace writes to us that she is going to marry him; but they say she has promised them [meaning she-devil Turner and Mrs. Satan Blair, and their criminal band] that she will kill him." She went on to tell her how I was writing a

THE CONSPIRACY. 301

religious book, and was talking of illustrating it, and said, "If he does illustrate it, he will have a picture in it showing Jim Blair, Arthur Lee, Bill Mayo and Gitchell trying to get into his room after midnight to murder him." The lady sitting by her immediately said: "As you and your husband know all about the attempts to murder the General, why does he not stop them?" "He would," said she, "but he is afraid it would break up some business relations he has, and he is afraid they would get somebody to kill him." "If he is afraid of that," said her companion, "he is not fit to be Governor." She then replied, "If the General ever comes back from Europe he will stop it." "It is his duty to stop it now," said the other lady. Mrs. Francis then said, "They say [meaning Rotten Lee and Satan Blair] the General will have the Legislature impeach the Governor if he gets back from Europe." She then went on to tell how, only two months before, she and the Governor were in New York City, and ex-President Cleveland and his wife had urged on them that the General ought to be the next Democratic candidate for Governor of Missouri; and how Cleveland had written to Senators Vest and Cockrell to the same effect; and how all of them had agreed to it. Cockrell and Vest had talked about it, and talked to some others about it, however, before the ex-President wrote to them concerning it. She then went on to tell how Jim Blair had stolen $5.00 from the General by taking it out of a letter belonging to the General he had intercepted, and also said that the Governor had sounded some of the politicians in different parts of the

State, and in every case he found that the corrupt politician, no matter what his antecendents were, whether Federal or Ex-Confederate, was against the General. She then went on to tell how she and the Governor had the written program of warfare against the General, of Rotten Lee and Satan Blair, and were also receiving from the bad postoffice in St. Louis, copies of all the General's letters to Grace and others and copies of all letters coming to him. The lady asked her if she thought that was right, and if it was not the duty of the Governor to stop that kind of work in the postoffice. She said it was not his duty, as the general government had inspectors assigned to that duty, but that he had a right to do so through the State detectives on the police force if he wanted to. She then went on to say that: "We have learned a great deal from reports of the General's conversations and what he is going to put in his book, that has been of a great deal of service to us in the discharge of our duties;" speaking of herself as though she was as much Governor as was her husband. So much did she speak in this style that the other lady said to her: "Being made Governor, I am afraid, has made you silly." Mrs. Governor then looked up and exclaimed: "Look at the people, how they are looking at us! I expect they have heard every word I have said, and if they have heard it he has too, for he is nearer us than they." This broke up the conversation between the ladies. The Governor all this while was sitting back of her, with only a lady between them, hearing all she was saying, and waitng for her to stop, but not know-

THE CONSPIRACY. 303

ing how to stop her. Mrs. Francis talked the entire programme that night, having thoroughly committed it to memory. I wrote to the Governor for the programme, and he wrote back to me that he did not have it, and as his wife was in Colorado he could not get it for me. He could have written it out from memory and sent it to me if he had been willing. Satan Blair claimed that he had furnished the Governor with a written copy of the programme, and the Governor's wife proved that to be true by talking it at the theater in the presence of the Governor. Blair said if he went to the penitentiary Francis would go along with him, for he was in it as much as he was. When Francis was President of the Police Board I called on him to help stop Blair from using the detectives to corrupt the postoffice. He neglected to do his duty in the premises. The programme had also been talked over in whispers in the rotunda of the Planters' House by a party of men behind my back, but having no intention whatever of going over to Europe, I made no effort to remember that part of it. Parts of it, however, I did remember, and other parts I did not remember, till the events happened to cause recollection to bring them back to me. Not believing that Grace had agreed to invite me over to Europe to see her and then poison me, but believing that she was going to come over to America in July, and would be glad to meet me in New York, on the 6th of July I started for that city to await her arrival there.

In New York I found the hotels set up against me according to program. In the Fifth Avenue Hotel an attempt was made by men to get into my room to murder me after midnight. I have since learned that John F. Lee, brother to Rotten Lee, was one of those men. I had been told that Grace would probably come over on the ship with Mrs. Brant and her beautiful daughter Tallie. If not on that ship, then on the French streamer of the next week, along with Mr. and Mrs. Ben Cable. The steamer, with Mrs. Brant and her daughter Tallie, came, but Grace was not with it. But both ladies who came brought some news, Mrs. Brant delivered to me from Grace. I was to come over, bringing but a small amount of money along, for she would furnish me all the money I would need ; to come to private parlor No. —, third floor, if I found any difficulty at the office of the Grand Hotel, Paris. Mrs. Brant went on to say that Grace had told her to say to me that I need not be afraid of her trying to play any tricks on me. But, said Mrs. Brant, I am afraid she has very serious tricks to play on you if you go over there. Maria, when she arrives, will tell you the same as I do. She will deliver Grace's message to you, and then she will have something further to say to you. She will tell you not to go over there, but to remain on this side and marry her mother-in-law, who has as much as Grace has, and who will divide with you. I had known Maria when she was the young, beautiful, talented and accomplished Miss Maria Benton, grandniece of the great Senator, Thomas H. Benton, who represented Missouri in the United States Senate for thirty years.

Tallie corroborated all her mother had said. They also told me that Miss Lionberger would be on board with Maria with a letter for me from Grace inviting me over. This was on Sunday, and the next Sunday Maria and her husband, who is a member of Congress from Illinois, arrived on the French steamer La Bretagne, and Miss Lionberger was on board. I went down on a revenue cutter and boarded the La Bretagne at the quarantine at the lower end of the harbor, and came up to the wharf with them. While coming up the bay I had a talk with Maria. So when Miss Lionberger attempted to hand me the letter of Grace inviting me over, I turned away and received not the letter. I went to the Victoria Hotel to have some more talk with Maria, but the first time I called the clerk of the hotel, who was set up to do so, reported to me that she and her party had just gone out, which was false. The next time he reported that she and her friend had gone to Rye Beach, which was also false. They remained there ten days waiting for me to call, and wondered why I did not call. Believing they had gone to Rye Beach and being urged by two gentlemen to go over and see Grace about it, and hoping that all I had heard of her bad intentions towards me was not so, I concluded to go over and find out all about it from her.

CHAPTER 25.

MY EUROPEAN TRIP.

So on Saturday at noon, the 9th day of August, I sailed on the La Bretagne for Havre, the seaport city for Paris, on the English channel. Seymour D. Thompson, Judge of the St. Louis Court of Appeals, was on board, according to programme of the criminal band. The criminals knew that I had always been a friend to Judge Thompson, and had always thought he was my friend. This is the reason they bought the Judge with trips to Europe for himself and his daughter, to push me overboard when none of the other passengers were looking, and claim that I fell over accidentally. The Judge selected the rear end of the vessel and invited me, his friend, back there to look with him over the stern of the vessel, at the peculiar shade of color the vessel gave to the water in its trail. While leaning over the vessel and looking intently at the beautiful effect on the water, the Judge treacherously tried to reach around me and push me overboard. I was too quick for him, and the Judge was very much afraid I would push him overboard. He proposed to me that we leave that part of the vessel, lest we should do each other some harm, which we did, and the Judge went to his stateroom and locked himself up there for nearly two days, for fear I might take a notion to shoot him. Other people were on board from different States to help put me out of the way, bribed to do so by the trips to Europe. They were all kinds of people, and the Judge was

THE CONSPIRACY. 307

very intimate with them on board. I sent a cablegram to Grace from New York, but to make sure that she would know that I was coming, and would meet me at the depot in Paris, as Mrs. Brant had said she would, I also sent her a dispatch from Havre. The cablegram was never sent to her, the clerk having been set up to withhold it and rob me of my money. The dispatch she received, but she did not meet me at the station.

PARIS.

About noon, Monday, the 18th, I arrived in Paris and went to the Grand Hotel. I had forgotten all about the number of Grace's parlor, so I inquired at the office for her. The clerk denied that she was in the house, and said that her name had never been on their books, all of which was a lie. Having taken my dinner, I retired to my room and sat reading "Clark's Ten Great Religions" when I heard a very faint rap at my door. Thinking it was somebody who had mistaken the room, I paid no attention to it. Just then I heard Grace say: "I will wait and see him another time." Her maid said: "You had better see him now or you may not get another chance." I went to the door and they had gone. I again inquired at the office and they again denied that she was in the hotel. The next morning I went to the bank, where her mail was always directed, and inquired for her. There I was told that she had left the city, and had not left any word as to where her address would be thereafter, which was another lie. Having told the clerk to tell me to come, Grace dressed herself in her best and sat down in her parlor to wait for me Tuesday evening, but the clerk failed to deliver her word to me, and I went down to the Hotel Normandy that evening to inquire after Lionberger, as I had been told that he was there and was going to be my friend. Instead of Lionberger I met Adams there, and he told me Lionberger had gone over to England, and was on his way home by way of Liverpool. Adams then told me that Boyle was not fighting me, which he knew to be false. I then asked Adams to send his wife and sister-in-law to Grace, to let her know how the hotel people were lying to me, and to take her to me. Adams said his ladies would not have the time, as they were going to be very busy shopping the next day and were then going to start for home. I had no sooner left the Hotel Normandy than Grace came there to ask Adams to bring me to her. Adams took particular pains not to have the time and left for home.

The next morning, while still lying in bed, but wide awake, the head of the bed being alongside of the door, I heard Grace's voice. She was talking about me to a gentlemen, telling him a great deal. She said she had come there to try and catch the General as he came out and ask him not to tell it, for, if he did, it would ruin her and all of them at home. And went on talking in a' way that proved that she had really agreed to poison me. I remained in bed till she went away from in front of my door. I then rose, dressed myself and went out. Then the question with me was what course to pursue. The first course that presented itself to my mind was

THE CONSPIRACY.   309

to get to see her, tell her that I had overheard what she said in front of my door and bid her farewell forever. The next was to see her, make it up with her, turn all her money against the criminals and send them to the penitentiary. I then wrote her a letter, telling her that the hotel was set up to prevent us from meeting, and if she wanted to see me she had better come to my room, as I did not know where her room was located. This letter I took to her bank, and, after telling them that I knew she was in the Grand Hotel, asked them to deliver that letter to her. They agreed to do so, and, having told her in the letter to leave her answer at the bank, after waiting several days and receiving no answer, I concluded to see as much of Europe as I could and return home. They had already corrupted the postoffice in Paris against me.

After having seen all the sights of Paris, on Friday night the 29th, I left for Rome. I was locked up on the train, according to program, in the apartment with an Englishman and a Frenchman. The Englishman was to start a quarrel with me during the night, and he and the Frenchman were to kill me. During the night the Englishman, who was supposed to have been asleep, stretched out very slightly, touching my hat which was on my head with his foot, apparently accidentally. I rose and gave him a very firm and determined look, as much as to say, if that was not accidental, do not repeat it. The Frenchman was fast asleep, and the Englishman did not stretch out any more that night. The Frenchman left the car at Chambery, about the first town in the Alps.

We passed through the Alps, through Mount Senis Tunnel, by noon; one end of the tunnel being in France and the other end in Italy, French troops being at the French end and Italian troops at the Italian end. We saw statuary on the top of mountains as we passed through the Alps. The villages in the Alps were very beautiful. Some of the Alps were covered with eternal snow. Turin was the first place of importance reached after entering Italy. There a rough man and his daughter were placed in the apartment with me according to program. At Genoa, two other girls were put in that apartment, according to program. And as the train dashed on toward Rome, the stars shone brightly over the glorious Mediterranean. They were to drink wine, try to get me to also drink it, and act so as to excite me and try to get me to make an advance towards some of them, and thus furnish the rough man a pretext to murder me. The rough man's daughter, the girl from Turin, laid down flat on her back on the seat opposite me, looked across at me with peculiar looks, and then made peculiar motions with her person, and shouted at the top of her voice, "Glory," all the time looking me intently in the eyes. After a while the great beauty from Naples threw her foot across onto the seat alongside of me, and the other two girls motioned to me to take advantage of the situation. The stars never shone brighter and the planets Venus, Mars and Jupiter were in plain sight. I pointed them out to the girls and talked to them so beautifully about Mars and Venus, our nearest neighbor worlds, and looked back at them with so much admiration and love, that I won the girls over to my side. After a while another man was put in that appartment, according to program, but I was still left room to lie down and sleep. While I was asleep, the buxom girl from Genoa laid down at the other end of the seat and placed her cheek against mine. We slept that way some time, when the girl removed her cheek, and I, in my sleep, involuntarily moved my face after hers, much to the amusement of the others. She kindly put her cheek back against mine. After awhile all were awake again and some went into the toilet apartment. Then I went to sleep again, and the rough man raised his dagger to thrust it into my side, when his ardent daughter caught his arm, exclaiming, "Oh, don't!" just in time to prevent the blade from entering my side. The other two girls joined her in the protest and the man desisted. I was woken up by the noise, but knew that I could not rise in time to defend myself, so I left that entirely to the girls and pretended not to have woken up. At seven o'clock Sunday morning, the last day of August, we arrived in Rome.

ROME.

After breakfast I took a hack and a guide and went around to see the sights. I put in the entire day in that way. The weather was delightful and nature never furnished a brighter or more beautiful Sunday. That beautiful day I saw many of the magnificent churches, the ruins of some of the old temples in which the ancients used to worship the imaginary gods, the Tarpean Rock and the Coliseum. At Rome I met Dr. Grammer, of Baltimore, a preacher; Mr. Champion, of New York, and other Americans. At Rome an attempt was made on my life at the Hotel Continental, according to programme. I also passed Monday and Tuesday wandering through St. Peter's Church, the halls of the Vatican, the Pantheon and other places of interest, and on Wednesday went by railroad down to Naples and around to Pompeii, which is on the southeast side of the mountain of Vesuvius, in company with Dr. Grammer and Mr. Champion, where we got our dinners and then walked up the hill into Pompeii.

POMPEII.

We paid fifty cents each to get through the gate into Pompeii. It was a beautiful afternoon. We first entered the museum, where we saw many interesting objects that had been taken out of Pompeii. Among other things human forms, and burnt bread taken from the oven just like our wheat bread of the present time, the crust of which had been burned, that had been buried under the ashes of Vesuvius for nearly two thousand years. We then went up into the streets and wandered through them. We saw the old court house, the roof of which was gone. As we stood in front of the platform, in the West end of the building, on which the judge sat, I thus soliloquized: There sat the judge, here the lawyers and their clients, there the jury and back yonder the audience, having their legal troubles two thousand years ago and now the earth gives no account, even of their ashes. Two thousand years from now others not now in existence will

THE CONSPIRACY.

come and stand where I am now standing, and have the same thoughts that I am now having. In time they, too, will be gone, and the earth will give no account even of their ashes. Oh, how insignificant is man!

We then went and saw the big theater and the little theater, both of which were insignificant, the theater being in those days not the great institution it is now. The ancients had no great actors like our great Edwin Forrest, and our now great Edwin Booth, and the great English actress Adelaide Neilson, to charm the hearts of the millions from the stage. We then saw the temples in which the ancients used to worship and pray to the imaginary gods Jupiter, Mars, and the goddess Venus. We also walked through the street of the tombs. This is a beautiful street, paved and sidewalked like any other street, on either side of which are beautifnl little houses with open fronts, through which the magnificent stone coffins of the dead could be seen before they were removed. For three days and nights the volcano of Vesuvius rained ashes across the valley over onto Pompeii, a city of 30,000 people, till the entire place was covered out of sight, fifty feet of ashes or more being above the house-tops. For nearly two thousand years farms were cultivated above this buried city, till one day, while sinking a well for a farm house, they struck the top of a house and concluded to explore, when they found a paved street in front of the house, and concluded that they had found Pompeii, the ancient watering place for the rich, fashionable people of Rome, Naples and the rest of

Italy. It was a watering place all the year round, it being perpetual summer there. Forty acres of it have been excavated, and ninety acres of it are still under the ashes of Vesuvius.

Having done Pompeii, we returned to the station, and on ponies, with a guide, started up the mountain to see the crater by night. Holding to the tail of each pony was an Italian on foot whipping the ponies to help us up the mountain. We passed through a village on the side of a mountain as we went up. We got near enough to the crater to get a pretty good uiew of it as it threw up its lava, stones and fire. At one time it appeared to be a column of fire about one hundred feet high. At times it would cease to throw out lava and be perfectly dark around the crater. Off to the right of us the lava flowed down the mountain in great quantities and looked hot enough to burn a hole all the way through the earth. Dr. Grammer became afraid to go any further up the mountain, as Champion told him that he was going to push me in the crater, where I would have been burned up in the twinkle of an eye. The Doctor declared that he would not witness such a horrible sight. The Doctor then helloed back to me: "General, will you go back with me alone down the mountain?" Champion having said that he would not go with him. I answered: "Yes, I will." Champion had been bribed by the St. Louis criminal band to push me into the crater. Coming down the mountain, it being too dark for us to see in front of us, we walked for some distance, leading our ponies. The Italian who whipped my pony up the mountain caught me by the left arm to help me down, the cinders being nearly ankle deep. Suspecting him of treachery, I drew my revolver and carried it in my right hand, which act kept the brigand, as he was, in order. Just after this a party of brigands, accompanied by American co-conspirators of this American mafia, led by Rotten Lee and Satan Blair, came up, meeting us with lighted torches. The Doctor and Champion were in front and they met them first. I overheard one of them say: "See, he has his revolver in his hand. Shall we do that now?" "No," said the Doctor, "wait till we get further down the mountain." We then mounted our ponies and followed the torches. I mounted my pony, and, as I did I so, looked back just in time to catch the brigand in the act of preparing to knock me in the head. Seeing he was caught, and fearing I would shoot him, he instantly desisted. I rode on and the brigands kept at a respectable distance in the rear of me.

When we arrived at the station on the side of the mountain, consisting of two houses, where refreshments were to be had, we all dismounted, paid the brigands for their torches, and the doctor interceded for me and saved my life. There we took a carriage, and as we drove away, the doctor waved his hat and shouted as though he had beaten the brigands; and I did the same. They rushed after the carriage, and the doctor yelled at the driver to whip up, whip up, and away we went down the mountain side at a break-neck speed, dark as was the night. We quickly drove on to Civita Vecchia, where the conspirators had sent a hard American boy to get with me, show me around, watch his chances and murder me treacherously. The boy was with me alone most of the time. I bought a lunch and divided it with the boy and treated him kindly. The boy became my friend, and when the train came and the doctor took a seat in it opposite me, the boy looked in and shamed him for being in such a thing against such a fine gentleman, and the doctor looked ashamed; as the train moved off around the bay to Naples. The brigands had seen so much of the English and Americans visiting the mountains they could understand and speak the English language. We passed Thursday and Friday seeing the sights in Naples, where, in the museum, in the room devoted to curiosities taken out of Pompeii, we saw the positive proof that the ancients had Phallic worship in rich, fashionable Pompeii.

At Naples we were put in rooms 1, 2 and 3, the Doctor being in 1, I in 2 and Champion in No. 3. The two nights we were there efforts were made by men trying to break through a partition door between the Doctor's room and mine to murder me. I stopped their attempts by yelling at them and covering the door with my revolver. Saturday morning we left Naples and arrived at Rome at one o'clock P. M. I stopped there, the Doctor and Campion went on to Florence. That aftertoon I rode through the Pincio, the park, the Gardens of the Borghese and saw the palace of the Cæsars. That Saturday night I went to Florence by rail and arrived there Sunday morning at six o'clock. I spent Sunday and Monday seeing the sights and went to a garden opera Monday night with Dr. Grammer and Champion. I left there Tuesday morning for Venice, bride of the sea, and arrived there about 4 o'clock P. M., in company with young Willie Grammer, son of Dr. Grammer, who got on the cars at Bologna. The next day Dr. Grammer and Mr. Champion arrived and we all went around Venice together.

VENICE.

We went all over Venice, both on the paved streets and the water streets in gondolas. Venice is unlike any other city. There is not a horse, a cow, a dog, or any other animal in the city. There are no street cars of any kind; there are no carriages. Everybody walks or goes in a gondola. In front of the harbor is a long island. From the city we went in a small steamer over to that island, and then crossed the island to its sea front on street cars drawn by horses. Their bathing houses are of cane, and are along the shore, a short distance from the water, and are only used for dressing purposes. This is the Coney Island of Venice, on the Adriatic Sea. Everything in Venice is of great interest, and every tourist ought, by all means, to see that "Bride of the Sea." We passed over the "Bridge of Sighs," which leads over from the prison to the Star Chamber Court Room, where the Doges of Venice used to condemn their political prisoners to death. The dungeon is still in the same condition, and I laid down on the plank platform on which the prisoners used to sleep. Lord Byron, the great poet, slept two nights in that dungeon on that platform, just for poetic effect. While at Venice, Dr. Grammer, Mr. Champion and I went to the opera. As we were returning to the hotel, the Doctor suggested that we go by way of a darker street than the one we were on. We had not gone far when a very rough crowd of Italians came rushing at us and demanded of the Doctor, "Where is that man?" I looked at the Doctor, as much as to say, "Now, you tell them, and I will let you have a bullet." The Doctor declared that he did not know. They had been bribed to murder me, and it was evident that the Doctor was taking me down that dark street to give them a chance. Champion did not go into that street, and cautioned me not to go, but I did not at that time understand the importance of his warning. I retreated back to the well lighted street as soon as possible, a rough Italian sticking at me with an immense knife till bystanders stopped him and his crowd.

At Venice I heard that some St. Louis friends of mine, Miss Maffitt and her party, had gone to Oberammergau from Paris, to see the Passion Play, a representation of the Last Supper and the Crucifixion of Christ, which is only played one summer every ten years, and that they would pass the next two weeks among the lakes of Switzerland, and then return to Paris on their way home. This caused me to return to Paris by way of the lakes, as I wished to see them. I left Venice Thursday morning for Milan, and arrived there that afternoon. I left there Friday morning, and went on the railroad to Como, and rode on a steamer up Lake Como to Men-

THE CONSPIRACY. 319

aggio, and from there across by rail to Lake Lugano, and up that lake by boat to the town of Lugano. I remained there Friday night, and Saturday went to Lucerne, on Lake Lucerne. I remained there over Saturday night, and Sunday went by rail to the city of Geneva, at the lower end of Lake Geneva, arriving there early in the afternoon. I failed to find my friends at any of the hotels at the lakes, but at Geneva I found enemies awaiting my arrival, that they might murder me according to programme.

I had been stopping at what were known to the tourists as the Cook hotels, but to avoid the would-be murderers I concluded not to stop at any more of those hotels. Accordingly, at Geneva I stopped at a different hotel. My enemies were at the Cook Hotel. After dinner I started out to try and find my friends. Going down the street facing the lake, on the opposite side, I saw Boyle, and overheard him say to a man I took to be Henry Hance, of St. Louis: "There he comes; go and do that now." Hance replied, "I will not." Boyle then said, "Why did you come over here, if you were not going to do that?" Hance replied, "To get the trip." This conversation was held in a very earnest manner by Henry Hance, and in a very angry manner by Boyle, his face turning very red. I passed down the street, and Hance left Boyle and went on up the street. I looked back and saw Boyle was alone and crossing the street. I immediately went back to face him, and Boyle avoided a meeting by passing down the middle of the street on the opposite side of an empty omnibus that was standing there. We had the street to ourselves, no other people being about. I then went about inquiring for my friends, and found that they were not in Geneva.

I left Geneva Monday morning for Paris in a second-class car. At Macon, about noon, all the second-class cars were dropped out of the train and second-class passengers were told that they would have to wait till the evening train came by. That afternoon I went wandering about the streets of Macon and loitered on the banks of the river Soane, where there were a lot of women washing clothing and hanging it out on boats. While talking to the men, up came an Englishman with a great red moustache and wearing two watch chains. I talked to him, when he became a little offensive, and Henry Hance came up just in time to prevent trouble between us. Later I wandered into a very fine cemetery and went to reading inscriptions on the tombstones. The Englishman followed me into that city of the dead for the purpose of murdering me, according to the programme of the criminal band, the American mafia. I saw him coming, and faced him, looking at him as much as to say: "I am ready for you," when the Englishman thought prudence would be the better part of valor, and passed on. I kept an eye on the English murderer, as he is known to be in England, while he remained in that grave-yard. I finally went back to the station and waited for the evening train. I had some conversation with a New York lady who had been dropped there with her maid and little girl, as I had been. Finally the evening train came and I was told by several that that train did not go to Paris; that the train for Paris would not be there for an hour and a half yet. Just then I saw the New York lady, her maid and little girl get into one of the cars. I went to her and asked her if that train went to Paris. She answered: "This car goes to Paris." I got into that car and one of the would-be murderers came and ordered me to get out of that car, intending to keep me there over night to murder me. I looked back at him, as much as to say: "If you attempt to take me out out of here I will shoot you." The would-be murderers then held a conference and Henry Hance told them if they attempted to kill me they would have him to kill. They told him they would kill him, too. Then another of them, with whom I had formed some acquaintance on the ship going over, told them they would have him to kill, too. They then concluded to give it up and all jumped on the train and went to Paris. The criminal band had declared that I should never return to Paris alive, and there I was, back in Paris, very much to the surprise of those who had tried to procure my death.

CHAPTER 26.

I arrived in Paris Tuesday morning, stopped at the Hotel Chatham, and was placed in a room according to the programme of the criminal band. Some of my pursuers were placed in an adjoining room, between which and my room there was a partition door, against which I piled the furniture in my room. The partition door was tried, but I woke up in time to cover it with my revolver, and the would-be murderers desisted. I went about Paris, seeing the sights, a few days more. Thursday night I told an American I was going to go to Brussels on Saturday, then to London, then via Liverpool home. He repeated it. So Friday night some American ladies who desired to see me, disguised themselves and took their stand up against the wall of the Grand Hotel, near the west end of it, and waited for me to come by. So well disguised were they, I did not know them, and used language to the first lady that accosted me, insisting that I should stop, that I would not have used had I recognized her.

GRACE'S CONFESSION.

Seeing she was not recognized, she announced herself. She was Grace January, and wanted to talk with me. Her heart was full, and she made a full confession to me. She told me that she had intended to kill me; that Mrs. James L. Blair and Mrs. Charles H. Turner had urged her to kill me, and had instructed her how to do it with poison; that Adams had come down to Rome to talk to her about it, but that she would not talk to him about it; that Lionberger's sister had come over to Paris and urged her to do it, telling her it was necessary to save their fortunes and to save themselves from the penitentiary; that Lionberger himself had come over there and urged her to do it, telling her that her sister had talked to her about what was necessary to be done; that Tom Tutt and Mrs. Tom Tutt knew all about it and wanted it done; that Boyle had urged her to do it; that Mrs. Blair and Mrs. Turner kept telling her in their letters that all the Granite Mountain people wanted it done; and how they kept telling her that I had kept out of the way of her carriage when she sent it to me to bring me to the house to go with her to her mother's funeral, and how they kept telling her that I had remained away from her waiting for Anna, meaning the good and noble Miss Anna L. Allen, to come to St. Louis, thus exciting her jealousy, till they finally got her to consent to kill me; but that she would not do it now; and wanted me to remain in Paris and go home with her and others in December. But if I would not remain that long, then not to go Saturday afternoon, but to remain over till Monday, and Sunday Mrs. Tom Tutt would come to my hotel to see me, and whatever sum of damages I said, she would cable to her husband, and it would be placed in bank to my credit. If I did not remain over Sunday, to make no fuss about it, and when I got home it would be settled there, even to the amount of $100,000.

She went on to tell me the names of all the victims who

had been swindled out of their fortunes by the Granite Mountain people, who were trying to have me murdered. She then told me all the programme of the criminal band against me for the future, which was inconsistent with the idea that they intended to settle with me in damages, and proved that they intended to murder me, and only intended to settle in case they could not possibly have me murdered. Believing that I would be in great danger of being murdered if I remained any longer in Paris, I left there Saturday afternoon, as I had intended, for Brussels.

Sunday morning I went out to the battlefield of Waterloo, twelve miles southwest, back on the railroad toward Paris. A young man got in company with me on the cars going out. We went up on top of the Lion mound, which is fully a hundred feet high, mounted by an immense bronze lion made out of the French cannon the English captured on that field, the lion looking southwest toward France. We took a guide up with us, who pointed out to us the positions that were occupied by all the troops that fought on that field on both sides of the battle.

At the foot of the mound, on the east side of it, there stands a little frame hotel called the Hotel Musee, one room of which is filled with relics from the battlefield. I was shown through that room alone, by an English young lady whose ancestors had fought on that field, the proprietor's daughter. In that room is every variety of arms used on that field, all old flint locks; also part of Napolean's personal bag-

THE CONSPIRACY. 325

gage that was captured on the field, his copper camp kettle, his silver spurs, one of his swords, his hat and other articles. There was an equestrian picture on the wall showing how Napoleon tried to commit suicide when the battle had gone against him, by trying to charge the enemy solitary and alone, two of his officers catching the reins of his horse and thus preventing it. The idea that through mortification at his defeat he tried to commit suicide, which was suggested by me, was evidently a new idea to the girl, and she seemed pleased.

THE BALL AT BRUSSELS.

I then told her about the grand ball at the house of the Duchess of Richmond, in Brussels, before the battle of Waterloo, at which were the Duke of Wellington and his staff and other officers of the British army; and how they heard the cannonading at Quatre Bras, a few miles southwest of Waterloo, indicating the approach of Napoleon, and the effect it had on the party; and then repeated to her Byron's description of it in his immortal poem "Childe Harold:"

> " There was a sound of revelry by night,
>   And Belgium's capital had gathered then
> Her beauty and her chivalry, and bright
>   The lamp shone over fair women and brave men.
> A thousand hearts beat happily, and when
>   Music arose with its voluptuous swell,
> Soft eyes looked love to eyes which spake again
>   And all went merry as a marriage bell.

> But hush ! a deep sound strikes like a rising knell.
>   Did ye not hear it ? No ; 'twas but the wind
> Or the car rattling o'er the stony street ;
>   On with the dance ! Let joy be unconfined.
> No sleep till morn, when youth and pleasure meet
>   To chase the glowing hours with flying feet.
> But hark ! That heavy sound breaks in once more,
>   As if the clouds its echo would repeat ;
> And nearer, clearer, deadlier than before !
>   Arm ! Arm ! It is—it is—the cannon's opening roar !
>
> Ah ! then and there was hurrying to and fro,
>   And gathering tears, and tremblings of distress,
> And cheeks all pale, which but an hour ago
>   Blushed at the praise of their own loveliness ;
> And there were sudden partings, such as press
>   The life from out young hearts, and choking sighs
> Which ne'er might be repeated ; who could guess
>   If evermore should meet those mutual eyes,
> Since upon night so sweet such awful morn could rise."

On dashed the officers to the field of Waterloo, some to return and greet those mutual eyes no more forever.

The young lady was delighted with the poem, and thanked me for repeating it to her, and said she was going to memorize it and repeat it to visitors when they came there to see the field and the relics. The battle of Waterloo was the most important battle ever fought in Europe. It settled the fate of Europe for many years.

THE CONSPIRACY. 327

BATTLE OF WATERLOO.

The Duke of Wellington was a defensive general and always waited for the enemy to attack him. He had never been defeated, and, consequently, had unbounded confidence in his star of victory. Napoleon was an offensive general. He never waited for the enemy to attack him, but always first attacked the enemy. He had never been defeated on any field, and, consequently, had unbounded confidence in his star of victory. The world has never produced two abler generals than were Napoleon and Wellington. At Waterloo the second line of the English army and its reserves were posted on a ridge running East and West and faced South. The first line was on the declivity, in front of the second line. The French army faced North and occuped a ridge parallel to the position of the English. Its first line was also on the slight declivity, in front of its ridge. The first lines of the two armies were not very far apart. These two ridges were about one-half mile apart, with a slight declivity between them. The flanks of the English army were well protected by deep ravines at the ends of the ridge it occupied. The battlefield consisted of beautiful farms, with fine houses and other good buildings. Nearly every farm had a name. Each army had two lines and a reserve in the rear of the second line. Just back of the extreme right of the second line of the English army was a small ridge from which artillery could have enfiladed the entire English army and driven it from its position, so Napoleon ordered his brother, Jerome Bonaparte, who commanded the left wing of his army, to drive back the right wing of the English army and take possession of that ridge. This Jerome attempted to do at eleven in the forenoon, but, after a desperate fight, in which most of the time he was successful, was finally repulsed. This was the beginning of the battle. Later Napoleon ordered Jerome to try that again while he, at the same time, ordered a general fight all along the line, and, while this was going on, ordered a particular effort to be made to turn the left flank of the English, which resulted in a desperate fight there, in which General Eugene Beauharnais, the son of Josephine, fought gallantly, and in which the French were repulsed. Napoleon then ordered the French cavalry, which was commanded by Murat, the husband of Caroline Bonaparte, the youngest sister of Napoleon, supported by infantry, to break through the center of the enemies' line, with the view of dividing the enemy and getting part of the army between the forces of Jerome and the French cavalry, and thus attacking that part of the enemy in both flanks, while the rest of his army to the East fought the left wing of the English.

The French cavalry and infantry succeeded in breaking through the English center and camé very near capturing or killing Wellington in the rear of the second line of the English. His body-guard, staff and cavalry, as well as reserve infantry, had to fight desperately to save him, Wellington himself exhibiting the greatest personal bravery. The French cavalry and infantry were finally driven out of the English

THE CONSPIRACY. 329

lines and back to their own lines. Jerome also fought desperately, but failed to get possession of the infilading ridge and was driven back to his own lines, although at one time, the cavalry, ordered to help him, got through the enemy's lines and had a desperate fight behind them, and the two armies substantially occupied their original lines. Next Napoleon commenced continuous attacks, principally on the English center, and, at the same time, had his three hundred cannons pouring their destructive fire on the British till Wellington exclaimed: "Would to God that Blucher or night would come!" Napoleon grew desperate at the desperate resistance of the British. Hearing that the advance guard of Blucher's army was approaching from the East, at first he did not believe it and declared that it was Grouchy's army coming to re-inforce him, but, on becoming convinced that it was true, he sent some troops to hold them in check while he could try and defeat the English before Blucher could arrive with the main part of his army. Accordingly, he ordered his cavalry to charge the English center. They broke through, but were driven back. Napoleon then went with Ney, whom he had always called the bravest of the brave, and his old guard, till they were within a short distance of the enemy, where he made a speech of encouragement to them, telling them how he always relied on them to wrest victory from the enemy in the last resort, and how they had never failed him. The old guard answered him with shouts of "Vive L'Empeuror."

He then ordered them to charge the enemy's center. With

a yell, they gallantly charged the enemy's center, but were repulsed by the united efforts of the terrible fire of the enemy's artillery and the sudden charge of a body of infantry from concealment, to which Wellington said: "Up, guards, and at them." Soon after, about four in the afternoon, Blucher charged his army in the right flank and rear, and caused his troops to waver, and, at the same time, Wellington's entire army charged him in front. No army in the world could stand that—to be charged in the flank and rear by one army, and, at the same time, be charged in front by another army, so Napoleon's grand army broke and fled, and it resulted in a rout. Blucher and Wellington met in the charge where the headquarters of Napoleon had been during the battle, embraced and congratulated each other on their great victory. Blucher pursued the fleeing Frenchmen all that moonlight night, refusing to capture them, and slaughtering them, till Blucher and butcher became synonymous terms.

Grouchy had been ordered by Napoleon to keep Blucher away from that field or to follow him to the field and help to fight him and Wellington. Grouchy was only five miles away to the East and allowed Blucher to march away from his immediate front, only firing a few artillery shots at him as he went, fully knowing that he was going to help the English, as it was a cleared country and he could see all the way to the field at Waterloo and knew that the battle was going on there. Grouchy's conduct can not possibly be explained on any other theory than that he was wilfully treacherous to Napoleon. Had

THE CONSPIRACY. 331

he followed Blucher to the field and helped Napoleon, or kept Blucher away from the field, the victory might have been with the French instead of against them. This great, but only, defeat of Napoleon resulted in his exile and death on the now famous isle of St. Helena.

The English account states that Wellington had only sixty-five thousand soldiers, while Napoleon had eighty thousand. Wellington, however, had the assistance of Blucher's army.

I bought a cane that grew on the field and a pamphlet describing the battle, and rode away to the station on the top of an omnibus. From the top of the omnibus I threw pennies to the children, who followed it asking for them. They went down on their all fours and scrambled for the pennies just like pigs after an ear of corn. As I rode up the street on a street-car drawn by horses in Brussels, my companion, the young Englishman, advised me to go to England by way of Antwerp. That suggestion immediately brought to my recollection that the programme provided that I was to be murdered at night between Antwerp and Dover. So I concluded not to go by that route. Looking closely at the young man and asking him a few questions, I discovered that he was the same young man that rode in the same apartment with me by night from Rome to Florence, and had suggested to me to go up into the belfry at Florence, the programme providing that the red moustached Englishman should meet me there and murder me. I did not go up into the belfry at Florence. I told the young man that he reminded me of a young man that took a night ride with me from Rome to Florence, in such a manner as to let him know that I remembered him. The young man kept away from me after that. I passed the rest of the day roaming about beautiful Brussels, for some time being on the boulevard Waterloo—seven streets in one, lined with beautiful trees, some promenade and some driving streets, the houses being only on the outside of all seven of them.

Monday morning I went to London via Ostend and Dover. On the same train from Brussels to Ostend, in the same apartment sat opposite me the red moustached Englishman. I looked definately at him and he looked a little nervous. Crossing the Channel, I kept an eye on that red moustached Englishman. From Dover up to London he was not in the same apartment with me. I arrived in London about 6 P. M., and stopped at the Hotel Metropole. I had been advised to stop at the Hotel Metropole by an old gentleman and his two sons, who claimed to be Londoners, at the Hotel Continental in Rome, who gave the advise according to program of the American Mafia. In less than thirty minutes after my arrival, while standing in front of the entrance to the hotel, Boyle came by and entered the hotel. As he approached I looked at him as much as to say, "I am ready for you, sir." He then dropped his head and passed in. That night an attempt was made by the gang to get into my room to murder me. I saw at the hotel the red moustached Englishman, the big black moustached Englishman and others who had been pursuing me on the continent.

THE CONSPIRACY.

The next morning I went to the office of the American Minister, Robert T. Lincoln, son of President Lincoln, and told him about the conspiracy against me, how I had been pursued over the continent and how I was now being pursued for my life in England, and asked him for the protection of the American government. Mr. Lincoln replied: "You don't look as though they had hurt you very much. You are a lawyer, and ought to know that when you entered England you became subject to the laws of England, the same as any of her citizens. If anything happens, then I can act." The idea that I had to be murdered before I could get the protection of my own government from the American Minister in England was not a very pleasant one to me; and was not in accordance with my understanding of the International Law. I parted with Minister Lincoln with the understanding that I was to call and see him again concerning the matter; and had I done so, would doubtless have received the full protection of the American government from that accomplished gentleman. He would undoubtedly have called on the English authorities to protect my life from the criminal band while I was in England. The conspirators intended to murder me in the barber's chair in the Hotel Metropole, but the barber saved me from that by refusing to shave me, and not allowing me to enter the shop. They also attempted to surrouhd me in the office of the hotel to murder me there, but two young ladies who had heard of it, came and stood between them and me, very near to me. So they let it alone there.

For four days I went about London seeing the sights, among the rest the battle of Waterloo cyclorama, Westminster Abbey, the British National Museum, Wellington's tomb in St. Paul's Church and other sights too numerous to mention. I left London Friday, September 26, at 2 P. M., and arrived at Liverpool at 6·30 P. M. the same day. Arriving at Liverpool, the first hotel I went to claimed to be full, so I had to go to another hotel. There they put up a cot for me in the bath room, which had a communicating door with another room, Some men made an attempt on the partition door that night. but desisted on my waking up and covering it with a revolver. The next day, about 5 o'clock P. M., Saturday, the 27th of September, I sailed on the Etruria. It was a glorious moonlight night and everybody on board enjoyed it as we steamed out from Liverpool. The next morning, Sunday, we arrived at Queenstown, Ireland, about 9 o'clock. Many of us went on shore and looked around that Irish city. Having taken on the mails, we sailed away from there, all day in sight of the Irish coast and the coast of Wales. By Monday afternoon recollection caused me to know that I had been placed in a state-room with a man, according to the programme of the criminal band, so I went to the purser of the ship and told him about the conspiracy against me and that I heard that there were two state-rooms empty and I would liked to be moved into one of them. He offered to so move me provided I would pay another full fare. I refused to pay that amount. About an hour after this interview a man came to me and

THE CONSPIRACY.

asked me if I was willing to go and have a talk with the doctor. "Certainly," said I, and went and had my talk with the doctor. The doctor informed me that he had heard that I was afraid of being harmed on board and assured me that nothing could possibly happen to me on board, as men could not escape from the ship as they can on land. He then went on to ask me if I ate morphine or drank intoxicants. I informed him that I did neither. He then said to me, if I did not want to remain where I was I could have the hospital all alone to myself and that I could lock that and I would not be disturbed. I told him that I would accept the hospital on those terms. I was shown to the hospital by the aforesaid villainous-looking assistant to the doctor. The sea was very rough and I was feeling unwell, so I laid down in my bunk. When night came I tried to lock the door and found that it had been fixed so it could not be locked.

Recollection then brought back to me that part of the programme relating to what was to take place on the ship, and I at once realized that I had been placed in the hospital strictly in accordance with the programme of the criminal band. By that time I was very sea-sick, and remained in the hospital for two days without leaving it, during which time the villain tried to poison me with opium in beef tea and another dish. He failed to put in the beef tea enough opium to have the effect desired. It only acted as a sedative, and quieted my nerves. The villian looked very much surprised when he entered the hospital and found me alive and appearing bright;

and receiving from me the assurance that the beef tea was just what I needed, the villain eagerly insisted upon my taking some more beef tea at once, but I emphatically declined. The next morning the villain came with a dish for me, at the sight of which my stomach revolted after having taken one bite. The villain urged me to eat it, and seemed very much disappointed when I refused to do so. Had I eaten it, I would never have gotten out of that hospital alive. Having failed to murder me by poison, the conspirators sent one of their number into the hospital to murder me by assassination. I faced him firmly and just then some deck hand who had heard of the conspiracy, appeared and ordered him out and told him if he came into that part of the ship again they would throw him overboard.

I slept in the hospital at night to the end of the voyage, protected by the deck hand and the fear of my revolver entertained by the conspirators. Boyle was on board and led the conspirators. His closest co-conspirators on board were Frank Hirchberg, and his wife, and her brother. The program provided that his wife should try to play a treacherous trick on me by night in some lonely part of the ship, out of sight of all others, and at the critical moment her husband, her brother and Boyle were to appear on the scene, she was to complain and they were to throw me overboard. I gave the lady no chance to play her treacherous trick. She is a daughter of General D. M. Frost, and as treacherous as her father, who sought my confidence only to betray it. He was first treacherous to the Union and then treacherous to the Confederacy. Jefferson Davis ordered him stricken from the rolls as a deserter. While traveling in Italy I heard Dr. Grammer tell Champion that Judge Clover had come over to look after the safety of the General, but that he was not going to speak to me or have anything to do with me; that the conspirators had sent him over to do so in order to manufacture a defense for themselves in advance of their having me murdered.

CHAPTER 27.

We arrived at the quarantine at 11 P. M. Saturday night, and went up and landed in New York Sunday morning. I remained in that city several days, during which the conspiracy was carried on against me. The conspirators had Ex-President Cleveland told that I had been abusing him over in Europe, hoping thereby to have him refuse to see me, but the lying trick did not succeed. I had been speaking of him only in terms of the very highest praise ; have never spoken of him in any other terms ; and never will speak of him in any other terms than those of the very highest praise. I had a very pleasant interview with the Ex-President, and left for Greenfield, my old home, in Indiana. There I stopped to see my relations and become thoroughly posted as to the future program of the criminal band against me.

There I learned that the conspirators had all the principal hotels in St. Louis set up against me, so there was but little choice as to which was the best for me to stop at. I went to the Lindell Hotel, not expecting to remain there long, arriving in the evening. At supper I was poisoned by rough-on-rats being put in my tea, which made the tea very red, caused me to nearly fall from my chair. After that I called for clear green tea, and would not drink it unless it was so, and always tested it before I drank much of it.

I determined to see Governor Francis and demand of him the protection of the law. I met the Governor on the street and told him that I wanted to have a talk with him. The Governor excused himself on the ground that he had no time to talk to me then, but the next time he came down from Jefferson City he would stop at the Lindell himself and have a talk with me He did not stop at the Lindell, as he said he would, and avoided me, and allowed the conspiracy to run on against me. He did not stop it as Mrs. Francis said he would to the lady that night in the theater, if I came back from Europe, for I had gotten back from Europe alive, and he had not stopped it, and when I finally asked him to stop it he told me that I must be mistaken about it. Twice the Governor made that hypocritical reply to me when I applied to him for protection, and when he person-

THE CONSPIRACY. 349

ally knew that I was not mistaken. Not till he was told by others that it was his duty as Governor to stop it at once, did he take any action whatever, and then only just enough to try and save his own reputation in case I was murdered, and let the conspiracy run on against me. He could have put an end to it at any time through his Police Board had he so desired, and the fact that he did not, proved that he did not want to do it.

Just before the Legislature met, I heard of a scheme on the part of Francis to get quite a number of the members of the Legislature who had been elected as Vest men to go back on him and elect him (Francis), to the Senate as the successor of Vest. I went to the closest friend of Francis and told him that I had heard of the secret scheme and read the riot act to him, and told him that it should not be done. Hence the willingness on the part of the Governor that I might be murdered. The Governor knew that his Chief of Police, Lawrence Harrigan, was in the conspiracy, because I, while a Police Commissioner, had voted to dismiss him from the force for failing to place in the relief fund money that had been placed in his possession for that purpose, and appropriating it to his own use. The chief performed the part assigned him by the written programme of the criminal band, namely : that whenever I should come to him for the protection of the Police Department, he should tell me that from his investigation of it, he did not think there was anything in it. That he would lie and play the hypocrite about it just like the Governor. Shame on such a Governor! Through Turner and Overall, Blair succeeded in perpetuating the conspiracy against me in the Police Department, and has thus far saved himself from prosecution.

Dr. Grammer said to Champion, in accordance with the written programme, in Italy, while traveling with me, so that I heard it, that Blair and Lee claimed that they would have the Criminal Court set up against any prosecution I might try to bring against them or any of their criminal band, should they not succeed in having me murdered. That they had both candidates for Judge of that Court secured, namely : J. C. Normile and Ashley Clover. That no matter which was elected they would own the Judge ; that if Normile was re-elected they would own the Judge and also the Circuit Attorney, as Clover, son of Judge Clover, was already that, and if he did not defeat

THE CONSPIRACY.

Normile he would have to hold his present office for two years longer; if he beat Normile, then they would own the Judge and would buy the new Circuit Attorney, whoever might be appointed to fill the vacancy caused by Clover's election to the Judgeship. Both Normile and Clover unwittingly gave me confirmation of the truth of the doctor's assertion. The Judge of the Court of Criminal Correction also performed a part assigned to him in the programme of the criminal band. The programme of the criminals also claimed that they had bought the Circuit Judges with trips to Europe and some with trips to the sea coast, so as to own the courts in case I should sue them for civil damages. Judge Dillon's confession subsequently made to me, confirmed this.

The 26th day of August, 1891, in the Governor's office at Jefferson City, I told him that Rotten Lee and Satan Blair were still running their conspiracy against me and asked him to stop it. In reply, the Governor said that he himself would kill me if I ever gave the facts to the newspapers or put them in my book. This he said in a low tone of voice, but still I heard it. Shame on such a Governor, everlasting shame on such a Governor!

THE CONSPIRACY.

In the early part of the summer, Thomas E. Tutt, who has twice tried to treacherously murder me, and others of the conspirators at different times, called Senators Cockrell and Vest to St. Louis, and told each that they had been damaging me in ways that it was not necessary to explain, and wanted them to fix it up with me for them; but wanted them to get me out of the race for Governor, telling them that they intended to pay me $60,000 in damages. Both Senators told me about it, and referred me to an old lawyer who was a friend of theirs, and who was out of the city at the time. When he returned to the city, Satan Blair got to him before I did and feed him ahead of me, and through his machinations prevented the settlement.

To head off the next attempt to settle, Blair murdered Frank Hicks, the lawyer, in a most cowardly and treacherous way, to prevent him from becoming my attorney. After having murdered him he had it falsely published in the newspapers that Hicks shot himself accidentally while trying to unload a revolver. It was in the written program of Rotten Lee and Satan Blair that Blair was to murder Hicks, and how he was to murder him and how he was to try to con-

THE CONSPIRACY. 353

ceal it, if Hicks attempted to become my lawyer, under the direction of Chris Ellerbe, whom Blair claimed as one of his secret attorneys to help clean me out. Blair carried out that part of the program, and poor Hicks is in his grave. Six weeks before Blair murdered Hicks, he, Blair, told Senator Vest that he was going to murder Hicks, and Senator Vest told me that Blair had so told him. Four weeks before the murder, in the Confederate ball, Mrs. Mary J. Cable, in the presence of many people, told me that Blair was going to murder Frank Hicks, and how he was going to murder him and how he was going to try to conceal the murder. Blair did it just as she said he was going to. Mrs. Cable said Blair's wife told her. Going into the office of Hicks, which was on the same floor as Blair's office, he talked in a friendly way to the unsuspecting Hicks for a short time, and suddenly drawing a revolver fired at his heart. Hicks fell over and Blair placed the pistol with which he had shot Hicks, alongside his victim, and ran out of Hicks' office and gave out that Hicks had shot himself accidentally while unloading a revolver, and got a man out at Ferguson to falsely say that he loaned Hicks that revolver. Before he died,

Hicks said that Blair murdered him. Blair has since reported to his co-conspirators that he did murder Hicks, and imagines that he is a great hero because he cowardly and treacherously murdered an unarmed, unsuspecting man.

They also had an attempt made to murder me in West Virginia on the train as I went to Washington City. During the night two rough country men, accompanied by a rough country girl, came on the train. One of the rough men occupied an entire seat opposite my own, which I occupied alone. On the seat back of the rough country man were seated the girl and her other companion. The rough man opposite me turned his back toward me and his face towards the window of the car, and then threw his sporting rifle across his left shoulder, the muzzle pointing towards me, and began to play with the hammer of it, intending to pull the trigger and shoot me, and claim that it was done accidentally. His companions, the conductor of the train and others were there by pre-arrangement to swear that the shooting was entirely accidental. I prevented it by moving from my seat and going forward in the car just in time to save my life. Just as I moved I overheard the rough girl say to him, don't do it now, he is

THE CONSPIRACY. 355

moving. The rifleman looked around and was very much surprised to see that my seat was unoccupied and that I was in a seat some distance in front of it. The rough party soon left the train. When I arrived in Washington, Satan Blair, who came there for the purpose, tried to assassinate me by slipping up behind me, accompanied by a crowd of men, and trying to shoot me in the back in Willard's Hotel. The crowd accompanied him to help him assassinate me, if necessary, and then swear that I was killed in self defence. Hon. Marshall Arnold, a member of Congress from Missouri, knocked his pistol to one side and prevented the assassination. When they found that there was one man there that would help me, the cowardly gang ignobly retreated from the field. The next morning I met the cowardly Blair on the street where there was nobody in the way, and offered him battle, and he, coward like, backed down and hurriedly sneaked into a house.

On the afternoon of the 24th of March, in the Senate Chamber at Jefferson City, I sat immediately in the rear of Mrs. Gov. Francis and a young lady who accompanied her, and overheard their conversation relating to myself. In that conversation Mrs.

Francis broke down and acknowledged to the young lady that both she and the Governor had given their consent that I might be murdered. She said that the Governor would support me for Governor, but he was afraid if I became Governor that I would have Blair tried for murdering Hicks, and that would expose all these matters; and that he was determined that these matters should never become public, for if they did it would ruin the reputation of his administration and he could never do anything more politically. That if the General published her confession or said anything about him or her concerning these matters in his book, that the Governor had declared that he, himself, would kill the General. And thus at last I also received the positive proof from the wife of the Governor that he was also in the conspiracy to murder me. Everylasting shame on such a Governor, who did not seem to have sense enough to know that the first duty of a Governor is to protect human life, not to destroy it or allow it to be destroyed. Mrs. Francis also said that her husband had certain State Senators bought to support him for the office of United States Senator. That he expected to buy it away from Cockrell, but that he was a little afraid some other man with more money than he had might come along and buy it from him. This proves that the Constitution of the State ought to prohibit the Governor from becoming a candidate for the United States Senate.

Mrs. Francis also said that Charles H. Jones, editor of the St Louis Republic, had promised Morehouse that he would support him with his paper for Governor, but that her husband had bought him away from Morehouse by buying $2,000 worth of his stock in the paper; but that the stock brings no dividend, and the Governor considered that he had lost just that much money. But, said the young lady, he got his political influence, and that is what he bought. Mrs Francis then went on to say that Jones had promised the General that he would support him for Governor, but had sold out to the criminal band who were opposing the General ; but that the sale of the stock was not to actually take place till after the campaign was over ; so if the General found it out he could not charge Jones with having been bought. And that was the reason that he is not now supporting the General with his paper. She said that Jones would promise anybody anything and then sell out right opposite to what he had promised. Everlasting shame on Jones for selling out. Mrs. Francis also said to the young lady that in the murder of Hicks, Blair was guilty of murder in the first degree, and that she and the Governor and all the rest of them were guilty of murder in the second degree, and seemed very much distressed about it. The young lady said to her : If it makes you feel so badly when you are only guilty of murder in the second degree, why do you want to go ahead and have the General murdered in the first degree ? She made no reply to that.

Rotten Lee and Satan Blair also succeeded in exciting considerable war prejudice against me, notwithstanding all the work I had done for the southerners, and both Cockrell and Vest and other Confederate officers were for me. In this connection I will say that both Vest and Cockrell acknowledged to me that they were wrong during the war, and that I was right. Vest said that men who were wrong during the war had been crowding out men who were right during the war; and that that was not right, but that he and Cockrell had been in the Senate so long and become so old that they would not know what to go

THE CONSPIRACY.   359

at now if they were turned out of there. Cockrell said this same thing to me, and added that one of the Senators ought to be a Union man, and if he found that he could not get a re-election, he would be for me for the Senate. He also said that he and Vest would urge Cleveland to put me in his Cabinet as Secretary of War. It was magnanimous in Vest and Cockrell to say those things, and I honor them for saying them. I honor them both in the highest for acknowledging that they were wrong on the war questions, for it was not only honorable and manly in them to do so, but it was also patriotic, when they became convinced that they were wrong. But as in the judgment of the author, those questions are settled for all time ; they are now of no importance except as matters of history.

Rotten Lee and Satan Blair also, whenever they found any man was friendly to me, immediately manufactured a lie to the effect that I had said something awful about him or some female member of his family. It always had the effect to turn him against me till the lie was corrected by some friend of mine. In no instance did any man ever come to me and give me a chance to say whether it was a lie or not. Reader, take warning from this and never condemn any person till you have given him a hearing. If you do condemn anyone without giving him a hearing, it will simply put it in the power of your worst enemies to turn you against your best friends and to turn your best friends against you. So do not allow villians to make a fool of you. Always allow everybody a free hearing before you go back on him.

Before the death of Governor Marmaduke, they got him into the conspiracy against me. The week before he died he spent in St. Louis drunk. Hearing that he was in the conspiracy, I went to the Southern Hotel to face him on it.

During the conversation between us he broke down and confessed that he had suggested to Blair to get up some false affidavits against me to furnish him a pretext to remove me from the Police Board. He had lied on me at West Point and was then going to lie on me in Missouri. He also said to me: "Gooding, you have saved me and saved me the Governorship by coming here and giving me this talk, and I thank you for it from the bottom of my heart, for I would have done it if you had not given me this talk, and, if I had done it, the Legislature would have had

THE CONSPIRACY. 361

a perfect right to come together of their own volition and removed me from the Governorship." The next week he died of the effects of dissipation. There died a man who had treated me meanly at West Point and whom I had forgiven and whom I had helped to save from defeat at the polls. I had also loaned him money many times and taken care of him when he had delirium tremens and concealed the fact from the world for him; but, in spite of all of it, he treated me meanly to the last. The Governor back of him was in a conspiracy to murder me and the present Governor is in a conspiracy to murder me. This is a bad record for our Governors to have made. One in a conspiracy to remove me from the Board on false affidavits suggested by himself and two in conspiracies to murder me. It is to be hoped that the next Governor will be an improvement on the last three.

They also had arrangements made in every part of the State to have me assassinated if I attempted to canvass the State for the nomination. In the beginning of this conspiracy Satan Blair said to Frank Gainni that Rotten Lee had said to him that he was going to spend his money hiring people to help him knock out Gooding with the widow and in politics, and if he succeeded in getting the widow's money, it would be as good an investment of his money as he could possibly have made.

The history of this conspiracy ought to be a warning to other people and morals can be drawn from it. Rotten Lee, although he has spent his money as aforesaid, has not, and never will, get the fortune of the widow, as she says she will never marry him, because he is a ROTTEN man. Moral: No rotten man ever ought to try to force himself on an unwilling widow.

Satan Blair has not yet, and never will, get the Governorship, for he is certain to be hung for the murder of Frank Hicks. Moral: Never commit a murder to carry your point against a political rival, for if you do you will be hung.

The Granite Mountain criminals are still in danger of having to disgorge and being punished under the criminal laws of our State. Moral: Get your fortunes honestly, and then you need not live under the fear that you may have to disgorge and be punished under the criminal laws.

Moral for public officials: Be honest in your official positions, and then you need not fear ex-

THE CONSPIRACY. 363

posures, disgrace and punishment. Through the fear of counter investigations and publications, the mothers of Rotten Lee and Satan Blair confessed their shame to them and implored them to quit making war on good people, meaning myself and my relations. Mrs. Satan Blair confessed her shame, as did also Mrs. She-Devil Turner.

Moral for all fools like Rotten Lee and Satan Blair: Before you investigate anybody else, and finding nothing wrong, make unjust war on good people, first be sure that you are all right yourselves and then investigate your own folks, and be sure that their records are all right, lest through fear of counter investigations and publications they confess their shame to you and implore you to quit making unjust war on good people, your betters.

The criminal band got Mayor Noonan, who also wanted to be Governor, to revoke my permission to carry a revolver to defend my life, so that Rotten Lee and Satan Blair might shoot me down without any danger to themselves; but I refused to give up my revolver when the detectives asked me for it. They then got his sister-in-law into the conspiracy to help murder me by giving her a trip to Europe.

Fearing, if I became Governor, that I would, through the police department, have him and his sister-in-law prosecuted as co-conspirators of Rotten Lee and Satan Blair, Noonan actively canvassed the city for one of my competitors from the country, to prevent me from having a chance to get a delegation from the city, and thus knocked me out of the race with the aid of the others.

Fearing I might, if I became Governor, through my power over the Police Department, have him and his wife prosecuted as co-conspirators of the American Mafia, led by Rotten Lee and Satan Blair, Governor Francis also helped to prevent me from getting a delegation from the city. When I found out the situation I stood aloof from the primaries, and retired from the race. The criminal band having prevented me from becoming Governor by the power of their money, spending more than a hundred thousand dollars bribing bad men to make war on me, their lies and their tricks, their crimes and the aid of Charles H. Jones, editor of the St. Louis Republic, and the aid of Francis and Noonan, in the interest of good government, I hereby demand of the next Governor of Missouri that he shall see that the Police Depart-

THE CONSPIRACY

ment of St. Louis, who are in possession of all the facts, do their duty, to the end that James L. Blair is tried, convicted and hung for the murder of Frank Hicks. I also demand that Arthur Lee, as the chief co-conspirator of Blair, shall also be hung for that murder. I also demand that their co-conspirators, the Granite Mountain criminals, and also their co-conspirator, David B. Francis, and all the rest of the conspirators, male and female, shall be punished according to law

Last February in Washington, D. C., I heard Hon. Ben T. Cable, of Rock Island, Ill., repeat to his wife the program of Rotten Lee and Satan Blair against me. In that program he repeated that they intended to have my noble friend, Judge Milton S. Robinson, of Indiana, murdered, if he did not cease his efforts to protect me from their efforts to murder me ; and have it done by poison in his own home at Indiana, and lay it to heat prostration. He also said they intended to have my friend, Ex-Governor Chas. H. Hardin, who was supporting me for Governor, murdered by poison at the Ringo House, in Mexico, because he was declaring that I was needed for Governor to put them through under the law. He also said they intended to have Judge Bennett Pike murdered by poison, if he did not cease denouncing their conspiracy against me. He said they intended to have all three poisoned at about the same time, so they would all be buried on the same day. Robinson died at Anderson at the time Cable said he would, and was reported as having died from heat prostration. Hardin and Pike died suddenly at the time Cable said they would, and all three were buried on Sunday, the last day of July, according to the program as repeated by Cable. Hardin died at the Ringo House in Mexico, and Pike died in St. Louis. I was also told in St. Louis all about these three murders, but was told at the same time that all three of these gentlemen would be duly warned of their danger. I was also told about them in Greenfield, Ind., by two prominent citizens, who assured me that they would see that Judge Robinson was duly warned of his danger; and that it would not do for me to attempt to go to Indianapolis to warn Judge Robinson of his danger, as arrangements had been made to have me assassinated there, and that it would not do for me to write him about it, as arrangements had been made in the Postoffice to have my letter intercepted if I wrote. Believing that the aforesaid prominent gentlemen would warn Robinson, I left it to them.

Those three gentlemen died martyrs to the cause of good government, and I demand of the authorities and all good citizens of Indiana and Missouri that their murderers be hung according to law. On with the enforcement of the laws. Let no guilty man escape. Judge Normile committed suicide at St. Louis the ninth of August. Poor Normile deserved a better fate than to have been ruined and programed to his death by such criminals as Rotten Lee and Satan Blair. Sitting at the tables of the Police Board, Satan Blair, while telling Gainnie how he was going to have me murdered, would frequently say with an air of great contempt for human life: "What is a human life when it stands in the way?" The murders he has since committed and had committed prove that he has as great a contempt for the life of a human being as he has for the life of a fly. This world would be better off without him. Rotten Lee and Satan Blair are human monstrosities without heart or soul. But for the noble conduct of Samuel M. Kennard, Charles R. Gregory, John H. Maxon,

Web Samuel, Jerome Hill, and others acting with them, in hiring men to protect my life, I would have been killed in St. Louis. I hereby return my thanks to them. Notwithstanding the dangers that have threatened me in war and peace, by land and sea, I still live to tell mankind the true story of a world.

CHAPTER 28.

THE TRUE STORY OF A WORLD.

From the past we have learned how the democratic truth concerning creation, life and salvation, has had to contend against the despotic forcing of the monarchic lie concerning creation, life and salvation, for the possession of the human brain on this globe. And now, I will tell the entire true story of a world, the entire truth concerning creation, life and salvation, and in doing so will tell whence came the earth, and whence came man, and whither goeth the earth, and whither goeth man.

CREATION.

The history of the past proves that from the beginning man has been asking, What is the true story of a world, or, Whence came the earth and whither goeth the earth, and whence came man and whither goeth man? To these questions I answer: Space. What is space, and how do we know that the earth and man came from and will return to space? Space is that shoreless ocean of everlasting matter so finely disintegrated not a single atom can be seen even through a microscope, through which revolve the many worlds we see. It is commonly called ether. We all know nature abhors a vacuum. So, space must be filled with something, although invisible. In this shoreless ocean of invisible matter float the invisible germs of all life. If invisible, how do we know they exist? The atmosphere we breathe is invisible, in a state of repose, even through a microscope, but we know we breathe it, and can feel it when we blow our breath. So we know that some things exist, even when they are invisible. If invisible matter exists, why not also invisible spirits?

When the invisible atmosphere is disturbed it condenses into currents, and the wind is said to be blowing. It is then visible. The currents meet and one rolls the other up somewhat into the shape of a ball which goes whirling around, and is commonly called a whirlwind. In a like manner the invisible ether in space is disturbed and condenses into currents, which run against each other, one doubling up the other, which rolls on through space, first as a nebulous mass, gathering matter and forming into the shape of a ball which, rolling on, enlarges like a snow-ball rolling in the snow, till it gathers all the matter and germs of life necessary to make up a world, and by attraction and repulsion of surrounding globes is forced into an orbit in a solar system; and moving around in its orbit cools off and condenses, first into the consistency of a liquid and then into that of a paste. After awhile it cools off to that condition in which the germs of vegetable life develop or evolute into vegetation. Then follows that condition suitable to the evolution of the germs of animal life, and finally it arrives at that condition when the germs of human life evolute man and woman into existence. They multiply and the earth becomes peopled. The very dissimilar personal appearances of the different varieties of man, as the white man, the Indian, the Chinese, the Japanese, and the negro, prove that they came from different varieties of germs, that is, different origins. But that is no reason why they should quarrel and fight. And it is not necessary that we should try to prove that they all came from a common origin to satisfy the doctrine of the brotherhood of man, for we all know, as a matter of fact, that doctrine is not proved, for even among brothers in the same family there is but little brotherhood, and often none whatever.

The dissimilar appearances of man and the monkey also prove that they did not come from the same origin, as was asserted by Darwin, but on the contrary that they came from different origins, different kinds of germs. Wherever the germ happened to lodge on the earth there it evoluted its kind into existence, whether that was a white man, a black man, a yellow man, a red man or a monkey. This proves that the climate does not determine the complexion. We all know that the Esquimau Indian, who is almost black, has always lived near the North Pole, which proves that a northern climate will not make him white. The fact that white people have always lived in the tropic climate on both sides of the Atlantic Ocean, and remained white people, is sufficient proof that a tropic climate will not change the white complexion.

There is a tribe of Indians on our northwestern border called the Welsh Tribe, who are very proud of the fact that their ancestors were white; but among them are a few who have red hair and blue eyes. This is a case of breeding back. Some Welsh people, who located in North Carolina in early times, were driven West and then inter-married with Indians. The half-breeds married Indians and their children married Indians, and their children married

Indians, and that went on till the white Welsh people disappeared and nobody but Indians were left, and they boasted that their ancestors were white. A nearly white Welshman might come now from that tribe but it would be a case of breeding back, and the climate would have no influence on the complexion. The same has been the case where other races have inter-married. This breeding back toward the complexion of the ancestor proves, not only that the climate has no influence in determining the complexion, but that the original germ determined the complexion of the several races, and that the different races came from different germs. This conclusively contradicts the idea that there was originally only one first couple called Adam and Eve and which asserts that all mankind came from them.

Undoubtedly, many first couples of the different races were evoluted into existence simultaneously, or nearly so. This is proven by the existence of every variety of people almost everywhere on the globe. Ancient statues prove that the white man, the negro, and the red man, lived in Yucatan, in ancient times. The natural casualties will account for the earth having not become too populous in the past

and will do so in the future. As all vegetable life
came from germs, and is now simply a question of
growth under certain conditions from germ seeds, as
will be fully demonstrated hereinafter, why not all
animal and human life also come from germs?
The question is sometimes asked: Why do not
people evolute into existence now from germs?
The answer is easily made: the germs that the earth
gathered up in space were exhausted when it
was in condition to evolute them. We know that
the supply of germs of life will never fall off in
space, no matter how many worlds come into and go
out of existence, as space is without limit, and,
therefore, the germs of life in it are also without
limit. Consequently, nature will never die out, for
nature is eternal.

All trees are trees, notwithstanding some of
them are oak, some beech, and some walnut, as well
as other kinds. The fact that they are all trees
does not prove that they all came from the same
origin. Neither does the fact, that all the different
races are all people, prove that they all came from
the same origin. An acorn can only grow an oak
tree. It can not grow a beach tree or any other
kind of a tree except an oak tree. The same may

be said of a beachnut and a walnut. They can only grow their own kind of trees. The different varieties of people came, like the different varieties of trees, from different origins. As an acorn can only grow an oak tree, so a white germ of life can only evolute a white person into existence. As a beachnut can only grow a beach tree, so a black germ of life can only evolute into existence a black person. The same may be said of all the other germs. A blonde germ evolutes a blonde person, while a brunette germ evolutes a brunette person and so on as to all the different varieties of germs. From the separate germs of animal life came all the different varieties of animals. From the different germs of vegetable life came all the different seeds that grow the different varieties of vegetable life; and each vegetable seed had its own separate vegetable germ. All germs of life are original elements in nature. All germs of life are therefore the origin or creators of all life, each germ being the creator of its own kind. Even the only God-germ being the creator of the true and only God.

NATURAL STATE.

All history proves that originally all were roving children of nature, electing their chiefs. That there was neither minister, priest nor legal authority to tie the knot. That nature alone brought them together. That many of the uncivilized tribes still existing on our earth are living proofs of this fact. That the will of man alone divorced him. That the woman was the slave of man and could not divorce herself from him. That in time one man went with another man's woman. That jealousy caused the husband to kill the offender. That two of the Ten Commandments were thus established: Thou shalt not adult. Thou shalt not kill. That after a while man acquired personal property and his fellow-man stole it, and that this gave rise to the commandment: Thou shalt not steal. That in a similar manner the other commandments came, and thus the moral law was established. That experience proved that those who lived according to the moral law, as a rule, kept out of trouble and were happy, which state they called happiness or heaven, while those who lived contrary to the moral law were, as a rule, in trouble and unhappy, mentally confined to a dark cave called hades, or hell. So at first their ideas of hell and heaven were confined entirely to this world, and so they urged the importance of living in accordance with the moral law if people wanted to be in a mental heaven in this life and keep out of a mental hell in this life. Hell was a dark cave in the earth called hades, in which the greatest criminal in the community was confined. They called him the Devil because he deviled or tormented the people so they could have no peace in the community while he ran at large. Finally they confined all bad criminals in hades or hell. In fact, hades or hell was simply a penitentiary in which they confined the criminals to separate them from the good people, but knowing that the bad man there called the devil would torment them.

NATURE WORSHIP.

The first people, having no ancestors to inform them concerning the manifestations of nature, looked off into space at the sun, the moon and the stars, and wondered what they were. Observing that the sun caused the vegetation to grow, in gratitude they worshiped the sun. As the moon gave them light when the sun was gone away, in gratitude they worshipped the moon. Because the stars gave them light and looked so beautiful they worshipped the stars. As the earth grew or bore all their food, in gratitude they worshiped the earth, and called it Mother Earth. This was nature worship.

PLURAL GODS.

In time they conceived the idea that it was not the sun that caused the vegetation to grow but some invisible power back of the sun, which they called the Sun-God. In the same way they arrived at the idea of a Moon-God. And so on they conceived the idea of a separate god for every object in nature. Finally they conceived the idea that there was a Supreme God over all these plural gods, as there were supreme chiefs over the subordinate chiefs in this world.

CREATION BY EVOLUTION.

Seeing everything coming and going according to the laws of nature, they concluded that with all life it was simply a question of conditions; and that when the conditions failed there was no life. And also seeing the different chemical elements uniting to form new objects, they concluded that the earth had come into existence from matter passing through different conditions—from chaos to the perfect world, and therefore believed in creation by evolution.

FUTURE LIFE.

In time dreams started the idea of a life after the death of the body. Before they began to bury dead bodies man saw the dead body of his fellow-man decay and become invisible, and subsequently dreamed of seeing him as he appeared in life. Having seen the body decay and become invisible he knew that it could not be the body appearing unto him in a dream, so he concluded that the body must have had a spirit in it that presented to him in a dream the same appearance that the body had presented to his eyesight when it was alive. Hence his belief in a soul.

They at first believed that the spirits they had seen in their dreams remained in the neighborhood as they saw them there in their dreams. They called them ghosts, and were afraid of them. And thus started the idea in religion of a spirit-life after the death of the body. After a while they found out that they did not remain in the neighborhood, as they could not see them when they awoke, so they concluded that they only came there when they appeared unto them in dreams. And as they could not see them about they concluded that they must have gone into space; that the spirits of the good people must have gone up into space to a place of life and happiness which they called heaven from comparison to their idea of heaven in this life, where the Supreme God would bless them: and that the spirits of the bad people must go down into a place called hell from comparison to the dark cave called hades or hell here on earth, and as there was a great and good spirit, the Supreme God, in heaven, to receive and bless the spirits of the good, there must be a bad spirit they called the Devil, in hell, to receive and torment the spirits of the bad people. And thus came their ideas of the soul, of heaven, of hell, of God, of the Devil. And thus came natural religion.

THE MONARCHIC TRICK!

For many generations they enjoyed liberty both in politics and religion, but their cunning old chief, who had been elected to his office by the people, observing the great superstition of the people, and being very ambitious to have his chieftanship descend to his own progeny indefinitely, for the glory of his own family, pretended to have received a revelation from

God telling him that he was a son of God, although he had a Chinese mother, and commanding that he and his progeny should rule over the Chinese and live in luxury, at their expense, forever. And whosoever disputed it was in revolt against the will of God, and should be eternally damned for it. The ignorance and superstition of the people caused them to submit, and the cunning old chief was worshiped as the son of God, and was not only the temporal, but was also the spiritual ruler. And ever since the monarchs have been falsely representing God as a king like themselves.

It was a sharp trick the old chief played on them politically and religiously. And thus man was first deprived of his natural right of self-government, both in politics and religion. Thus was monarchy, in both politics and religion, established on the overthrow of free government by that lying trick of pretended revelation in favor of that fraud called divine right monarchy. It was the overthrow of all liberty, political and religious. Other chiefs got the idea and played the trick on their tribes. And later kings in most cases used the priests for the purpose of playing that trick on the people.

And since then man has been struggling at times

to recover his natural right of self-government, both in politics and religion.

That old lie of pretended revelation started the issue of Republican Politics *vs.* Monarchic Politics, and the issue of Republican Religion *vs.* Monarchic Religion, which will remain the issues till republican politics and republican religion shall be triumphant all over the earth.

For centuries the Chinese king pretended that he descended from God, and away back, if not now, was worshiped as a descendant of God, and was religious as well as political ruler, he claiming as a lineal descendant of God. The Chinese claimed to have had thirteen lineal descendants of God as their kings. Since the Chinese people have become so highly educated and intelligent they are ashamed that their ancestors ever believed any such a lie, and now put it fine by simply saying their kings were of celestial origin, which is only a new way of putting the old idea, God being the only celestial being in heaven. The Chinese themselves are now sometimes called celestials, on account of that old lie, so, in any form, it is the same old lie.

While under free government, their natural right, as we have already seen, they enjoyed perfect liberty, both political and religious, thinking and choosing for themselves, both in politics and religion, and believed in natural creation, creation by evolution.

But the old arbitrary chief thought his dynasty was more likely to be perpetuated if all free thought both in politics and religion was suppressed. Hence he told them that he would let them know what the truth was in regard to creation and salvation, that he had gotten it from God, and told them that their idea of creation by evolution was all wrong. That instead of nature creating them and everything else, God had created nature, created them, the earth, the stars, and everything else. That God having created them, He alone had a right to rule them. That they had no right to rule themselves for all authority came from God, and that God had authorized him to deliver his commandments to them, and they must obey them, or God would punish them in hell forever.

From all of which we see that religion, like politics, is either republican or monarchic; that under free government religion was republican, and under monarchy it was monarchic. Under free government politics and religion were separate and distinct;

that by the trick of pretended revelation overthrowing free government, politics and religion were united in monarchy, and free thought among the people suppressed in both.

SO-CALLED NECESSITY MONARCHY.

Ambition is never without a lie and a trick to overthrow free government and on its ruins establish itself in power and luxury at the expense of the people. Wherever the fraud of the so-called divine right monarchy has no longer been able to deceive the people, the ambitious monarch and his adherents have always come forward with another lie to try and retain monarchy. They have asserted that monarchy was necessary to protect life and property; but when the history of republics proved that life and property were just as safe in republics as they were in monarchies, that lie was exploded, and the plea of necessity for monarchy was gone, and the republics came as a natural consequence, as well as a natural right of the people.

SO-CALLED PLEBISCITE MONARCHY.

Whenever the fraud of the so-called divine right monarchy and also the fraud of the so-called necessity monarchy both played out with the people, the ambitious monarch, or would-be monarch, submitted his claim to the throne to an election by the people, but took particular pains to use his army to see that the election went in his favor, and proclaimed that he ruled by the will of the people—another lie.

If it had been a fair election it would have been wrong and a fraud, for one generation has no right to elect or force on succeeding generations hereditary rulers.

So plebiscite monarchy is also a lie and a fraud. When the kings could no longer play the trick of so-called divine right monarchy on the people, through themselves, they played it through Christ. Republican government, in both politics and religion, is the only rightful government on this earth. Wherever free government has been overthrown, ambition has done it every time.

And when ambition and avariciousness could no longer impose any kind of monarchy on the people, they have always imposed Patrician, that is, aristocratic, republican government, with favoritism to the few at the expense of the many, on the people, in contradistinction to a people's republic, in which all had equal rights before the law, with favoritism to none, with equal and exact justice to all.

We have also learned from history that in time temples to God were built, schools established, and learning carried to the highest point by some races, while other races have still remained uncivilized and in their native ignorance; that wars between tribes and nations, as well as civil wars, came. We all know now in our own time all about the great progress that has been made on our globe in everything, including learning, railroads, cable lines under the ocean, so that any news can be sent around the earth within a few hours. Finally, intellectuality of the masses will put a curb on the ambition of monarchs and would-be monarchs, and will bring back to all mankind true republican government, and the people will be as happy as it is possible for mortals to become.

Thousands of years this will go on, and finally the waters will disappear from the surface of the earth. All life will then disappear, as no life can exist without water. Passing inwardly the water will finally come in contact with the gases, oils and other explosives, create a steam and explosive power which, coming in contact with the fire in the interior of the earth, will explode the earth, casting it off into space so finely disintegrated not one particle will be seen, even through a microscope, thus returning the earth to its original condition, nature having no permanent use for a dead body undisintegrated. And thus it may be said to a world: From dust thou camest, and unto dust thou shalt return. And this is the true story of the material world. And it is the republican account of the birth, life and death of a world. Such will be the fate of our world in time.

But do I hear some one say that can not be so, for if a world were to explode it would break up the entire solar system to which it belonged? It would do nothing of the kind. A slight change in the relative positions of the planets, caused by attraction and repulsion, would make the system go on as though nothing had happened, and the world would not be missed any more than a man is missed when he drops out of this life. And this reminds us that when the earth shall explode and go back to space invisible matter to help make up new worlds, that there will be no people here to know anything about the greatness of any man that may have lived on this earth, and that people on other planets know nothing of their greatness. O, how vain is ambition!

BUT WHAT EVIDENCE IS THERE IN SUPPORT OF CREATION BY EVOLUTION?

From what they saw going on before their eyes, the primitive races had good reason to believe in creation by evolution. They saw everything coming and going according to the laws of nature, that with all life it was a question of conditions. They saw that a hen-egg was matter without life or action. What it would become was entirely a question of conditions. If let alone it would decay, disintegrate, pass away and become invisible. If placed under a hen for three weeks it would, under the action of heat, evolute into a chicken, a thing of life and beauty and splendid food for man.

That as to what a grain of corn would become was a question of conditions. If left exposed to the weather it would decay and become invisible. If planted in the ground in the proper season and properly tilled it would evolute into a corn-stalk and ears of corn. That a grain of wheat would similarly produce wheat.

MAN.

That as to whether man comes into this world or not was entirely a question of conditions, and as to whether he lived or died was also a question of conditions. If his supply of air was stopped his lungs collapsed, he died, decayed, disintegrated and became invisible. If his food was stopped the same result followed. If he had no water to drink the same result followed. If his blood ceased to flow the same result followed. That disease would cause the same result. From all of which they concluded that life was the result of matter under certain conditions and when the conditions failed there was no life.

Seeing the chemical elements uniting to form new bodies they concluded that the earth had come into existence from matter passing through different conditions, from chaos to the perfect world. Modern geology has proven that belief to be true.

ASTRONOMY.

Astronomy has also proven it to be true. Astronomers tell us that through their telescopes they can see worlds in every state of evolution, from the nebula to the perfect world; that to suppose that our little world is the only peopled globe would be the quintessence of self-conceit.

Astronomy informs us that Venus is better adapted to sustain human life than our own globe; that Mars is also a perfect world. The astronomers have made a map of Mars showing that one-half of its surface is water and the other half land; that Mars has water-ways that are believed to be canals; that Jupiter, fourteen times as large as our little world, is now in the condition of a paste not yet in a condition to evolute any kind of life, thus furnishing us the positive proof in our own solar system that worlds come from nebula.

The Jewish Bible also sustains this truth of natural conditions. It says the earth was void and without form. Void means nothing, or matter so finely disintegrated that it can not be seen even through a microscope. The Jewish Bible also says the earth shall be destroyed by fire. The natural or republican account of creation as we have already seen explains how it is to be destroyed by fire, by explosion. Thus the Jewish bible and the republican account of creation sustain each other; that is, that the earth came from nebula.

FROM CHAOS TO COSMOS.

Last, all religions, republican and monarchic, unite in declaring the earth came into existence by evolution, republican religion declaring that it came from the power of matter to form all the bodies of nature by evolution, monarchic religion declaring that its Monarchic God is all-powerful, and that he ordered nature to evolute it into existence, and that any body who doubted that should be eternally damned.

All races of men have believed that the earth came from chaos. From chaos to comos, organized worlds, has always been the belief of all men, nobody ever believing that the worlds have always been organized as they are now. Mankind have only differed as to who caused the evolution, the majority believing in the republican account of creation, that nature, matter of its own powers, caused entire evolution, while the rest of mankind have been forced to believe in the monarchic account of creation which was started by a pretended revelation, that there is an all-powerful supreme being, independent of nature, matter, who caused nature to evolute everything into existence. Our Jewish Bible account of creation teaches that the earth itself came from space chaos, but that the Monarchic God caused it to evolute into existence, and that he made a special creation of man.

HOW DO WE KNOW THAT WORLDS EXPLODE?

Twice I have witnessed that sight. Once during our late civil war, as I was riding at the head of my command, a cavalry brigade in the Union Army, on a night march in Louisiana, looking to the southeast tropic sky, I saw a world, commonly called a star, explode. At that time I thought nothing of it. But three years after the war I was going up the Pacific ocean on my way to California when, one beautiful night, all nature seemed to blush for its own loveliness. As I stood on the deck with a beautiful young lady stargazing in the southwest tropic sky, I again saw a world explode. "Why, that star exploded," exclaimed beautiful Pauline Lamoine. "Pauline, that was a world," said I, "many times larger than our own." Otherwise we could not see it at its great distance, so many million miles away. Such will be the fate of our earth in time. And this is the true story of a material world. Usually the world drops out of its orbit before it explodes, in which case it is dismissed with the remark: "Oh, that is nothing but a shooting star." Well, what is a shooting star but a world that has burned out its interior parts by volcanoes, and its substance has passed off into space in gases till it no longer has sufficient mass to hold it in its orbit by attraction and repulsion, when it drops out of its orbit followed by a train of fire and explodes.

Having learned the true story of a material world let us now learn the true story of a spiritual world. And this brings us to the question:

IS THERE A GOD?

As we have learned from history that the imagination of man has created so many imaginary gods in India, Egypt, Greece, Rome and elsewhere, what proof is there of the existence of any God at all? First, the almost universal belief that there is a God; that all religion, republican and monarchic, have taught it. That the Greek and Roman republican religions taught that a Supreme God as well as subordinate gods of the Greeks and Romans were evoluted into existence by nature. That he was not a creator and dictator, but a dispenser of happiness to those who proved themselves worthy of it. Monarchic religion has taught that there is a Supreme Being, or God, independent of nature, self-existent, that ordered nature to evolute everything into existence; that He is a creator and dictator, and will eternally damn anybody who disobeys His orders. Monarchic religion also teaches that the machinery of the universe is so perfect that it must have required a great intelligence, or architect, called a Supreme Being, or God, to have made it, as a house made by man required intelligence to make it.

In reply to this, republican religion asserts that nature itself, of its own powers, is the greatest architect of all, and capable of making any organized universe. That it is the nature of matter to assume all these different forms and organizations. That the mighty works of nature, the systems of worlds without number, are not to be degraded by comparison to a common house made by man.

The positive proof that there is a God is the fact that He naturally draws the brain of man to Him. In all ages the brain of man, cultivated and uncultivated, naturally feels itself drawn off into space after God, and mentally sees a form, a personal God. If one God, then, why not many Gods? The only knowledge it is possible for us to acquire is by impressions made on our brains by nature external to our brains, through the senses, sight, hearing, touch, taste and smell, and also impressions made on our brains by the reasoning power of the brain. From the impressions made on their brains by external nature, and their reasoning power, the greatest intellects of all times, from the earliest priests in the Order of Sacred Mysteries to the greatest intellects of our times, have all concluded that there is a God, and only one God.

This cumulative evidence furnished by the greatest intellects of the world in all ages ought to be considered conclusive evidence that there is one God and only one God.

The fact that the imagination of man has created so many imaginary gods, is no proof that there is no God at all, for the mind of man on other subjects generally wanders in the dark some time before it arrives at the truth. It has been so in regard to this subject of a God and a soul. In the person of the author the mind of man has at last arrived at the truth in regard to both God and the soul.

The monarchic religionists claim that their God is unlimited in his powers. The republican religionists claim that their God is limited in his powers.

The plural gods were imaginary gods; and as it is an impossibility for any god to make one plus one make three, it necessarily follows that the monarchic god, whom the monarchists claimed to be all-powerful, is also an imaginary god.

There is only one real God, and he is a democratic God, the God of the people, and the God of love. History proves that all the ancient republics, as a rule, had republican religion, and that the monarchies had monarchic religion. Monarchic religion is out of place in a republic. Republican religion alone is appropriate to a republic. Republican religion is the only rightful religion anywhere on the earth.

The history of mankind proves that a God to pray to is as necessary to the brain of man as food is necessary to the stomach. So why doubt the existence of the true and only God?

But the fact is there was only one God-germ in all space and it evoluted the true and only God into existence in the beginning of creation to exist forever and to bless man for all time, on all the planets, and to receive immortal souls after the death of the body.

Some of the ancients believed that a God was in the beginning evoluted into existence to bless man for a long time and was then absorbed into space and gave way to a new God, who in time was also absorbed, and so on.

Some of the ancients believed that the soul after many centuries in heaven was absorbed into space and ceased to be a soul. This was believed to keep heaven from becoming too crowded with souls. They seemed to forget that heaven is capable of indefinite expansion.

Next, has man a soul, and whence his belief that he has?

SOUL.

We have already learned that before they began to bury dead bodies, man saw the dead body of his fellow-man decaying, and subsequently dreamed of seeing him as he appeared in life. Having seen his body decay, he knew it was not the body reappearing unto him in a dream, so he concluded that the body must have had a spirit in it that presented the same appearance as that presented by the body in life. Hence his belief in a soul. They at first believed those spirits remained about the neighborhood, calling them ghosts, and were afraid of them.

It has been asserted that man has a self-consciousness that he himself is a spirit or soul independent of his body, that is, simply living in the body.

Nearly all men, uncivilized as well as civilized, and most highly cultured, believe they have souls. If man has no soul why this almost universal belief in it, in men of almost all races and conditions?

ARGUMENTS AGAINST THE EXISTENCE OF A SOUL.

In reply to the arguments in favor of the existence of a soul the infidel materialists declare there is no soul and furnish the following arguments in favor of their position: That as soon as the blood ceases to flow through the brain there is no life. In reply to which the religionist says there is a soul, but it will not remain in the body that does not furnish blood enough to the brain. That declaration says the infidel materialists assume that there is a soul. That assuming there is a soul does not prove it. That it is a fact well known that when the blood ceases to flow through the brain in proper quantity man has no mind till the blood again begins to flow through the brain in proper quantity as in the case of a swoon, when his eyes open and he again has mind or intelligence, which is sometimes confounded with the soul.

This confounding of the soul with mind or intelligence has fooled the infidel materialist and caused him to think that he has proven that man has no soul because he has intelligence only while the blood flows in proper quantities through the brain. The soul being an existence separate and distinct from mind or intelligence this only proves that a soul is not necessary to physical human life, but does not prove that there is no soul.

In reply to the assertion of the religionist that he himself is a spirit proven by self-consciousness, the infidel materialist says that self-consciousness or proof only exists while the blood continues to flow in proper quantities through the brain, which proves that the self-conscious spirits have no existence.

The infidel materialists have also asserted that spirit is only matter in space so rarified as to be invisible, and that self-consciousness is only a self-consciousness of origin, evolution having already proven that man's body came from space, rarified invisible matter, and that there is no spirit, but all is matter in one condition or another. Nature is sometimes called God and therefore everything that emanates from nature is said to emanate from God.

That man at the time he was convinced of the existence of a soul by his dreams, had not studied the law of the brain so as to learn that a dead person reappearing to him in a dream was only the image of a dead man that had been impressed on his brain during life, being brought up within the brain during sleep by that power of the brain called recollection, which sometimes acts during sleep as well as waking hours. That it was all in his own brain. That neither body nor spirit had appeared unto him in a dream. That the image of the body was simply revived in his own brain where it had been lying dormant.

ARGUMENT IN FAVOR OF THE EXISTENCE OF GOD AND THE SOUL.

The human brain is the highest development of material nature on the earth. And when it is operated on by material nature, other than itself, thought is the result, says the infidel materialist. Then religious thought must be the result as well as any other thought. If religious thought be the offspring of the brain when operated on by material nature by what right does the infidel materialist deny the truth of it? To do so is to proclaim nature itself in its highest development religious thought, a failure or a lie. If that offspring of material nature, religious thought, teaches man that he has a soul, and that there is a God, by what right does the infidel materialist deny the truth of it when he himself asserts that all thought is the result of matter acting on the brain? The infidel materialist believes in all the developments of material nature till he reaches its highest, religious thought, and then declares that a failure or a lie. The believer, on the contrary, considers that highest development of material nature, religious thought, no failure; on the contrary, only the beginning of a still higher development, the certainty of the development of the quality of immortality in the soul.

When the material nature through its highest development, religious thought, tells man that he has a spiritual soul that may be developed into an immortal soul, and that there is a God somewhere in space to whom that soul will go after death, by what right does the infidel materialist deny that great truth spoken by nature itself through all the ages to every race of mankind?

It has already been stated that in the shoreless ocean of space float the germs of all life. The fact that we are all here proves that there were physical germs in space. If physical germs, why not also spiritual germs in space?

Within each male physical germ there was a soul-germ; and within each female physical germ there was also a soul-germ; and when the male physical germ evoluted the male into existence its soul-germ at the same time evoluted the soul into existence. This may also be said of the female germ and its soul-germ. But how about the posterity of the evoluted male and female. Whence came their souls? The answer is easy. We know whence came their physical bodies: from the uniting of the seed of the male and the seed of the female: which are nothing more nor less than the germs of physical life. Within the seed of the male is a soul-germ: and in the seed of the female is also a soul-germ. The physical germs of both parents unite to create the physical body; and the soul-germs of both parents unite to create the soul. The development of the quality of immortality in the soul by religious thought and consequent religious conduct, would be no more wonderful than is the development of religious thought from material nature, the brain.

It requires religious thought, the highest development of material nature, the brain, and consequent religious conduct, to develop the quality of immortality in the soul after any mortal has sinned.

So if you would have an immortal soul and live after death, you must be good in this life: at least the general tenor of your life, the majority of it, must be good. Otherwise you will not have developed the quality of immortality in the soul; and death will be the end to you. Choose ye between eternal death and immortality beyond the grave.

TRANSMIGRATION OF SOULS.

In Egypt they finally imagined that the soul had to transmigrate through every animal from the lowest to the highest, man, in this world and in the next world, had to make a similar transmigration through all the animals before it could ever reach the final paradise. This was the foolish idea of the evolution of the soul. From this came to Darwin the equally foolish idea that the body evoluted from a common origin with the lower animals. Neither the body nor the soul of man ever came from the lower animals, nor a common origin with them.

The body of man came from his own physical germ in space, and his soul from its own soul germ, which was inclosed within his physical germ.

All nature proves that the animals were placed in this life by Nature solely for the use of the people in this life, and not to furnish souls to them. As they were placed here only for the convenience of the people, it follows that they have no souls. The senses and some intelligence were given to the animals, that they might take care of themselves till the people should have use for them. The fact that they have intelligence only proves that they have physical life. The fact that they can not comprehend the abstract qualities, as truth, virtue, etc., proves that they are incapable of considering the question of spirituality, and consequently have no souls. When you talk to them about the physical objects in nature, they can understand you, but when you speak to them of truth or spirituality, they can not understand you, and can not be made to. The power to comprehend abstract truth and spirituality is the dividing line between human beings and animals; between spiritual life and physical life; between people with souls and animals without souls.

And this is the true story of a Spiritual World.

The republican and democratic churches will help you to be good, happy in this life, and reach immortality beyond the grave. So sustain those churches of the people, and the people's God forever. But keep Church and State separate and distinct from each other forever.

DIFFERENT RELIGIONS.

Republican religion is the only true religion, and there is only one real God, and he is the republican God. The God of the People, the God of Love. Monarchic religion is the religion of eternal hate, and having originated in fraud, pretended revelation, and been perpetuated by tyranny, has no rightful existence anywhere on the earth, and ought to be abandoned by all mankind.

History proves that the ancient republics all, as a rule, had republican religion, and that the monarchies had monarchic religion.

Monarchic religion is out of place in a republic. Republican religion alone is appropriate to a republic.

Republican religion declares that nature was the creator and that nature created man to be a source of happiness to woman, and created woman to be a source of happiness to man, and created God to be a source of happiness to both.

Republican religion declares that redemption is the right of every child of humanity. Monarchic religion on the contrary consigns the millions to eternal damnation.

Republican religion has erected as splendid temples to the republican God as monarchic religion has ever erected to the monarchic God, and republican religion has done as much for Art as has ever been done for it by monarchic religion, as was fully proven by the magnificent temples at Athens and Rome, and the sculpture and paintings in the same.

There is but one limitation on the right of man to think and choose for himself in religion, and that is this: He has no right to establish monarchy in religion, for that denies to man the right to think and choose for himself in religion.

True republican religion never brought trouble to any people. Wherever in the republic of religion trouble has come, it has always been brought on by some of the people trying to force some monarchic idea on the rest of the people.

Republican religion ennobles the human brain, and says to it: Think, for nature created you to think. Monarchic religion, on the contrary, degrades the brain by denying to it the right to think, and says to it, you shall not think, but blindly obey the orders given to you.

Republican religion came first and existed for centuries when monarchic religion came by fraud and stole all its good ideas where it has any, from republican religion. The monarchies of Europe for centuries forced the people to believe in monarchic religion by burning them at the stake and murdering them in the inquisition and massacres. A monarchic religionist is one who wants monarchy in religion and wants to be the monarch himself and force everybody to believe as he believes.

In the order of nature God was created before man that he might be ready to bless man when he came into existence.

The advocates of republican religion have geology, chemistry, astronomy and all science and nature to sustain them in the truth of what they advocate, while the advocates of monarchic religion have only the false assertion of the tricky old chief and equally tricky men since his day to sustain their religion which originated in fraud and has been perpetuated by tyranny, denying to man his natural inalienable right to think for himself in religion and politics.

The monarchic religionists are infidels to the only true faith, republican religion, and deserve the fate of all who deny to the people the right to think for themselves in religion and politics, eternal death; that is, that death will be the end for them.

The first worship was nature worship in the groves; the next the worship of the imaginary gods, Jupiter and others, that were supposed to preside over the powers of nature, in the grand temples that were erected to them in Athens, Rome and elsewhere; and last, the worship of the only true God, the republican democratic God, the dispenser of happiness to mankind in answer to prayer.

The worship of the different powers of nature and the worship of the imaginary gods were simply nature leading the mind of man to the one only true God, the republican God, the people's God, the dispenser of happiness to mankind.

That God is not an all-powerful Creator and dictator is proven by the fact that this life has so many wicked slanderers, poisoners and murderers and would-be murderers who try to murder good people while they sleep. If He had possessed the power of creation He would never have created such. And if He were an all-powerful dictator He would not allow such to live, slander, poison and murder innocent people. If He had the power to prevent such crimes and would not exercise it to protect innocent people He would be meaner than the criminals.

Nature can be excused for creating such criminals,

for we all know that she sometimes makes miscarriages and brings forth human monstrosities without heart or soul.

DEFENDS RELIGION TO THE LAST.

If there was no God, and man had no soul to save, and it was all simply matter, in one condition or another, from chaos to cosmos, and back from cosmos to chaos, to help make up new worlds, why would a religious nature have been impressed on man by matter? All admit that man has a religious nature. In that case it is plain that a religious nature would have been impressed on man to make him lead a better life here. But there being a God, and man having a soul to save, it is plain that matter has given him a religious nature, not only to make him live a better life here, but that he may also develop the quality of immortality in his soul, that he may avoid eternal death and live forever beyond the grave.

So in either case it is plain that his religious nature ought to be cultivated. But the question naturally arises how ought it to be cultivated? But first we will consider how it has been cultivated. In the historic part of this book we have already learned how it has been cultivated all around the earth, both in republican religion and monarchic religion. So we will now consider how it ought to be cultivated.

HOW SHOULD THE RELIGIOUS NATURE OF MAN BE CULTIVATED?

As to whether or not religion is good for a man, depends entirely as to how his religious nature is cultivated.

The right to worship God according to the dictates of his own conscience is one of the natural, inalienable rights of man, and any cultivation of his religious nature that deprives him of that right is plainly an improper cultivation of it, as forcing monarchic religion on him.

Republican religion, or religious liberty, is the natural, inalienable right of man, and is the soul of our republic, and ought to be the soul of every country in the world.

"O Liberty, how many crimes have been committed in thy name!" was the exclamation of Madame Roland as she stood on the scaffold to be guillotined during the French Revolution.

O Monarchic Religion, how many crimes have been committed in thy name! In thy name the martyrs were burned at the stake in violation of the commandment: Thou shalt not kill.

In thy name thousands of innocent people have been murdered on the altar as useless sacrifices to imaginary gods in violation of the commandment: Thou shalt not kill. In thy name thousands were murdered in the Crusades and Inquisition and in the massacre of Saint Bartholomew. In thy name innocent blood has been shed, but in the name of true democratic religion no crimes are ever committed, for in that every human being is accorded the right to think and choose for himself.

Any cultivation of religion which causes wars or the taking of human life as sacrifices, or as martyrs, or in any way, other than for crimes according to the criminal law of the land, is plainly wrong, and deserves the denunciation of mankind in all ages.

Any cultivation of the religious nature of man that causes man to hate man, or fails to restrain him from manufacturing lies about his fellow-man, or having him secretly poisoned or assassinated, while awake or asleep, is plainly wrong, and deserves the denunciation of mankind in all ages. Any cultivation of the religious nature of a man that prevents the destruction of human life inculcates the moral law and prevents man from hating and slandering his fellow-man and encourages him in the hope of eternal happiness beyond the grave, is plainly right, and should be encouraged by all mankind in all ages, for:

> " 'Tis religion that can give
> Sweetest comfort while we live,
> And after death, joy
> Lasting as Eternity."

Obey the Golden Rule: Do by others as you would have them do by you, and you will never do a mean thing to anybody, and immortality will be yours.

As hope is better than despair, so republican religion is better than infidelity. As life is better than death, give me the hope of immortality. As republican religion is the religion of love, and monarchic religion is the religion of eternal hate, give me the republican religion. As I breathe my last let the music of "Sweet Bye and Bye" sound in my ears, as I hope for immortality.

And if it be all a dream, let me dream it forever. But it is not all a dream, it is a reality, for in each physical human germ, there was a spiritual germ to evolute into a soul and reproduce its kind for all time in the order of nature.

And somewhere in space Heaven will be found and weary souls gain rest, for:

"There is a land that is fairer than day,
 And by faith we can see it afar,
For the father waits over the way
 To prepare us a dwelling-place there.
  In the sweet bye and bye,
  We shall meet on that beautiful shore.

"We shall sing on that beautiful shore
 The melodious songs of the blest,
And our spirits shall sorrow no more,
 Not a sigh for the blessing of rest.
  In the sweet bye and bye,
  We shall meet on that beautiful shore.

"To our bountiful Father above,
 We will offer the tribute of praise,
For the glorious gift of His love,
 And the blessings that hallow our days.
  In the sweet bye and bye,
  We shall meet on that beautiful shore.

ERRATA.

On page 23 in the fourteenth line, the word *Brahman* should be *Brahm*.

There is an interregnum of nine pages between pages 337 and 347. This mistake was caused by having different parts of the book printed by different printers, and miscalculating the number of pages that the manuscript would make. The chapters and matter are all in their proper places however.

www.ingramcontent.com/pod-product-compliance
Lightning Source LLC
Chambersburg PA
CBHW022121290426
44112CB00008B/765